Making Chaucer's
Book of the Duchess

NEW CENTURY CHAUCER

The works of Geoffrey Chaucer are the most-studied literary texts of the Middle Ages, appearing on school and university syllabuses throughout the world. From *The Canterbury Tales* through the dream visions and philosophical works to *Troilus and Criseyde*, the translations and short poems, Chaucer's writing illuminates the fourteenth century and its intellectual traditions. Taken together with the work of his contemporaries and successors in the fifteenth century, the Chaucerian corpus arguably still defines the shape of late-medieval literature.

For twentieth-century scholars and students, the study of Chaucer and the late Middle Ages largely comprised attention to linguistic history, historicism, close reading, biographical empiricism and traditional editorial practice. While all these approaches retain some validity, the new generations of twenty-first-century students and scholars are conversant with the digital humanities and with emerging critical approaches – the 'affective turn', new materialisms, the history of the book, sexuality studies, global literatures, and the 'cognitive turn'. Importantly, today's readers have been trained in new methodologies of knowledge retrieval and exchange. In the age of instant information combined with multiple sites of authority, the meaning of the texts of Chaucer and his age has to be constantly renegotiated.

The series New Century Chaucer is a direct response to new ways of reading and analysing medieval texts in the twenty-first century. Purpose-built editions and translations of individual texts, accompanied by stimulating studies introducing the latest research ideas, are directed towards contemporary scholars and students whose training and research interests have been shaped by new media and a broad-based curriculum. Our aim is to publish editions, with translations, of Chaucerian and related texts alongside focused studies which bring new theories and approaches into view, including comparative studies, manuscript production, Chaucer's post-medieval reception, Chaucer's contemporaries and successors, and the historical context of late-medieval literary production. Where relevant, online support includes images and bibliographies that can be used for teaching and further research.

The further we move into the digital world, the more important the study of medieval literature becomes as an anchor to previous ways of thinking that paved the way for modernity and are still relevant to post-modernity. As the works of Chaucer, his contemporaries and his immediate successors travel into the twenty-first century, New Century Chaucer will provide, we hope, a pathway towards new interpretations and a spur to new readers.

NEW CENTURY CHAUCER

Making Chaucer's *Book of the Duchess*

Textuality and Reception

JAMIE C. FUMO

UNIVERSITY OF WALES PRESS

2015

www.uwp.co.uk

British Library Cataloguing-in-Publication Data
A catalogue record for this book is available from the British Library.

ISBN   978-1-78316-347-2
eISBN   978-1-78316-348-9

Typeset by Marie Doherty
Printed by CPI Antony Rowe, Chippenham, Wiltshire.

*To Vincent, for giving the push,
and to Rocco, for leading the way*

CONTENTS

Acknowledgements   ix
List of Abbreviations   xi

Introduction   1

1   Reading the *Book* (I): Critical History – An Overview   7
2   Reading the *Book* (II): Themes, Problems, Interpretations   49
3   All This Black: Reading and Making   79
4   Rereading the *Book* (I): The Materials of Transmission   105
5   Rereading the *Book* (II): Literary Reception up to
    the Sixteenth Century   131

'Now hit ys doon': Conclusion   175

Notes   181
Bibliography   213
Index   235

ACKNOWLEDGEMENTS

Combing through the entire critical history of even a supposedly 'minor' Chaucerian poem is a daunting task for the twenty-first-century scholar, and in this I benefited enormously from several valuable scholarly resources. I must record my debt to the generous and informative interpretative guides to the *Book of the Duchess* provided in Helen Phillips's 1982 critical edition and Colin Wilcockson's Explanatory Notes in *The Riverside Chaucer*, as well as A. J. Minnis's overview of the poem and its backgrounds (with V. J. Scattergood and J. J. Smith) in the 1995 Oxford Guides to Chaucer volume on *The Shorter Poems*, and Will Roger Knedlik's 1978 University of Washington PhD dissertation on 'Chaucer's *Book of the Duchess:* a bibliographic compendium of the first 600 years'. I am grateful to Stephanie Downes for sharing work in progress on Chaucer's French reception, and to Ben Barootes for numerous inspiring conversations regarding the *Book of the Duchess*, the fruits of which appear in a McGill University doctoral dissertation from which I profited in the later stages of this study. I would also like to record my sincere appreciation for the support this project received at University of Wales Press. Finally, my deepest thanks go, as ever, to this study's dedicatees, without whom there probably would have been no book, and certainly no dream.

LIST OF ABBREVIATIONS

ChR   *Chaucer Review*
EETS   Early English Text Society
MED   *Middle English Dictionary*
OED   *Oxford English Dictionary*
SAC   *Studies in the Age of Chaucer*

Individual works by Chaucer are abbreviated in accordance with *The Riverside Chaucer*, p. 779.

INTRODUCTION

Sometime after September 1368, during the reign of Edward III, a young courtier named Geoffrey Chaucer composed a poem in English that has variously been titled 'The Deeth of Blaunche the Duchesse', 'The Dreame of Chaucer', and, most commonly today, 'The Book of the Duchesse'. Around this same time or shortly before, Chaucer was translating into English some or all of Guillaume de Lorris and Jean de Meun's *Roman de la rose* and experimenting with a range of lyrical forms in English and, very likely, French. Although Chaucer refers in his *Retraction* to certain compositions now lost, some of which may have been early, the *Book of the Duchess* (hereafter *BD*) traditionally has been accepted as Chaucer's first major narrative poem and the earliest instance in his *oeuvre* of what would become a favourite literary form: the dream-vision. Although by no means monochromatic in its literary affiliations, the poem is heavily coloured by the style and poetic effects of the popular French forms in which Chaucer had thus far been schooled. A study in melancholy, *BD* features an artful narrative structure that interlaces a first-person narrator's semi-comic struggle with depressive insomnia, relieved by the soporific exercise of reading a book, with a poignant dream-plot concerning the death of a beloved lady and the despondency of her grieving husband. The knight and his lady in the dream are allusively identified as John of Gaunt, in whose army Chaucer would serve in a 1369 expedition in France and to whose household his wife Philippa would in 1372 be connected as *domicella*, and Blanche of Lancaster, who died of the plague in 1368, possibly at the age of twenty-three. The poem thus interweaves the narrator's seemingly mundane private frustrations against the public spectacle of a loss suffered by a member of the royal family – one of the most powerful men in England and father of the future king Henry IV. The *Book* ends with a brief account of its own composition in the voice of the now refreshed and alert narrator, whose experience awake and asleep has given us our first sustained encounter with the 'Chaucer-persona' that would become a hallmark of many of the poet's works. The poem now being completed, the narrator briskly declares, 'This was my sweven; now hit ys doon' (1334).[1]

This much is generally agreed upon. However, beyond this, little consensus exists regarding precise date and occasion, thematic unity and even such basic matters of artistic purpose as John of Gaunt's actual connection to the circumstances of the poem's writing and the extent to which it offers a consolation for Blanche's death. As Chaucer's first serious act of literary invention, *BD* has been regarded at different points in its reception history as both a juvenile effort and a nuanced expression of the subjectivity of grief, as an autobiographical reflection and a study in narrative fragmentation. The part played by *BD*, furthermore, in the early modern development of Chaucer's canon in the blackletter editions was by no means insignificant. Although *BD* has received steady critical attention in the form of articles and book chapters, it remains the least thoroughly examined of all of Chaucer's dream-visions, to which – *BD* excepted – several monographs apiece have been devoted. Only one book-length study of *BD* exists, published over forty years ago: James Wimsatt's still highly valuable *Chaucer and the French Love Poets: The Literary Background of the* Book of the Duchess (1968), which situates the poem in French traditions of courtly verse. Wimsatt's focus is naturally quite selective, and he does not offer – nor does there otherwise exist – a thorough overview of scholarship on the poem. No Variorum edition or volume in the Chaucer Bibliographies series has been devoted to *BD* to date, and the only chapter-length surveys of criticism available, such as D. W. Robertson, Jr's contribution on the poem in Beryl Rowland's *Companion to Chaucer Studies* (1979), are outdated and often argumentatively biased. While *BD* has, of course, been represented in those monographs of recent decades that treat Chaucer's dream-visions as a group, attesting to a healthy critical interest in placing Chaucer's early poetry in its literary context, the monumental studies of Chaucer's poetry that have been formative for the current generation of Chaucerians – investigations of history, gender, reception, style and politics, by critics such as Lee Patterson, Carolyn Dinshaw, Seth Lerer, C. David Benson, David Wallace and Paul Strohm – have generally refrained from integrating *BD* with the important patterns they identify. This critical elision of *BD* is curious in light of the undeniable importance of *BD* in Chaucer's poetic development, his political connections and his reception as an English author.

Clearly, there is a need for a rigorous and critically balanced assimilation of *BD*, the story of its reception and dissemination, and the major trends in its interpretative history into the fabric of twenty-first-century Chaucer studies. The present study aims to provide such a resource, and it is hoped that what follows will prove valuable both for newcomers to the poem and for seasoned scholars seeking a consolidation of and fresh perspective on the critical possibilities offered by *BD*. The present critical moment, with its commitment to recontextualizing Chaucer in his own sociopolitical context and attending to the material circumstances of his works' transmission, is an ideal one in which to assess and reorient traditional lines of debate concerning *BD* (for example, its consolatory tactics, Boethianism, secular vs. Christian perspective, and other issues).

Towards this end, the following chapters provide a panoramic view of critical trends in *BD*'s interpretation as they develop over time, and – complementarily – assess the importance of *BD* within contemporary understandings of Chaucerian authorship and the culture of book production in the later Middle Ages and early modern period. The thread that integrates the five chapters of this study is the construction and value of *BD* as a *book*, a material artefact. By exploring Chaucer's concern with the act of writing and the multiple textualities through which experience is mediated, this study places *BD* in the context of broader concerns with authority, reading practices and the vernacular circulating in the late fourteenth century. It furthermore argues that these concerns associate this first major act of Chaucerian book-making with the poet's increasingly intricate apprehension, in his later works, of books as agents in their own right. In the broadest sense, this study attempts to establish the relevance of *BD* to the construct of English authorship in the particular form in which it was to emerge from Chaucer's own reflections on his output and responsibilities as a writer – reflections which, newly applied by his poetic and scholarly successors, contributed to the 'idea' of a canon.[2]

The key word 'Making' in my title refers both to Chaucer's own 'makyng' of the *Book* – echoing his self-designation as 'I, that made this book' (*BD* 96) – and its continual (re)making by fellow poets, readers and critics over time. 'Making' unites and integrates all of the textual processes with which the present study is concerned: writing, reading and reception. *BD* is a study in poetic communication and collaboration (between an English poet, French love poets and Ovid; between the Chaucer-persona and the Man in Black) that is simultaneously about loneliness and poetic individuation. By yoking issues of creative and scholarly reception with those of book production and materiality, this study investigates acts of collaboration stemming from *BD*'s status as a textual, imaginative act. It seeks to dislocate the rhetoric of closure by which *BD* may appear to seal itself off from perpetuation – 'now hit ys doon', as the last line has it – and to locate Chaucer's strategies of *inventio* in a resonant setting of critical response and poetic appropriation in which the poem is far from tidily completed.

An implicit concern of the following analysis is how a poem that has been relegated to Chaucer's 'minor' works, or that has been presumed less valuable than Chaucer's mature accomplishments to a theorization of his poetics, can at the same time so doggedly elicit opposing interpretations and impertinent claims, both from its early readers and its modern critics. In part because of its tantalizing, but ultimately precarious, connection to Chaucer's own biography as a courtier serving the royal household, *BD* has been deemed both too important and not important enough, stubbornly resisting a firm historical footing. In certain respects, *BD* constructs and introduces the 'Chaucer' that is an organizing principle of the corpus we now study under that name, yet for all its importance to Chaucer's canon from an early stage, the work is difficult to place in a critical narrative that is not overdetermined

by Chaucer's mature accomplishments. *BD* is in fact a highly resistant – and resilient – poem among whose central preoccupations is its
own making: here, long before Shakespeare's play-within-a-play, was
Chaucer's book-within-a-book. As such, *BD* has much to offer twenty-
first-century readers for whom the interplay of media, the projection
of the self into alternative lives and the artifice of personal discourse
are familiar concepts in contemporary experiences of textuality. In
fact, the highly interactive nature of *BD* as a text that is transformed by
contact with other texts – both the French and Latin models it engages
in the course of its narration, and the subsequent literary creations that
appropriate it – makes it especially germane to twenty-first-century
textualities, with their newly dynamic avenues of communication, destabilization of authority through subjective response, and complication of
linear temporality. In viewing high culture through the lens of desultory
experience, in re-mixing an ancient story – an Ovidian fable read in
bed – into a living chronicle and in finally claiming all this for extem-
porary dissemination, *BD* is oddly prescient of the participatory culture
of writing that dominates new media today. In a contemporary world
suspicious of institutionalized authority, the irreverence in Chaucer's
tribute to a fallen noblewoman towards 'quenes lives, and … kinges, /
And many other thinges smale' (58–9) is increasingly our own.

To capture these dynamic aspects of textuality in *BD*, this study follows an arc from reading to writing to rereading, at the same time that it
suggests the overlapping nature of these textual practices. The first two
chapters map the critical terrain of *BD* from the beginnings of the professional study of English literature in the late nineteenth century up to the
present day. Chapter 1 provides a diachronic overview of broad trends
in scholarly opinion; debates over dating, occasion and revision; and the
range of generic affiliations that have been brought to bear on the poem.
Chapter 2 then narrows the lens to a number of key interpretative issues
in *BD* that have prompted recurrent debate and continue to preoccupy
critics today: problems of communication, consolation and Boethianism,
the performance of gender roles, the poetics of illness, and the creative
friction between French and English discourse. Shifting to a consideration of *BD*'s own inscription of textuality, the third chapter scrutinizes

Chaucer's vocabulary of 'making', focusing in particular on resonances of the word 'book' in the poem and its title. It then contextualizes *BD*'s self-conscious evocation of reading and writing within vernacular discourses of authorship in the French traditions that informed the poem and in differently oriented visionary texts produced by some of Chaucer's English contemporaries in the late fourteenth century.

The final two chapters investigate the reception of *BD* over time – how the 'book' was received and repackaged by Chaucer's early editors, readers and poetic followers. In doing so, these chapters address a significant gap in scholarship to date, which has devoted only scattered attention to the late medieval and early modern dissemination of Chaucer's first narrative poem. Chapter 4 focuses on the material 'book', detailing what is known of *BD*'s manuscript preservation and its journey into print beginning with William Thynne's 1532 edition of Chaucer's *Works*. Examining this phenomenon from an interpretative rather than strictly textual angle, the chapter draws attention to the integration of *BD* in early modern biographical narratives and highlights several instances of annexation and supplementation that shaped the meaning – and canonical value – of *BD* for early readers. Chief among these is a long-lived collocation of *BD* with *Envoy de Chaucer a Bukton* that forms a forgotten thread in the early poem's reception history. This study concludes with a fifth chapter that provides, for the first time, a detailed and sustained analysis of early creative responses to *BD* by John Gower, John Lydgate, Charles of Orleans and Edmund Spenser, as well as the poets responsible for the *Isle of Ladies*, *The Floure and the Leafe* and the *Kingis Quair*. The spectrum of early responses to *BD*, which include prequels and sequels, reversals and corrections, interpolations and emendations, testifies not only to the currency of the poem beyond what the surviving manuscripts attest, but also to its incitement of irreverent appropriations in its own right, as befits a poem so richly attuned to its own textuality and intertextuality.

To apprehend these dynamics of reading, writing and rereading, and to reconstruct the textual encounters that have shaped this seminal literary effort, we must now reopen the *Book*, beginning with the story of its 'making' by professional readers.

1

READING THE *BOOK* (I)

Critical History – An Overview

O n the face of it, Chaucer's *Book of the Duchess* is an unprepos-
sessing, even simple poem. Its central matter consists of a largely
one-sided conversation between two strangers, leading to a wholly
predictable revelation expressed in three short monosyllables: 'She ys
ded!' (1309). There occurs no real action to speak of, unless one counts
the forest hunt that is kept offstage for most of the narrative. Human
drama hangs on the awkward structure of the poem like an ill-fitting
mantle: the poem's only genuinely endearing character is a lost puppy,
and he vanishes after ten brief lines. *BD* ends quaintly – one might
even say naïvely – with the Chaucer-persona placing the completed
poem, as if tied with a shiny ribbon, in our hands to enjoy and be done
with. 'Thin prettiness', sniffed the great early Chaucer critic and editor
J. M. Manly regarding *BD* in his 1929 Warton Lecture, *Chaucer and the
Rhetoricians*. The stiff artificiality Manly detected in Chaucer's use of
rhetorical convention in the early *BD* led him, rather astonishingly, to
express relief that we have a limited stock of Chaucer's juvenilia over
which to spill ink: 'Unfortunately – or perhaps fortunately – most of
his early writings have perished.'[1]

Manly was not alone among distinguished early Chaucer scholars in
disdaining *BD* as a meagre, amateurish, imitative or at best rough-hewn
work whose chief relevance is its demarcation of how far Chaucer's
genius had yet to evolve. Writing in 1871, the indefatigable Victorian

scholar Frederick James Furnivall, whose seminal contributions to Chaucer studies include his establishment of the Chaucer Society and coordination of the Six-Text Edition of the *Canterbury Tales*, regarded *BD* as a patchy experiment. Furnivall endorsed William Godwin's view, advanced in his 1803 biography of Chaucer, that *BD* jumbled stylistic promise with more than occasional 'trite, vulgar and impotent' passages which attest to 'the crudeness of taste of the times in which Chaucer wrote'.[2] Particularly offended by the oddly paced ending, Furnivall conveyed his hope that 'Chaucer felt ashamed of himself for this most lame and impotent conclusion ... every time he read it: he ought to have been caned for it.'[3] Similarly, C. S. Lewis in his *Allegory of Love* (1936) found the overall effectiveness of *BD* as an elegy marred by rhetorical indulgence in 'the old, bad manner' which Chaucer, unlike his early poetic followers, would eventually outgrow.[4] For Robert Kilburn Root, writing in 1922, *BD*'s artistic potential crumbled into 'mediocrity' and 'weary reading', especially when weighed against Chaucer's later poetry (rather irrelevantly, Root noted that John Keats evinced much greater poetic maturity at a young age than did Chaucer).[5] Even Charles Muscatine, one of the most sensitive students of Chaucer's creative imitation of French source materials, offered faint praise for this narrative poem of Chaucer's most fully steeped in the French tradition, referring to it politely as a 'competent courtly elegy' diminished by 'conventionalism'.[6]

That such negative opinions did not finally dominate the scholarly history of *BD* owes much to George Lyman Kittredge, who defended the poem as 'charming and generally underrated' and a 'lovely and pathetic elegy'.[7] Kittredge's foundational work on *BD*, in articles minutely tracing the poem's sources in various *dits* of Guillaume de Machaut, and in the interpretative analysis developed in *Chaucer and His Poetry* (1915), set the terms of investigation and debate for the remainder of the twentieth century. The lines of critical discussion opened by Kittredge, centred especially upon the motivation and consistency of the narrator and the thematic coherence of the poem, engendered over time a dazzling array of interpretative perspectives on key issues of genre, characterization, literary relationships and the poetics of consolation, among others. The diverse (and sometimes divisive) history of scholarship on *BD* attests to the richness and elusiveness of a poem once thought wholly without guile, debunking Muscatine's claim that among Chaucer's early poems, *BD* is 'the most homogeneous in style and the clearest in meaning'.[8] In point of fact, this 'happily depressing', restively eclectic poem about death, literature, featherbeds, hunting and feminine beauty raises enduring problems of interpretation that cast into relief both the formative narratives of Chaucer scholarship and its patterns of development to the present day.[9]

Twenty-first-century scholars occupy a very different conceptual space from the earlier critics whose views have just been rehearsed. Those literary historians, philologists, editors and textual scholars were the learned architects of Chaucer studies as an academic discipline; theirs was the fundamental work of standardizing, contextualizing and disseminating Chaucer's works for an increasingly professionalized academy, one for which Chaucer carried the authority (for English literature) of a founding father. Today's more diverse and decentred academy, by comparison, is sceptical of canonical imperatives and irreverent towards its 'father figures'. Simultaneously, it is critically contemplative of its own institutional history – a trend, for Chaucer studies, well represented by the interrogations of Chaucer's critical and popular reception by Steve Ellis (2000), Stephanie Trigg (2002), Kathy Cawsey (2011) and others. From this vantage point, the momentousness of Chaucer's first major narrative poem is enfolded, as Elizabeth Scala has observed, in an 'overdetermined sense of origins'. For Scala, *BD* is a kind of authorial *Bildungsroman* centred upon Chaucerian self-invention: as the narrator transforms from reader to writer over the course of the narrative, he emerges as 'what we now recognize as *Chaucerian*' (Scala's italics).[10] When the passive and anonymous persona who struggled to sleep and dream recounts his resolution, at the end of the poem, to 'put this sweven in ryme' (1332), he enunciates the 'author-function' known ever after as 'Chaucer', creator of the *Book of the Duchess*. In Steven Davis's view, what emerges from *BD* is not only the idea of Chaucer as an author (a fresh 'brand', in late-capitalist terms) but of a newly identified Chaucerian *audience* of which we are inscribed as members – a market, so to speak. In Chaucer's attempt, in *BD*, to 'create and embrace a new reader', he thus inaugurates and models a critical tradition for his poetry, collapsing his own acts of reading and interpretation within the poem (i.e. the book the narrator reads in bed, which prompts his dream) into our own, future efforts to parse Chaucer.[11]

The originary status of *BD* pertains not only to Chaucer's corpus and his expressions of authorship but also to English literature itself, insofar as it is the first poem written in English substantially to appropriate French courtly tradition,[12] thus contributing to the growing empowerment of English as a language of cultural respectability in the second half of the fourteenth century, when ongoing war with France made this on one level a nationalist gesture. The consciousness and canniness of *BD*'s English intervention in French registers of language, style and subject matter have led some critics to regard *BD* as, far from a servile or derivative practice run for Chaucer's more 'original' later poetry, no less than a linguistic 'manifesto' in which Chaucer is 'highly conscious of the linguistic, poetic, and political implications of his project'.[13] In this view, English literature, reflective on itself as such, first takes shape when *BD* ends by announcing its own composition.

Much institutional, canonical, and cultural weight thus comes to rest on what once seemed an unassuming early poem innocent of grand designs. As twentieth-century criticism on *BD* flourished, lines of continuity from this first substantial poem to Chaucer's mature poetry were frequently emphasized, marking a shift from the earlier marginalization of *BD* towards its assimilation into a steadily realized artistic vision. The assumption of consistency between *BD* and Chaucer's later poetry – its evidencing of the same Chaucerian 'author-function' that certifies *Troilus and Criseyde* and the *Canterbury Tales* as masterworks – expresses in different terms the assertion, discussed above, that *BD* is a poem very much within the control of a recognizably Chaucerian Chaucer, even if this perspective only comes full circle at the end.

Argumentative circularity has marked much scholarship on *BD* as a result of the premise that Chaucer's later poetic practices can guide our interpretation of puzzles presented by his first major poem. It is telling, for example, that John Livingston Lowes should begin his appreciative analysis of *BD* not by confronting the poem on its own terms but by invoking the framework of Chaucer's mature genius: 'It was no less inevitable – Chaucer being Chaucer – that from the first his work should bear his individual stamp.'[14] Similarly, Nevill Coghill finds in *BD* confirmation of poetic features – the matter of love, the art of storytelling – for which Chaucer's later works are justly famous.[15] Even less favourable assessments, such as that of J. S. P. Tatlock, reflexively deploy later evidence to evaluate this early poem: so, the central characters of *BD* are flat 'patrician ideals' rather than dramatically fleshed-out portraits, and the dreamer's inconsistencies are clumsily sketched in contrast with the subtle complexities through which the mature Chaucer reveals character.[16] Especially riskily, Chaucer's mature poetry has been invoked to adjudicate cruxes in *BD*, for example the problem of the dreamer's overhearing, yet appearing unaware of, the Man in Black's early reference to his beloved's death. According to W. H. French (who draws on *Troilus*, the *Canterbury Tales* and the *Legend of Good Women* for evidence), Chaucer elsewhere values clarity of motivation, and so must not intend ambiguity here; furthermore, critical confusion over the Man in Black's later chess analogy is belied by the fact that 'Chaucer usually kept his imagery clear and sharp.'[17]

More recent critics have made, if anything, more sweeping claims for *BD*'s affinity with Chaucer's later poetics, endorsing by implication the relevance of the mature writings as a measure of artistic design in *BD*. Louise O. Fradenburg represents this trend in arguing that *BD*'s 'elegiac poetics' are foundational for the rest of Chaucer's poetic career, which in her view is absorbed with problems of loss and remembrance.[18] Charles W. Owen, similarly, discerns in *BD* Chaucer's trademark 'confidence … in implicit relationships' and polyvalence, claiming that the poem 'foreshadows his mature triumphs'.[19]

No doubt it is critically healthy, and has often been productive, to integrate *BD* within the totality of Chaucer's poetic achievement (as chapter 3 of the present study will further attempt), and to see its enduring relevance to Chaucer's expression of authorship rather than presuming its immaturity or unworthiness of Chaucer as we wish to define him. It is important, however, to be conscious of the danger of freighting *BD* – for better or worse – with foregone conclusions regarding Chaucer's 'usual practices' based on later works produced under different cultural and personal circumstances. Although the point may seem academic, it is not quite right to read *BD* as a poem written by the author of *Troilus and Criseyde*, the *Canterbury Tales*, and so on, because the author of *BD* is *not yet* that author, not yet an inhabitant of those (still non-existent, or at least inchoate) imaginative worlds. He certainly is not yet the author publicly identified with a renowned and influential corpus, or with the valorization of English letters, or with the discipline upon which we receive degrees or draw a pay cheque. The fact that the Chaucer of *BD* writes from a historical moment that is in important ways unimaginable to us releases an air of open possibility and disorientation in the poem that we would do well to weigh against the historical pressures of overdetermination that condition our experience of *BD* and its interpretation. To adapt a remark by Jacques Lacan, from a consideration of language and temporality, we must negotiate in *BD* 'the future anterior of what [Chaucer] shall have been for what [he is] in the process of becoming'.[20]

This and the following chapter identify various 'nodes' of interpretative discussion that have occupied *BD* scholarship over the twentieth century and into the twenty-first while proving especially provocative of continuing debate. It is neither possible to be comprehensive in the selection of topics and representation of criticism (limitations of space preclude this) nor to offer a linear interpretative guide to the poem (readily available in several excellent handbooks and editions[21]). In consideration of the great quantity of scholarship that exists on *BD*, and its exponential increase in the last twenty years (from which period roughly as many articles and book chapters were published on *BD* as had been in the period from 1900–90) – making it all but impossible for a critic publishing on *BD* today to familiarize herself with all criticism on the poem – it is hoped that the following will serve as a *vade mecum* for students, instructors and researchers seeking an up-to-date interpretative digest of scholarly opinion on key critical issues in *BD* studies.

BD Scholarship: A Historical Overview

A diachronic itinerary of broad patterns of development 'be processe of tyme' (*BD* 1331) will be of practical use before proceeding to the synchronic, topic-based perspective offered in chapter 2. In general, scholarship from the beginning of the twentieth century up to around 1950 approached *BD* through the lenses of biography and source study. Debate revolved around possible historical bases of the narrator's love-sickness (as the eight-year sickness, cryptically mentioned at *BD* 36–7, was typically interpreted), the most extravagant of these being Margaret Galway's proposal that Chaucer, identified autobiographically with the narrator, suffered unrequited love for Joan of Kent, wife of the Black Prince.[22] Of more lasting relevance was the foundational work on the French and Latin literary sources of *BD* accomplished in the first half of the century by Kittredge, W. Owen Sypherd, Constance L. Rosenthal, Edgar Finley Shannon, Haldeen Braddy and others; intellectual and cultural materials informing the poem (apart from specific source relationships) were also mapped, e.g. medieval travel lore and hunting practices.[23] When literary-critical (as opposed to philological) interpretations of *BD* were executed in this period, as touched on above, they tended to regard the poem as jejune, uninspired or artistically imbalanced – Kittredge being an exception here, as already observed. The poem's extensive basis in prior (French) sources rendered it, for early critics, less than authentic, more of a poetic exercise than a richly original poem; its uneven successes (the first 450 lines were thought superior to the long dialogue with the Man in Black) betrayed a lack of steady artistic control. A later articulation of this perspective, by Ian Robinson, conveys the point succinctly: 'before his inspiration became fully effective Chaucer wrote in a way that is *only* traditional ... [H]ere a tradition is speaking through him rather than *vice versa*'.[24]

Against these views, mid-century Chaucer scholarship, methodologically buoyed by formalism and New Criticism, identified various forms of structural coherence in *BD*, especially on the levels of thematic development, imagery and characterization. Earlier generations' concern with *BD*'s sources – related to the interpretative emphasis on derivativeness – was, with few exceptions (notably, the work of James I. Wimsatt), supplanted by an approach to the poem as very much Chaucer's own, with his artistic mastery and psychological realism cohering an ostensibly disjointed narrative. Typical here is Donald C. Baker's praise of Chaucer's 'architectonic ability' in weaving recurrent motifs, in and out of the dream frame, resulting in 'an admirably evolved structural and poetic achievement' that is far more polished than typically 'interminable' medieval visions.[25] No longer seen as the odd man out among Chaucer's early narrative poems, *BD* came to be standardized and codified by respectable literary classifications, such as Robert O. Payne's formula of the 'combinative structure' poem (representing the 'book-experience-dream formula'). Payne perceives *BD* as the 'most satisfactory' among Chaucer's poems in this category, its unifying thematic constitution (in Payne's reading, the centrality of nature) leading to closure without any major disruptions by irony.[26]

The commonly encountered notion of the Man in Black as a projection or alter ego of the dreamer, and their conversation as a psychologically faithful working-through of melancholy – seminally formulated by Bertrand H. Bronson in 1952 – further streamlined readings of the poem, even to the extent that the dreamer's experience (and the possibility of consolation) could be collapsed into that of his noble interlocutor, resulting in a neat resolution.[27] The tactics of consolation, and the extent to which it is satisfactorily achieved in the poem, concerned nearly all post-war critics of *BD* in one form or another. The view of *BD* as structurally coherent and artistically polished may be said to have reached its high-water mark in Muscatine's 1966 reading, remarked upon earlier, which noted the poem's stylistic homogeneity and thematic clarity not as indications of its success but, surprisingly, of its deficiency in comparison with Chaucer's later poetry. *BD* suffers, for Muscatine, from its being the 'most finished' as well as the most conventional of Chaucer's dream-visions, leaving, as it were, little of substance to talk about.[28] John Gardner, writing in 1969, carried this point further in remarking on the 'neatness' of *BD* as an arrangement of 'an extraordinary number of repetitions, or echoes: words, phrases, images, and dramatic situations', allowing scarce room for 'various interpretation'. Taking licence from this apparent simplicity, Gardner proceeds rather immodestly to offer 'what will prove the definitive explanation of Chaucer's method in this poem and elsewhere'.[29]

Needless to say, *BD*'s continual provocation of divergent interpretations disproves such claims of tidiness, and 'definitive explanations' have been met with well-deserved scepticism. Indeed, critical elucidation of *BD* was not as unruffled an enterprise around mid-century as these comments suggest. Even as Muscatine and Gardner were voicing these opinions in the 1960s, starkly different readings of the poem, challenging the premises of most existent criticism, were being advanced by D. W. Robertson, Jr, in solo publications and a study jointly authored with Bernard Huppé; a wave of 'Robertsonian' readings would follow. Writing in 1963, Robertson and Huppé (whose approach is treated in more detail in the section on Boethianism in chapter 2) essentially maintained that *BD* is not a vindication of courtly love, or even an encoding of the experience of John of Gaunt, but a tableau of Christian consolation in which the dreamer and the Man in Black, allegorically representing two sides of a single mourning self, achieve spiritual reintegration through the memory of White's immutable virtues. The poem thus cautions against the dangers of irrational desire for worldly things, and redirects the grieving subject towards superior spiritual rewards aligned with reason.[30] A work once admired for its fresh and realistic eschewing of allegorical didacticism as practised by its French sources turns out, in this reading, to be centrally driven by allegory.[31]

Regardless of one's position on Robertson's polarizing methodology, which insisted on an Augustinian value system for medieval poetry evinced through exegetical (often allegorical or iconographic) interpretation, it is difficult not to find such readings – at least initially – refreshing when taking a long view of the history of scholarship on *BD*. Cutting through the stagnancy of received lines of analysis regarding the narrator's obtuseness, the celebration of courtly love, psychological verisimilitude and the workings of elegy and consolation, Robertson's readings of *BD*, like his interventions in Chaucer studies more generally, were a maverick 'affront to everything postwar critics agreed on'.[32] Robertsonianism was a veritable game-changer in

BD criticism, focusing and re-charging subsequent scholarship; as the claims of the so-called exegetical school were advanced or, as the case may be, devastated, new vistas of interpretation emerged that ultimately generated a deeper historicism. Rather ironically, as Steven Justice has noticed, 'What Robertson rejected in mid-century scholarship is now generally rejected: assumptions about progress and invariant human nature; breathless appreciation of erotic sentiment combined with embarrassment in its bodily apparatus; confidence in the transparency and goodness of art; the cultivation of the sensitive soul.'[33] Even as post-Robertsonian readings polemically opposed the literary assumptions of exegetical critics, insisting on the poem's secularism, they tended to adopt a less placid view of *BD*'s courtly harmonies than did their predecessors and increasingly entertained the tools of 'theory' (of which exegetics, of course, is a forebear).

The shifts of emphasis in post-1970 criticism on *BD* developed not only from the ideological gulf opened by exegetical interpretations but also, paradoxically, by what formalist and exegetical programs had in common.[34] In particular, Robertson and Huppé substituted one critical uniformity for another in their assertion – analogous to Gardner's above – that the 'thoroughly coherent' nature of the poem can be revealed by means of 'one key' to interpretation, namely 'the clear and inevitable unfolding of the truths of Christian consolation'.[35] Dissatisfied by such normalizations, a new generation of critics adapted poststructuralist methodologies to identify what it perceived as the poem's fundamental lack of unity – an observation that in some ways resurrects early twentieth-century interpretations, with multivalence now framed as artistically admirable rather than as a sign of immaturity. The first sustained interpretation along these lines was that of Robert M. Jordan, in a 1974 article later incorporated into his 1987 book *Chaucer's Poetics and the Modern Reader*. Jordan characterized the compositional technique of *BD* as one of 'aggregation' of disparate elements, precluding any reading in terms of continuity. The history of debate over the narrator's motivations, by this interpretation, testifies to the essentially rhetorical, as opposed to dramatic, logic of characterization in the poem: thus, the narrator is not 'a unified consciousness, developing consistently through experience', and his function is 'multiple rather than unitary'.[36]

More explicitly theoretical readings soon followed, among the most trailblazing being Judith Ferster's 1980 article, revised for inclusion in her 1985 book *Chaucer on Interpretation*, which draws on phenomenological hermeneutics to explain the centrality of communication and self-consciousness regarding audience in *BD*.[37] Particularly in the 1970s and until the 1990s, *BD* came to be regarded as a study not in the closure that post-war critics discerned, but in inconclusiveness;[38] as a poem that defines itself against readers' structural expectations of literary patterns;[39] and as a deeply self-reflexive poem about poetry itself (particularly the inadequacies of courtly language).[40] No longer an unfolding of profundities of human experience or a vindication of Christian truth, *BD* became a mirror of the postmodern condition, thematizing disjunctiveness and miscommunication while revelling in 'irony at the expense of utterance itself'.[41] Multivalence and irresolution, of course, risk becoming monolithic 'keys' to the poem as much as the constructs they replace, as *BD* once again – thanks to its interpretative commodiousness – finds itself remade in the image of its readers' cultural and ideological investments. Formulated sensitively, however, the view that *BD* declines to 'provide definitive answers or reassurances to the issues about mutability, death and desire that it raises' appears to be confirmed by the variegated history of scholarship.[42]

So, to adapt the climactic question asked of the Man in Black by the dreamer, where are we now? Scholarship on *BD* has increased prolifically in the last fifteen years: at the time of writing, approximately seventy-five articles and book chapters substantially treating *BD* have been published since 2000. Although the poem's critical journey into the twenty-first century is in many ways eclectic, three dominant critical trends – attended to in individual sections in the next chapter – may be isolated. First, starting in the 1990s, there has been an accumulation of feminist and queer-studies approaches to *BD*, often shaped by psychoanalytic methodologies; these have been as subversive of received readings of the poem (as a touching memorialization of a noble lady) as was Robertson's exegetics in its own way. Second, previous generations' defences of the poem's thematic coherence and, later, its challenge to hegemonic artistic structures, have shifted towards arguments for its concerted intellectual seriousness. Scholars including Kathryn L. Lynch, Peter W. Travis and Peter Brown have productively exposed *BD*'s conversance not just with literary precedents and expectations, but with late fourteenth-century fields of learned discourse, especially philosophy and optics.[43] This brings *BD*, importantly, into line with Chaucer's 'mature' poetry in its aptitude for, and intervention in, the scholarly debates of his own day. Finally, the literary relationships informing *BD* – marginalized, after the spadework of early 'source study', for much of the poem's critical history – have been remobilized in the study of intertextual dynamics, which resists older models of subservience and apprenticeship in the practice of *imitatio*. Of particular interest here is the cultural dialogue between Englishness and Frenchness animated by the poem, a topic that has been richly studied by Ardis Butterfield, Deanne Williams and others on the level of discourse as well as style. Chaucer's first 'original' narrative poem, precisely because it is so freighted with priority in Chaucer's *oeuvre* and in English tradition, increasingly appears pivotal for our understanding of the ideological formation of the English vernacular, a phenomenon whose social, political and religious impact in late medieval England is of great moment in medieval studies more generally.[44]

With these coordinates of *BD*'s critical reception in view, we turn now to a digest of particular sub-threads in the modern scholarly history of the poem.

Date and Occasion

Surprisingly little can be stated with any certainty regarding the date of *BD*'s composition, its performative context and its intended first readership; scholarly opinions to this day vary widely on these issues. While such uncertainty surrounds virtually all of Chaucer's works, it is especially frustrating in the case of *BD*, given that this is the poem of Chaucer's most grounded in historical reality, so that it can (almost) be called 'topical'. There is no real doubt that *BD* memorializes the death of Blanche, Duchess of Lancaster, named 'White' in the poem, from plague in 1368, and that the dream-protagonist, the Man in Black, is a poetic correlative of Blanche's husband, John of Gaunt. The poem makes this much apparent through its riddling, but not really obscure, allusions to Lancaster ('long castel', 1318) and Richmond ('ryche hil', 1319), of which Gaunt was earl until 1372, in conjunction with 'walles white' (1318, another likely reference to Blanche). Chaucer himself refers to the poem as 'the Deeth of Blaunche the Duchesse' in the Prologue of the *Legend of Good Women* (F 418, G 406), a designation repeated by John Lydgate in the *Fall of Princes*.[45] This already gives a much more historically circumscribed picture of the poem's *raison d'être* than we have for Chaucer's other poetic productions – for which topical allusion is less of a certainty – and it would not seem difficult to square with Chaucer's life as a young courtier in the king's service and, in 1369, accompanying John of Gaunt on a military campaign in Picardy and several years later receiving a life annuity from him.

Beyond this, a great deal is unclear, both because of vagueness in the historical records and critical disagreement over how to correlate the pieces of the puzzle. Complicating matters is the fact that any elucidation of *BD*'s historical purpose is necessarily implicated in an interpretation of what the poem is about, and what it sought to accomplish for its first audience (if that, indeed, was Gaunt) – and on these matters there is little consensus. Although modern editors and annotators generally concur that *BD* was composed before 1372 (reasons for this date, with dissenting opinions, are reviewed below), its most recent editor, Kathryn L. Lynch, rightly observes that '[t]here is little, finally, that links the *Book of the Duchess* securely to any specific point in time, though the general historical reference of the poem is not in doubt'.[46] An index of the problem of dating is the fact that until forty years ago, scholars did not even have the year of Blanche's death right, and hence were working with the wrong *terminus a quo*;[47] the *terminus ad quem*, we shall see, turns out to be much more difficult to fix. In a 1974 article, the historian J. J. N. Palmer unearthed clinching evidence – a 1368 letter addressed to Queen Philippa, wife of Edward III, concerning John of Gaunt's prospective remarriage – that proves Blanche could not have died in September 1369, as had traditionally been supposed. Palmer traced the error in dating to a faulty chronicle tradition deriving from a single authority, and he collated evidence from previously overlooked chronicles that supply a September 1368 date for Blanche's death, consistent with the various historical circumstances at play.[48] This adjustment of date immediately affected problems connected to the poem, such as the belief (mistaken, as it turns out) that Gaunt could not have been at his wife's side when she died because he was on a military campaign in France in which Chaucer himself took part:[49] in fact, Gaunt was thus occupied in 1369, but not in 1368. No longer, too, could it be said that 'the news of [Blanche's] death did not ... reach John until he returned home from his campaign in November [1369], when he discovered his double loss, for his mother, Queen Philippa, had died a month before his wife';[50] nor could it be supposed that Gaunt did learn of his wife's death but mysteriously declined to return home for the funeral.[51]

That such concerns once did circulate underscores the larger question of Gaunt's formal relationship, if any, to *BD*. It has often been assumed that Gaunt in some way commissioned the poem and that Chaucer composed it under his patronage, but evidence for this is shaky at best, deriving ultimately from a notation made by the Tudor antiquary John Stow next to the title of *BD* in Oxford, Bodleian MS Fairfax 16, describing the poem as having been made at 'ye request of ye duke of Lancastar', and 'pitiously complaynynge the deathe of ye sayd dutchesse blanche'.[52] This remark, dating from two centuries after the poem's composition, may well be a romanticization of topical clues provided in the text, and Derek Pearsall rightly cautions against the assumption that 'every one of Chaucer's writings turns upon some event in his supposed patron's exciting life'.[53] On the other hand, the possibility, thoughtfully delineated by Lynn Staley, that Gaunt in fact crafted his 'public identity', in his divided position as uncle to Richard II and father to the man who would next claim the throne, through patronage of authors including Chaucer, provides ballast for a reading of Gaunt's involvement.[54] Did Gaunt request an English poem in commemoration of his late wife, perhaps for delivery at one of her annual memorial services?[55] Was Chaucer then rewarded for his efforts with the life annuity granted in 1374? Or did the young Chaucer himself hit upon the idea as a way of asserting his courtly presence and gaining favour with the most powerful man, after the king, in the royal household?[56] If so, did he do this soon after Blanche's death, in the immediacy of Gaunt's grief, or was the poem fashioned later as a subtle encouragement to Gaunt to move on and remarry?[57] Might it even have been written after Gaunt did remarry?[58] Is *BD* an accurate reflection of Gaunt's special devotion to his first of three wives,[59] or is it intended as damage control for a public image marred by the scandal of his affair (which began during his second marriage, although rumours may have placed it earlier) with Katherine Swynford?[60]

Such a range of possible scenarios arises because *BD*, if it was historically intended as an elegy for Blanche, for public performance or otherwise, is an exceedingly odd elegy.[61] This is only partly because of its hybrid form, which blends the memorializing rhetoric proper to elegy with a consolation for the widower, whose ordering and survival of grief form part of the poem's trajectory. It is also, as an elegy, rather tactlessly structured: before we are given any hint of its central subject, we must endure over two hundred lines of the narrator rambling evasively about his own problems (insomnia, a mysterious eight-year sickness), then, the mood lightening, laugh at his jokes surrounding the framework of the dream-vision proper (the heterodox prayer to Morpheus, the offer of the featherbed). Within the dream, wherever our critical sympathies lie, it is difficult to shake the feeling that neither the Man in Black (the Gaunt figure, let us remember) nor the dreamer comes off particularly well – the one is self-involved and frequently exasperated with his interlocutor, the other is bumbling in his attempts at counsel. As soon as White's death is openly aired – the central point of the elegy, after all – it seems that Chaucer cannot end the poem quickly enough: virtually nothing is said (since, it seems, nothing can be said); the dream ends; and the narrator brings the whole experience back to himself, reflecting on it as a novelty that will, through the composition of the poem, advance his poetic career. Even that eventuality, according to some critics, is sequestered in self-referential irony if we finally understand *BD* as a vindication of plain speech – the blunt truth of 'She ys ded!' cancelling out all the courtly circumlocutions that preceded it – which amounts to 'a poet's condemnation of poetry'.[62] Hard indeed it is to fathom how 'a self-defeating poem about the impossibility of writing poetry about love and death' – written in the yet-marginal language of English, no less – could either console John of Gaunt or distinguish a fledgling court poet.[63] Even if we suppose this to be a strategy of self-insulation, by which Chaucer negotiates his delicate social position vis-à-vis Gaunt through a creative elaboration of the humility topos,[64] the poem seems too diffuse to function chiefly as a public tribute, too idiosyncratic to be explicable entirely in terms of a historical (as opposed to imagined or self-projected) audience.[65] Its essential commitments seem to lie in the world of fiction, resulting in a poem that is only tangentially 'about' John of Gaunt, or even – as feminist critics contend, in arguments to be reviewed in the next chapter – Blanche of Lancaster.[66]

Many of the key critical insights that have come to frame the poem's interpretative context thus rest awkwardly with attempts at dating; where literary interpretations have been attempted in tandem with specificity regarding historical occasion, the results have often been curious, as we shall see. Given these difficulties, it is not surprising that a great many literary critics offhandedly supply the barest and most derivative of temporal anchors for the poem (e.g. 'around 1368', 'before 1372' or even – in a critical lag still seen occasionally – '1369' (assuming this to be the year of Blanche's death)) before rushing headlong into interpretative analysis. Passing assumptions that *BD* was produced 'for John of Gaunt', dedicated to him, or performed for him similarly surface undefended. The matter is not helped by the fact that whatever tantalizingly datable minutiae the poem does contain have not generated anything approaching critical consensus.

A case in point is the reference, at the end of the dream, to 'this kyng' riding homeward to the 'long castel with walles white, / Be Seynt Johan, on a ryche hil' (*BD* 1314, 1318–19). These lines, thick with identifying markers topically linked to Gaunt, raise the question of what is meant by 'this kyng'. According to some critics, this must allude to the fact that Gaunt, a duke in his own country, acquired the title of King of Castile and León beginning in 1371 (formally, in 1372) by virtue of his marriage to Constance of Castile. Thus *BD* could not have been written before 1371 or 1372, well after Blanche's death, unless the lines in question represent a later addition.[67] Although this explanation seems tidy, it is compromised by a number of mitigating factors. First, the logical connection of 'this kyng' both to the preceding and the following text seems tenuous. As Helen Phillips points out, it would be odd for Chaucer to juxtapose 'references to the titles of the second marriage with a pun on the first wife's name [i.e. 'walles white' linked with Lancaster in line 1318]'.[68] It is not, in fact, certain that 'this kyng' even refers to the Man in Black (hence Gaunt) as opposed to the emperor Octovyen (last seen at lines 368–86), whose presence implicitly resurfaces with the return of the hunting party at lines 1312–13. If Octovyen is the figure evoked by 'this kyng', the regal title is more fitting, especially if we grant a possible allusion to Edward III.[69]

Nonetheless, the looseness of Middle English syntax and terminology may well allow for an identification of 'this kyng' with the Man in Black, in his status as knight (and irrespective of Gaunt's royal title in 1371): as John Gardner points out, 'Chaucer calls Scipio a king in the *House of Fame*, and the *Gawain*-poet speaks of Bertilak as a king.'[70] This would be poetically appropriate, if not logically immaculate, if we grant the intensification of language and symbolic reference that characterizes this climactic section of the poem, with the dream on the precipice of dissolution (a dream that has not been beholden to strict logic thus far).[71] Thematically speaking, the figurative promotion of the Man in Black from knight to king might be related to his maturation in perspective over the course of his conversation with the dreamer, his new-found dominion marked by his return to the castle and the conclusion of the h(e)art-hunting (1313).[72] Another symbolic register potentially active here involves the rhetoric of chess, which the Man in Black earlier invoked (to the dreamer's confusion, it would seem) to figure his loss of White to Fortune (lines 652–741). Having lamented Fortune's chessboard capture of his 'fers' (654; in context, 'queen'), the knight, having regained his dignity, exits the poem as the king and master he truly is – reflecting, at the same time, the dreamer's completed understanding of the chess allegory.[73] In the final account, there is good reason to see, as two of *BD*'s editors have, 'this kyng' as an evocative figure not simply synonymous with Gaunt, Octovyen or anyone else; instead, Octovyen, the Man in Black, and the unnamed king all represent different aspects of the mourning Gaunt, summoned to point up different emphases in the course of the narrative.[74] An allusion to Gaunt's title of king of Castile and León, with the foothold in historical time that it affords, simply is not necessary for the passage to make sense, and it seems reductive by comparison with other interpretative contexts available to the reader.

Other allusions in *BD* to topical matters and aspects of chronology lead to similar stalemates. The reference to the castle on a 'ryche hil', a pun on Richmond, would appear to impose a *terminus ad quem* of 1372, since Gaunt surrendered his title as earl of Richmond in that year. However, the Richmond title (like that of Lancaster, lost upon Blanche's death) 'could be suitably recalled for the married lovers on a commemorative date'.[75] Similarly, the characterization of the Man in Black as '[o]f the age of foure and twenty yere' (455) only complicates attempts at dating, since it is certain that Gaunt was twenty-eight years old in 1368 when Blanche died. The discrepancy here is often supposed to derive, not from an oversight on Chaucer's part, but from a scribal error introduced early in the transmission of the archetype, with 'xxiiij' a corruption of 'xxviiij'. This assumes that Chaucer means to portray Gaunt a year after the event, necessarily a matter of speculation, and one which seems awkward considering that the Man in Black is described as having '[u]pon hys berd but lytel her' (456). It is possible, alternatively, that the younger age was intentionally supplied to increase pathos;[76] that total verisimilitude in such matters was not a medieval literary expectation;[77] that Chaucer strategically skewed the age in order to present the Man in Black as a fictional construct rather than a faithful mirror of Gaunt;[78] that the number twenty-four has symbolic properties intrinsic to the poem's thematic structure;[79] or (a recurring sub-theory) that twenty-four was Chaucer's age at the time of writing, not Gaunt's.[80]

The numerically precise eight-year sickness with which the poem teases us at lines 36–7 further perplexes chronology: if it is simply a rhetorical exaggeration (meaning something like 'a very long time') or, more plausibly, a creative displacement from a differently situated passage in Machaut's *Jugement dou roi de Behaigne*,[81] it lacks any value for *BD*'s dating. Alternative theories have included allusion to Chaucer's supposedly unhappy married life or, still more fancifully, to a hopeless love affair. Huppé and Robertson, in one of their more reviled proposals, detected an allegorical pun invoking Christ's cure of humanity's spiritual ills.[82] More suggestive is the possibility that the eight years registers the length of time between Blanche's death and the composition (or completion) of the poem, though this demands what seems a surprisingly late date (1376) for the poem – so late, in fact, that it would no longer enjoy clear priority as an inaugural narrative in Chaucer's canon (something that many critics believe the poem itself dramatizes). Edward I. Condren, in a series of heterodox studies to be considered further in the next section, argues that *BD* as we have it is a revision of an earlier, differently directed elegy, and that the eight-year sickness refers to the long-term difficulties of writing the poem, which Chaucer offered to Gaunt in 1377.

A hypothesis that has proven more generally attractive is that of Phillipa Hardman, who dates *BD* to 1374–6 on the basis of its appropriateness to the occasion of the completion of the double tomb commissioned by Gaunt for Blanche and himself. Adopting the iconography of memorial funerary art as a point of reference for the stylized poetic structure of *BD*, as well as its concerns with representation and image-making, Hardman concludes that as a 'verbal equivalent of the tomb erected by John of Gaunt as a memorial to Blanche and to his own grief', the poem would have made a fitting contribution to the annual memorial service coinciding with the dedication of the double tomb. This explanation has the virtue of justifying a date for the poem well after Blanche's death – making it a record of the event's lasting significance rather than its immediate impact – and illustrating why it may have been of moment in the mid-1370s. Regarding the eight-year sickness, Hardman suggests that it could plausibly situate the poem eight years after Blanche's death, in 1376 (after the tomb would have been completed), or that eight may be a dummy-number, substituting for another figure that could have fitted the metre and indicating that the poem may have been revised to suit an occasion later than its original completion.[83]

It is, of course, possible that *BD* does rhetorically appropriate funerary sculpture in its literary texture – a point that emerges compellingly from Hardman's study – without necessarily being anchored historically in any particular memorial service, fortuitous as the conjunction with the double tomb's completion would have been. Such iconography must have been well known to Chaucer, and would naturally have suggested itself in the composition of a poem whose alternative Chaucerian title is 'the Deeth of Blaunche the Duchesse' (*LGW* F 418). Arguments of an internally literary nature should make us cautious of a dating as late as 1374–6 (the earlier end of which surfaces, alternatively, in arguments connecting *BD* to the life annuity granted to Chaucer by Gaunt that year). In addition to the fact, remarked upon above, that *BD* has often struck its readers as a poem about Chaucer's birth as a poet – as a first poem, that is, celebratory of its own firstness, an effect that would be compromised by the later dating – it cannot be ignored that *BD* is wholly lacking in Italian influence: surprising if it postdates Chaucer's first diplomatic journey to Italy in 1372–3.[84] A poem such as the *House of Fame*, by contrast, seems almost giddy in its creative reinvention of the new-found Dante; Chaucer surely would not have submerged his exposure to Italian poetry, had he gained it by this point, into total invisibility in *BD*.

The most promising lead regarding the dating of *BD* is one that has commanded little critical interest, and is deserving of further investigation: the impact of *BD* on contemporary writers. The only Chaucerian who has given this issue serious attention is James Wimsatt, who argues that *BD* is not only steeped in French literary precedents, but that it reciprocally influenced French poetry composed by courtiers who, like Chaucer, frequented Edward III's court and esteemed the Machaut tradition. Wimsatt discerns early borrowings of *BD* in two poems by Oton de Granson, the *Complainte de Saint Valentin* and the *Complainte de l'an nouvel*; in the anonymous *Songe vert*; and in Jean Froissart's *Dit dou bleu chevalier*, leading him to claim that *BD* must have been composed quite soon after Blanche's death, by 1369–70, in order for it to serve as a model for these French poems.[85] The dating of these French poems is not, however, indisputable, and Wimsatt's reorientation of received lines of influence regarding many of these poems – where it has been acknowledged at all – has not always been accepted.[86] Nonetheless, those who have challenged Wimsatt's chronology have tended to engage only superficially with his detailed analysis of borrowing patterns, which issues from a profound immersion in the literary relationships among the numerous representatives of the *dit amoreux* tradition – work that remains foundational for any study of *BD* as 'Chaucer's most visibly "French" piece of writing'.[87] If Wimsatt is correct in suspecting that *BD* 'grew out of a French literary development and became an integral part of that development'[88] – a hypothesis that is corroborated by Ardis Butterfield's important recent study of Chaucer's participation in an interactive and collaborative model of authorship across rival vernaculars[89] – then further attention to contemporaneous French poems with which *BD* found itself in dialogue, and which it may in part have inspired, may facilitate progress in matters of dating that have been stymied by the poem's elusive historicity.

The *Book* that Wasn't: Shadows and Avatars

This section, a satellite of the previous one, considers how problems surrounding dating and occasion, together with inconsistencies perceived within the poem, have led many critics to highlight the protean aspects of *BD*'s composition. The stories told here – all scholarly hypotheses regarding the poem's stages of composition, some more colourful than others – if not always representative of mainstream critical opinion, are nonetheless important to the story of *BD*'s making. These narratives are presented as a corrective to standard accounts offered in critical editions and guides which tend to treat *BD* as a fixed artefact rather than a mobile imaginative construct, as it inevitably must have been for Chaucer as a young poet – and as it certainly was for those 'clerkes …[a]nd other poetes' (*BD* 53–4), from Lydgate to Spenser, who would later re-make Chaucer's *Book* as their own.

The notion of a shadow-text – forms of the poem that may once have existed, cancelled or repurposed – is not sheer literary-historical conjecture: Chaucer himself famously contemplates alternative lives for his texts, for instance at the end of *Troilus* when he confides that he would rather have written a different kind of poem, and may yet do so some day. This signature habit (which may well be a tongue-in-cheek promotional strategy for projects in the pipeline) combines with gaps and inconsistencies in authorial lists such as the *Retraction* to open Chaucer's corpus to future invention, as the early modern apocrypha illustrate. *BD* is a poem whose compositional history is obscured, paradoxically, by the generosity of Chaucer's own comments on it. Chaucer mentions the work in some form three times, more than any other single work:[90] in the *Legend of Good Women*, among the poems claimed by Alceste to serve the God of Love (F 418; G 406); in the Introduction to the *Man of Law's Tale*, where it is apparently identified as 'Ceys and Alcione', made 'in youthe' (II 57); and in the *Retraction*, which revokes the poem among other 'translacions and enditynges of worldly vanitees' (X 1085). Of these references, the Man of Law's is the most problematic: is 'Ceys and Alcione' to be understood as a synecdoche for *BD* as a whole? Or does it refer to a free-standing poem about the two classical figures – as early references by John Lydgate and John Bale imply – that perhaps was absorbed at one stage into the larger framework of *BD*?[91] If so, was this free-standing work substantially the same as the Ovidian story told at what is now *BD* 62–217, or might it have been more closely related to the *Heroides* template (abandoned women proving their faithfulness to the point of death) structuring the remainder of the Man of Law's list, which centres upon the *Legend of Good Women*?[92] Complicating matters is the fact that part of the section of *BD* devoted to the Ceys and Alcione story (lines 31–96) is missing from all three MSS and must be supplied from William Thynne's 1532 printed edition. The authenticity of the missing lines – which also contain mention of the curious eight-year sickness – has been questioned by N. F. Blake, who believes they were forged by Thynne himself, and that what Chaucer actually intended for this section was lost to posterity through an accident of transmission.[93] While the debate is unlikely to be resolved definitively, Helen Phillips, in her edition of *BD* and a related article, has defended the authenticity of these lines, and her position has been accepted by most critics.[94] Phillips plausibly suggests, moreover, that textual problems surrounding the Seys and Alcione episode might ultimately derive from Chaucer's own process of revision: 'If these were points where Chaucer had dovetailed a version or a section of an earlier work into the new narrative they might have been particularly subject to revision or cancellations which could have left their mark on the transmitted texts.'[95]

These and other considerations have led a number of critics to postulate alternative versions of *BD* at different points in what may have been its compositional history. In some cases, these owe a debt to interpretative puzzlement over *BD*'s tonally varied elements, as for example Furnivall's remark, in 1871, that the substance of the poem up to the encounter with the Man in Black may have been 'written for another ending, and then used for the piece of deathwork ordered by John of Gaunt'.[96] Others have felt, similarly, that the early parts of *BD* read as if 'Chaucer forgot that it was after all an elegy which he was writing'; it is only a short leap to suppose that, initially, he was not.[97] A different set of theories, drawing on the poem's historical references, attempts to account for its development in relation to its public uses. Howard Schless, opining that the reference to 'this kyng' must refer to Gaunt's royal title current from 1371–2, allows that the rest of the poem – that is, everything up to its conclusion – could in theory have been composed any time before this, closer to Blanche's death and before Gaunt's remarriage.[98] Phillipa Hardman also suggests that *BD* may have been formally adjusted over time, in this case to suit different occasions (i.e. different annual memorial services); thus, the eight-year sickness might at earlier points have been a two- or four-year sickness – a possibility, of course, that must be entertained in the absence of manuscript evidence, since the line in question survives only in Thynne's edition.[99]

The most elaborately developed of such theories is that of Edward Condren, who interprets *BD* not as figuring Gaunt through the Man in

Black, but as sustaining a dramatic confrontation between two aspects of the Chaucerian narrator himself – an approach not unrelated to Robertson and Huppé's reading of the two central characters as an allegorically 'split self'.[100] Specifically, in Condren's reading, the dream's disruption of linear time causes the Man in Black to represent the narrator in his emotional state immediately after Blanche's death, i.e. around 1368, while the narrator in the frame of the poem (outside of the dream) represents Chaucer at the time of writing, in 1377, eight years after the tragic event. Fastening on what he regards as the surprising fact that Chaucer did not produce an elegy for Queen Philippa, wife of Edward III, who died a year after Blanche, Condren posits that *BD* initially was intended as a tribute to Philippa, but that Chaucer abandoned this effort only to refashion the poem, completed eight years later, as an elegy for Blanche. The reason for this shift, Condren argues, is that in 1377, the year of Edward III's death, Gaunt's patronage would have been politically opportune and the savvy Chaucer would have sought ways to gain it. To effect this, Chaucer added the topical references near the end linking the poem to Gaunt, and assembled the rest of the poem as we know it, though he failed to adjust certain earlier allusions to Queen Philippa (such as the loss of the 'fers', or queen).[101]

BD thus exemplifies, in Condren's reading, Chaucer's maturation as a poet not only because the narrator, by the end, progresses past emotional numbness towards a sense of poetic purpose. It also does so because Chaucer critiques his own youthful poetic inefficacy in the person of the Man in Black – inefficacy that stalled the completion of the poem for eight years (!) – and celebrates his hard-won literary accomplishment in the newly directed poem now completed.[102] The poetic disequilibrium that has troubled many readers coalesces, in this approach, with shifts of political circumstance as well as Chaucer's own writerly development. The resulting lines of argument make for a good story but frequently strain credulity: 'Edward III may well have asked Chaucer to compose a poem to the queen's memory, not realizing that the poem would take eight years to complete, and even then have its direction altered so as to eulogize his daughter-in-law instead.'[103] It is tempting to remark that a poet who took eight years to write a public tribute, then reflected on his own previous inadequacy in a poem designed to supplant that tribute, would have been fortunate indeed to gain favour in the household of Gaunt, even as his future brother-in-law. More to the point, perhaps, is the tendency of *BD*'s subtleties – here, the failure of the Man in Black to constitute a perfect surrogate for Gaunt, and the mystery surrounding the eight-year sickness – to bleed into critical conjecture, to the extent that scholarly ingenuity vies with the creative energy of the poem itself.

Other historically based accounts of *BD*'s poetic evolution similarly engage what Stephanie Trigg has called the openness of Chaucer's writerly signature, 'countersigning' his poem with critical supplements – at times even conspiracy theories – that shape a new, virtual narrative.[104] Three examples will serve to illustrate this point, each in its way radically subversive of received wisdom regarding audience, motivation and chronology; each impelled, if towards unlikely ends, by genuine cruxes presented by the poem and its topicality. The first, a reading developed by Alfred L. Kellogg in 1972, triangulates Chaucer's composition of *BD* with his wife Philippa's duly rewarded service in Gaunt's household and her sister Katherine's status as Gaunt's mistress and future wife. Kellogg's approach reminds us of the importance Philippa bears to the relationship between Chaucer and Gaunt – it was she who had, it seems, the closer connection, serving Gaunt's second duchess Constance and receiving an annuity of her own from Gaunt before Chaucer did. This leads Kellogg to surmise, echoing an old rumour still entertained by some popular biographers but generally seen as fanciful, that Philippa at some point had an affair with Gaunt. *BD* then emerges as a poem shaped by class tensions and sexual intrigue, at once fraught with Chaucer's angst over Gaunt's intentions regarding his wife and driven by his sense of duty in writing an elegy for Blanche. Kellogg concludes, remarkably, by bringing this social awkwardness to bear on the interpretative difficulties of *BD* as an unconventional elegy: 'The situation', writes Kellogg, 'could hardly be considered conducive to the elegiac mood.'[105]

No great leap takes us from this analysis to the even more sensational reading, published in 2000, by Ian Robinson and Doreen M.

Thomas, which rejects the very premise of most studies of *BD* since the Renaissance: that it is an elegy produced for John of Gaunt on the occasion of his first wife's death.[106] The Man in Black's recollection of his courtship of White concerns not only Blanche, in this reading, but also Katherine Swynford, whose presence in the poem is submerged in verbal ambiguity and sexual euphemism. Such an approach, tendentious as its details often are, meshes with the recently proffered observation that Philippa Chaucer's connection to Gaunt's court and Gaunt's incipient affair with Katherine (both dating from the early 1370s) justifiably shape our reading of the poem and its historical moment.[107] To the question of why Chaucer would have written a poem detailing Gaunt's marriage to Blanche as well as his extramarital relations with Katherine, and indeed why Gaunt would have rewarded Chaucer with an annuity had he known of it, the authors respond that such an exposé may have attracted 'hush money'.[108] Once again, *BD* becomes the template for a narrative that is at odds with its apparent constitution, at least as most readers have understood it, and the resulting avatar of Chaucer's poem is empowered to say things to and about history that the medieval work itself, with its suggestive but finally unproductive purchase on contemporary events, cannot.

A final expression of this phenomenon, a 1995 article by Zacharias P. Thundy, follows the precedent of Condren and others in positing two distinct stages of *BD*'s composition. The first of these dates from the usual window of time after Blanche's death (Thundy does not commit himself to the earlier or later part of the years spanning 1369–74), while the second – in the most radical argument for dating yet presented – is placed in 1399. Like Robinson and Thomas, Thundy identifies supposed verbal allusions that shift traditional lines of interpretation, here resulting in a pro-Lancastrian poem directed to the new king Henry late in Chaucer's life. Neither genre nor recipient is left intact in this revisionist approach, which thoroughly de-romanticizes *BD* as a piece of political propaganda – 'a celebration of the homecoming of Henry IV' – legitimized by perceived inconsistencies explicable by the later political context (e.g. the puzzles of the chess allegory, read as 'Gaunt's failure in keeping Henry from exile').[109]

What these diverse readings have in common is a determination to fill in the poem's lacunae, to muscle its uncertain dating and occasion into alternative historical scenarios – in this last case, a partisan investment in the Lancastrian regime, anticipating the Henrician political appropriation of Chaucer's vernacular authority in the fifteenth century. Implicit justification is drawn from the probability of the poem's revision, implied by the Introduction of the *Man of Law's Tale*, as well as its momentousness as Chaucer's first original narrative. Of course, interpretative multiplicity and critical disagreement characterize the scholarly topography of all of Chaucer's significant poetry, but certain proprieties seem more than usually agitated in refractory readings like those just reviewed. As a poem that is at once historically anchored and free-floating, which seems to stage a convergence of 'public' and 'private' Chaucer, *BD* has empowered many readers to make its author into the Chaucer they would like him to be, properly situated in history. Whether a jealous husband and social climber, an investigative journalist, or a brilliant political strategist, the Chaucer who emerges from these readings satisfies the critical need for a more fleshed-out, socially material progenitor of English literary tradition. Here critical elucidation merges with creative reception, and Chaucer, like Seys in *BD*, becomes newly ambulatory as other voices speak through, and for, him.

Genres at Play

The interpretative pliancy of *BD* witnessed in the previous section raises the problem of genre: just how should one classify this half-comical, self-involved, imbalanced, courtly, dialogic poem about death? Can it be identified within a single, recognizable rubric of genre that would afford it a historically specific literary context? If it is, as generally (though, as the preceding readings illustrate, not universally) assumed, an elegy for Blanche of Lancaster, how do we account for what appear its breaches of elegiac propriety, its indirection, its dilation? These questions may be approached through a synoptic investigation of the various genres and generic registers brought to bear on *BD* over its critical history: these include, singly or in combination, elegy, *dit amoreux*, dream-vision, debate, pastoral and commentary, together with internal elements such as lyric and *chanson d'aventure*. The sheer abundance of these formal categories has suggested to some critics that *BD* – not wholly unlike Chaucer's much later virtuoso send-up of literary forms in the *Nun's Priest's Tale* – is a sceptically 'playful manipulation' of generic expectations, a 'serial presentation of genres' that 'explores the capacity of certain literary forms to convey information or express truth'.[110] With this possibility in view, the relative merits of these interpenetrating generic registers, understood as living (as opposed to immutable) frameworks of interpretation by which an author activates a set of expectations in the reader,[111] will now be considered.

I. *Elegy*

Chaucer was not the only court poet to memorialize Blanche. Jean Froissart, who was attached to the English royal court from 1361 until his fellow Hainaulter Queen Philippa died in 1369, laments in his *Joli buisson de jonece* (1373) that Blanche's death has filled him with 'melancolie', and that she died 'jone et jolie … Gaie lie frisce esbatans / Douce simple dumle samblance' (young and beautiful … Gay, pleasing, lively, full of joy, / Sweet, simple, of humble demeanour).[112] This poignant description occurs in the midst of a long, philosophically inflected and artistically introspective *dit* about love and authorship. Although the *Joli buisson* as a whole mirrors the generic complexity of *BD*, the simple pathos with which it frames the duchess's death (admittedly, in a list of other deceased nobles) contrasts sharply with the indirection of Chaucer's poem regarding its central subject. It seems significant, as Robertson observed and recent critics have reinforced, that Chaucer, rather than Froissart – whose ties to the royal court were even closer at this time – produced a formal elegy for Blanche, and that this elegy was executed in English rather than French.[113]

Chaucer lacked a solid model for elegy in English: the native genre of Anglo-Saxon elegy disappeared after the Norman Conquest, and continental traditions of funereal laments and monumental elegies had no counterpart in England. The term 'elegy' itself does not surface in English until 1514, according to the *Oxford English Dictionary*.[114]

Furthermore, Chaucer appears to have resisted what precedents for elegiac writing were supplied by French poetry. In an important article that positions *BD* within a 'familial tradition of elegiac poetry' including Froissart's commemoration of Blanche as well as Jehan de la Mote's *Regret Guillaume Comte de Hainault*, Butterfield underscores the peculiarity of *BD* as an oblique, non-public expression of the tradition. In this, she argues, *BD* intervenes critically in a discourse which is defined by its social function, one that assumes the power of poetic expression – particularly as crystallized in inset lyrics – to perform and articulate the experience of loss.[115] The obscurity of *BD*'s public occasion and dissemination only intensifies its failure internally to assert a public or political voice, or a mimetic relationship to real-life events.

To be sure, *BD* conveys the sorrowful impact of the beloved's death, but the evasion and circumlocution practised for the bulk of the poem, combined with the absence of explicit Christian consolation, for example regarding the soul's heavenly reward, result in a finished product that coheres unconventionally around the inadequacies of linguistic representation. By avoiding neat closure, and offering as the anticlimactic last words on White simply that her 'los' is 'routhe' (1310) – a pity – *BD* short-circuits the fulsome rhetoric of mourning expected of an elegy. Similarly, the poem suppresses, in the prefatory narrative of Alcione's grief over her drowned husband, 'what she sayede more in that swow' because '[h]yt were to longe for to dwelle' (215, 217): as if talk of sorrow is dispensable for the present purpose. At the same time as it avoids direct confrontation with the fact of death – such that, as late as lines 1140–2, the narrator can presume that Black's loss stems from a lovers' quarrel rather than mortality[116] – *BD* offers no easy way out of the impasse of grief. If it seems, on the one hand, to revivify White through poetic remembrance and to give her an aesthetic afterlife, on the other, it implicates us in a resistant 'pathology of grief', unbinding an emotion that cannot (and perhaps should not) be fully mastered. In Steve Ellis's view, the recollection of White's vitality explodes in a second loss, one that we as readers viscerally experience: 'The poem is thus a reenactment of Blanche's death: when it does come [i.e. in the Man in Black's final admission], it comes with extraordinary and shocking abruptness.'[117] For others, the very obduracy of grief, the poem's lack of commitment to an unambiguous 'moving on', limns a 'creative melancholy of loss, desire, and discontinuity' that becomes a 'potentially visionary' – as opposed to therapeutic – resource for poetic power.[118] Similarly, Fradenburg interrogates readings of *BD*, and elegy more generally, as 'fundamentally reparative', suggesting that in our quickness to assume that 'the grieving subject does not want to talk to us' – that mourning should reach closure, and life go on – we mask the deeper possibility that 'we do not want to talk to the grieving subject'.[119] In its studious avoidance of a public register, its attention to artistic development and its delicate yet finally untransmuted voicing of melancholy, *BD* is perhaps best understood as a critical examination, even a deconstruction, of elegy.

2. Dit Amoreux

BD's affiliation with the fashionable medieval genre of the *dit amoreux* – French love-narratives popularized by Machaut and further developed by Froissart, Deschamps and others – has been studied rewardingly, the most thorough investigation remaining Wimsatt's 1968 *Chaucer and the French Love Poets*. The multivalent *dit* tradition, which originally took shape in response to Guillaume de Lorris and Jean de Meun's *Roman de la rose*, crystallized around the following features identified by Wimsatt: a developed first-person narrator who functions as an observer rather than a direct participant in the central love-adventure; a concern with poetic virtuosity enacted through inset lyrics and complaints; a high degree of artistic self-consciousness regarding the construction of the *dit*; an imaginative cross-pollination with the genre of dream-vision; a deployment of allegorical personifications, developing towards realism; and a pronounced philosophical (specifically, Boethian) element yoked to the subject matter of erotic love. At least superficially, *BD* adheres to all of these features, making it the first discernible conduit through which French love-narrative and courtly style infiltrated English verse.[120]

The more subtle ways in which *BD* does *not* perfectly fit the template of the *dit amoreux* have led some critics to see it not only as 'a poem within a tradition' but also as 'a poem about that tradition'.[121] As was the case with *BD*'s relation to elegy, here too this first articulation of a genre in English appears to talk back to that genre: as R. Barton Palmer argues, *BD* effects 'a critical examination and at least partial rejection of the values inherent in love vision poetry'.[122] It does this in part by resisting the Machauldian amalgamation of 'Boethian idealism' with amatory values[123] – the *Remede de Fortune* (among the minor sources of *BD*), for example, consoles the Lover by conflating erotic satisfaction with the 'greatest good', and advancing the very un-Boethian idea that Fortune should be appropriated, rather than overcome, to achieve happiness. In *BD*, Chaucer adheres instead to 'the Boethian distinction between the limited goods of earthly existence and unlimited Goodness', for instance in reframing the Seys and Alcione story – inherited from Ovid's *Metamorphoses* by way of Machaut's *Dit de la fonteinne amoureuse* – as an illustration of 'the brittle mutability of earthly happiness'.[124] This more sober emphasis, of course, is appropriate to a poem about death, one in which the power of love cannot conquer Fortune. An alternative critical view holds that the *dit amoreux* tradition is in fact systematically ironic in its distortions of Boethian counsel, and that French love-narratives appearing to endorse sensual pleasure over reason actually parody the genre of philosophical vision that develops out of Boethius' *Consolation of Philosophy*. The *dits amoreux*, understood thus, are morally serious rather than frivolously 'courtly' works, and they contribute to received medieval wisdom regarding the folly and deception inherent in love. *BD*, then, is a 'straight' participant in this tradition, using the example of the distraught Man in Black to warn against the destructive excesses of passion – a line of argument that intersects with Robertson and Huppé's exegetical interpretation.[125]

However these issues are decided, what may be most compelling about Chaucer's engagement with the *dit amoreux* tradition is the creative vocabulary it offered in the shaping of narrative perspective and authorial voice. This is especially true if, here too, Chaucer challenged rather than simply replicated the subsumption of Machaut's narrators into the 'emotional extremism' of courtly discourse as a noble distinction.[126] A. C. Spearing, discussing the English afterlife of the *dits* in relation to the critical construct of 'autography', a kind of text 'written in the first person and (to a greater or lesser extent) about the first person, but [which is not] auto*bio*graphic because its purpose is not to narrate the life of an individual behind the text', discerns an enabling mode of subjectivity which, rather than imposing a strict division between narrator and author, facilitates the development of a poetic 'I' 'as a means of evoking proximality and experientiality'.[127] *BD* is among the first poems to instantiate autography as a new kind of writing in English; what Chaucer learned from the *dits* about authorial perspective, in Spearing's view, would shape the major poetic efforts, across genres, of Chaucer's entire career (Spearing focuses especially on *Troilus* and the *Canterbury Tales*). This broadening of a generic classification into a poetic procedure or sensibility relevant to a range of writings aptly reinforces Wimsatt's remark that Chaucer's later poetry does not extirpate the influence of French love-narrative but instead 'absorbs and subsumes it'.[128]

3. Dream-Vision

That *BD* is exceptionally sensitive to the imaginative potential of the dream conceit upon which it rests has long been recognized. Kittredge in 1915 admired the poem's accurate depiction of the 'irrationalities of dreamland', epitomized by the associative comings and goings of locales, characters and motivations from the start of the dream up to the meeting with the Man in Black.[129] Although it has variously been objected that irrationality as an aesthetic effect was not an available construct in medieval dream-visions, based as they were in intellectual models quite distinct from Freud's theory of the subconscious,[130] and that courtly allegories in general display an 'incoherence of plot sequence' that need not be related to the dreaming mind,[131] general opinion holds that Chaucer exploited the capacity of the dream as such – that the fundamental ambiguity of the poem on so many key issues emanates from the multivalence inherent to dreams (as lines 276–89 teasingly remind us). Indeed, *BD* exemplifies what Steven Kruger, in his influential study of late-antique and medieval discourse on dreams, describes as the 'doubleness and middleness' of many literary dreams – their fidelity to more than one category of interpretation (reliable or unreliable, revelatory or somatic), and their hermeneutic fertility as 'an important way of exploring "betweenness" itself'.[132]

A frequently cited example of Chaucer's attention to the oneiric medium is his intricate correlation of the waking and dreaming states, showing the residue of conscious concerns to be transmogrified within the theatre of sleep. It is, of course, not uncommon for medieval dream-visions to imply a connection between a narrator's waking mindset and the content of his dream: in *Pearl*, for example, the narrator's obsession with his lost pearl leads to a vision that elucidates the significance of the pearl through dramatic colloquy, and in William Langland's *Piers Plowman* the serial alternation between waking and dreaming 'remind[s] us of the waking world running alongside [the dream world] and interacting with it'.[133] In *BD*, however, the reconfiguration of quotidian details within the dream, the nuanced relationship between the narrator's bedtime reading and the dream content, and the renovation of subjectivity that some detect in the progression of the dream all position Chaucer's poem as uniquely invested in the dream form. The narrator's casual dismissal of chess as a leisure activity at lines 50–1, for example, is displaced in the dream to the Man in Black's deployment of a chess analogy for matters of life and death (lines 652–741). Similarly, the description of the book read by the narrator as treating of 'quenes lives, and of kinges, / And many other thinges smale' (58–9) hints both towards the Man in Black's chess analogy (which centres upon the loss of a queen) and the cryptic reference to 'this kyng' at the end of the poem (1314). In both cases, game is turned to earnest as what once seemed trivial, or at least someone else's concern, is brought home to the dreamer's own emotional actualization. Within the dream, a complementary intensification and transposition of imagery occurs, aligning the narrative energy of the inner frame with modern understandings of 'dream-work'. The pun on 'hert' – as simultaneously the hart pursued by the hunting party, the heart as locus of emotion, and the physical 'hurt' associated with the poem's hearts – is a supreme instance of dreams' play on linguistic polysemousness, with the first 'hert' leading, through an associative chain of narrative events, to the second and third.[134]

Even very different interpretations of *BD* tend to concur that the Man in Black is not simply a representation of a historical figure, the putative recipient of the poem, but also in some way a dream projection of an aspect of the narrator himself. Whether we understand this phenomenon allegorically (as in the Robertsonian view of a self split oneirically between its rational and sensual capacities) or psychologically (i.e. Black as the suicidal melancholy fought by the insomniac narrator; the dreamer as the functional, resilient inner man who still enjoys life), we cannot help but perceive the dream's complex purchase on subjectivity, its performance of a self-in-process. In staging 'a dialogue between the self and sorrow', and in offering the narrator a 'vision of himself as he should be', the dream holds therapeutic potential not primarily for the Man in Black, whom the dreamer resolves to 'make ... hool' (553), but for the broader matrix of experience that is the narrator and, at the end, the author.[135]

Authorship itself stands at the precipice of dream experience in *BD*, first when the book read in bed, featuring the story of Seys and Alcione, supplies a portal into the dream, via the prayer to Morpheus that it inspires. Then, in the dream, a bedroom with walls engraved with the stories of Troy and the *Roman de la rose* enfolds the dreamer as if within the pages of an illuminated manuscript anthology, leading to a dream that projects and inverts the slumber-inducing Ovidian narrative about a severed marriage. Capping this book/dream sequence is the transformation, upon waking, of the dream into a new book, for our own bedtime perusal. It is well recognized that the reciprocal association between books and dreams is a signature characteristic of all of Chaucer's dream-visions, and it is generally agreed that this programmatic bookishness is a Chaucerian innovation, one that signals the poet's particular investment in issues of literary authority and authorship in relation to dream form.[136] In Piero Boitani's assessment, the significance of this is great: beginning with *BD*, Chaucer 'consecrates [the book] as the key and integrating element of the dream experience ... and of the creative process itself'. Even before his exposure to the high claims for poetry advanced by Italian humanists, therefore, Chaucer's affirmation of the book as imaginative impetus shows 'literature becom[ing] one of the driving forces of European civilization'.[137]

It is possible, however, that Chaucer's originality in framing his dream with reading in a book has been somewhat overemphasized. As William Calin argues, Machaut's *dits* provide a precedent of sorts for such a tactic: in several of these narratives, dreams or visions are preceded by rehearsal of 'the author's own lyrical or narrative creations' (lays, overheard complaints, or references to Machaut's previous works). These 'self-referential autotexts', rather than the productions of external authorities such as the clerks and poets to which Chaucer's narrator refers at *BD* 53–4, supply for Machaut the substructure of the imaginative content which in turn glosses or situates them.[138] The difference, of course, is significant. Rather than celebrating his own poetic virtuosity, as Machaut does with transparent sleight-of-hand, Chaucer invokes other writers' texts as inspiration for his dreams. But of course, in doing so, Chaucer represents these seemingly inviolable masterbooks in his own (English) words, with his own selective emphases, and thus obliquely enunciates them as his own. An even more concrete precedent for Chaucer's book-dream sequences has recently been identified, by Stephanie A. Viereck Gibbs Kamath, in Guillaume de Deguileville's *Le Pèlerinage de la vie humaine* (mid-fourteenth century), from which Chaucer's *An ABC* also derives. In the three recensions of this spiritual allegory, which like the *dits amoreux* creatively issues from the *Roman de la rose*, Deguileville in different ways connects his dream with the reading of a book, most specifically in the first recension, when the narrator's study of the *Rose* itself 'plus m'esmut a ce songier' (moved me most to have the dream).[139]

As a dream-vision, *BD* participates in a venerable tradition of first-person writing featuring an adventure with personal, social or cosmic implications; an authoritative guide or guides; the trajectory of a lesson learned; and a closing reintegration with historical reality. Here as elsewhere, *BD* defies many expectations of the genre. As a poem of mourning, *BD* could well have followed the path of *Pearl* as an otherworld vision, in which the deceased is encountered in glory and a lesson in eschatology is offered; instead, Chaucer's dream features only

White's surviving mourner, the sole revival that takes place is in the imperfect arena of the imagination, and revelation is absent.[140] Instead of defining a voice of authority, the dream seems to be compromised by somatic pressures, governed by a fallible dreamer whose own waking concerns, as we have seen, colour the dreamed encounter. 'Through his dubious presentation of the dreamer', states Colleen Donnelly, 'Chaucer has deliberately muddled the potential significance of the vision to follow, dashing any assumptions about deriving a definitive answer to the narrator's waking preoccupations.'[141] *BD*'s lack of true closure – its ambiguation of any clear lesson learned – leaves us with a sense of 'incompleteness' that contrasts with the 'closed experience of revelation' expected of traditionally enlightening visions.[142] While on the one hand this avoidance of neat answers would seem to make *BD* 'true to life', on the other it reflects historically specific conditions that align *BD*, as Kathryn Lynch has compellingly argued, with a sceptical epistemology connected to late medieval nominalism. *BD* may be understood as a creative instance of a larger philosophical trend that stressed particulars over universals, and thus rejected the validity of abstract principles in favour of plural and partial ways of knowing. If 'the theme of frustrated knowledge' is structurally integral to *BD*, and the 'problems and limitations in interpretation' part of its thematic focus, then its apparent irregularities as a dream-vision are neither accidental nor damaging, but an index of the poem's seriousness as an intervention, from an amatory angle, in the subgenre of the 'philosophical vision'.[143]

4. Other Generic Registers: Debate, Pastoral, Chanson d'Aventure, Lyric, Commentary

If elegy, *dit amoreux*, and dream-vision variously define what we may call the macro-genre of *BD*, diverse micro-genres circulate within it, likewise contributing to its formal disposition. One of the most salient of these micro-genres is debate. A reader who approaches *BD* expecting a poem of gentle commemoration and consolation may well be surprised by the degree of friction that emerges in the dialogue between the dreamer and the Man in Black, who are frequently at cross-purposes despite the dreamer's polite efforts.[144] Some critics have seen the dynamic between the two characters as Socratic in complexion, with the dreamer probing the Man in Black through 'inductive questioning' towards restorative memory and self-knowledge.[145] Others have discerned a growing emotional connection leading towards 'true dialogue'.[146] More frequently, critics are struck by the awkwardness and failures of communication between the two interlocutors, interpreting this as a reflection of social inequality, distinct sensibilities, and even competing linguistic registers (this last topic is reserved for the section on 'Interlingualism' in the next chapter). As the dreamer tries but continually fails to understand the significance of Black's sorrow, his conversational good will is rebuffed many times over, suggesting a series of *faux pas*: the nobleman thrice scolds the dreamer, 'Thou wost ful lytel what thou menest' (743; cf. 1137, 1305) – in short, you don't know what you're talking about – and he recurrently fastens on the dreamer's well-intentioned words to show how far they fall short (1045, 1052, 1115, and – tragically – 1299). Because the dream-dialogue involves a contestation of words and wills, a struggle over understanding and meaning, it is appropriate to look to traditions of literary debate as an influence on this section of the poem.

Several narrative models of debate were available to Chaucer as he shaped the diverging viewpoints of his central characters. One literary-historical context for debate is outlined by Raymond P. Tripp, Jr, who classifies *BD* among other English 'big debates', such as the Old English *Solomon and Saturn*, that possess a 'dialectical structure' centred upon pressing existential issues that are not easily resolved. By attributing different worldviews to his two interlocutors, Chaucer stages a debate between 'radical alternatives to life' more profound than 'psychological mechanisms of consolation'.[147] The *Roman de la rose* supplies a different model: the debate between Raison and Amant, introduced in Guillaume de Lorris's section and elaborated in Jean de Meun's, which is more akin to a 'vertical debate', in contrast to what Tripp describes, since one participant possesses superior knowledge (even if contrasting worldviews are at stake). In F. N. M. Diekstra's opinion, the occasionally comic divergences between the dreamer's and Man in Black's assertions may be inspired by 'the absurdities between the Lover and Reason' in the *Rose*, although neither Chaucerian figure is as flatly characterized as his predecessor.[148]

Of greatest significance is a model of debate supplied by a direct literary source for several passages of *BD*: Machaut's *Jugement dou roy de Behaingne*. In this *dit*, the narrator overhears a lady and a knight debate which of them has suffered the greater loss in love: the one, through her beloved's death, or the other, through his lady's inconstancy (the matter is decided, by the king, in the knight's favour). Reworking this French source in *BD*, Chaucer combines attributes of – and specific lines spoken by – both characters in the Man in Black; at the same time, he displaces the debate structure onto the colloquy between the dreamer and the grieving knight. The intertext of the *Behaingne* is cued, in effect, by the dreamer's uncomprehending query, at lines 1141–2, concerning whether the knight's sorrow results from his lady's severance of their relationship (as it did for Machaut's knight), when the truth is that death is the culprit. What in the *Behaingne* was formal debate, presented for adjudication as a *demande d'amour*, in *BD* becomes dialogue, and Chaucer's narrator emerges as 'more a comforter than a dialectician'.[149] Important differences too surround the social inequality that shapes the conversation in *BD*; in the semantics of debate form, what ensues is more 'vertical' than 'horizontal' (in contrast to the situation in *Behaingne*).[150] In all, however, the capacity of the literary debate to give voice to alternative perspectives and to frame a predicament of interpretation – something Chaucer will develop further in the *Parliament of Foules* and, more broadly, the *Canterbury Tales* – sharpens *BD* as a poem that offers no easy answers.

The tradition of pastoral, related to the medieval French genre of *pastourelle* (typically involving a contest of wills between a knight and a shepherdess), supplies another register of debate, one with particular relevance to the *dit amoreux* genre. As Butterfield has demonstrated, *pastourelles* and *dits* share a number of formal and thematic characteristics, often featuring scenarios of debate, encounter and complaint placed in an idealized natural setting, as well as a fascination with social levelling and inversion, in which 'a clash between the courtly and the natural ... releases (at least fictively) all kinds of usually repressed social tension'.[151] Reading *BD* in relation to pastoral tradition, Butterfield argues that the poem's backdrop of morbidity, particularly as connected in a fourteenth-century context to plague (the cause of Blanche's death), establishes it as a 'counter-pastoral', that is, a work that draws on, and critically resituates, pastoral motifs inherent to *dit* tradition in order to grapple with historically pressing concerns. A related analysis, by Nicolette Zeeman, considers *BD*'s natural setting and its focus on song and dialogue in relation to the literary framework of the *chanson d'aventure*. This originally lyric form, which evolved into 'a narrative unit inserted into longer narratives' (including *pastourelle*), typically frames an encounter experienced by a poet-speaker in a rural setting, involving a dialogue that forms the substance of the larger poem. Beginning with the narrator's attempt to follow the hunting party on its adventure, *BD* adheres to this model: 'it involves an intensely emotional encounter in a landscape with a person who sings a song; this song becomes in a very real sense the "text" of the poem, to which it repeatedly returns.'[152] This device of embedment finally serves, for Zeeman, as a mechanism of authorial *inventio* and vernacular literary theory.

BD's central crux, both for the history of criticism and, it seems, for the dreamer himself, is embodied in the Man in Black's first lyric utterance, presented simultaneously as a spectacle and, in the perplexing terms in which it is introduced, an enigma: 'He made of rym ten vers or twelve, / Of a compleynte to hymselve / ... a lay, a maner song, / Withoute noote, withoute song' (463–4, 471–2). Although this lyric does employ some degree of poetic embellishment, it makes clear enough that the knight's lady is dead (critics who interpret it otherwise tend to ignore the apostrophe to death that makes the point abundantly clear[153]). Nonetheless, this lyric is inadequate to convey the full scope of the knight's meaning, which appears to be lost on the dreamer – although there has been much disagreement over how much he does understand and perhaps tactically suppresses – and the lengthy remainder of the poem, as Zeeman's remark above registers, takes shape to elucidate it. Lyrical set-pieces, often with intricate rhyme schemes and musical annotation, were characteristically intercalated into the long French love-narratives that form such an important literary context for

BD. The Man in Black's first lyric, however, lacks several of the distinct-ive features that render lyrical interludes so pivotal in the *dits*: instead of being musical, it is 'withoute song'; instead of being performative, it is clandestine; instead of giving scope to consolation, it wallows in pain.[154] For all the lyric's clarity, it is presented as inarticulate, lead-ing some to conclude that *BD* constitutes a rejection of lyric, which is 'devoid of temporal context', in favour of narrative.[155] In more nuanced terms, *BD* appropriates lyric towards narrative ends, using it to propel the narrative forward rather than, as occurs in the French poems, to 'reflect the psychological history of the narrator and/or some authority figure' and to provide 'an ostentatious display of technical virtuosity'.[156]

It may be more constructive, rather than assuming a clear dividing line between lyric and narrative, to view these as mutually reinforcing registers, with a suppleness that need not be constricted to precise formal criteria. It has been argued, for example, that the Man in Black's two inset lyrics effectively pause the narrative to facilitate a 'revelation and distillation of feeling', crystallizing his progress from solipsistic grief to constructive memory. In doing so, they at once stall, amplify and advance the poem's action.[157] If we broaden our definition of lyric to encompass complaint more generally (a register not necessarily marked by a special verse form, but lyrical in perspective), we can discern in *BD* a narrative consisting of 'several layers of complaint', including the narrator's opening lament over his melancholy state, Alcione's grief over Seys, and the Man in Black's complaints on death and Fortune.[158] It is even possible to see *BD* as primarily lyric in character: as Wimsatt has argued, the narrative consists of 'a succession of more or less lyric pas-sages' – in addition to the complaints listed above, this includes much of Black's recollection of White and their courtship. In this view, *BD* is thus 'primarily an elegiac meditation on human loss rather than a story of the narrator's experience'; the narrative simply provides an 'explicit dramatic setting for the essentially lyric passages'.[159]

We may finally consider how *BD* may be understood not only as a sustained act of exegesis on the Man in Black's first lyric – really, of course, Chaucer's own invention – but also as 'an extended gloss on Ovid'.[160] Drawing attention to the material layout of medieval commentary on the classical *auctores*, Martin Irvine proposes that *BD* uses the creative licence afforded by dream-vision to fashion a commentary of sorts on the Ovidian narrative of Seys and Alcione, the structuring presence of which we are reminded when the narrator awakens at the end with book still in hand. Much as the commentaries produced by medieval schoolmen functioned as 'supplementary text(s)' whose textuality encrusts and reframes ancient sources in the margins of manuscripts, *BD* may be said to stage an interpretative dialogue with the Ovidian episode at its conceptual core.[161] As an intellective dilation upon an ancient specimen, then, Chaucer's dream not only draws meaning from Ovid's story, but adds meaning to it. The dream becomes a vernacular opportunity to distil significance from an ancient core text.

The variegated scholarly history of *BD*, its relevance to apprehensions of Chaucer's canon and critical narratives regarding Chaucerian authorship, and its capacious accommodation of disparate genres all confirm that this early work, despite its occasional roughness, is far from simple. Indeed, the dynamism of critical responses prompted by *BD* associates it with what Umberto Eco, discussing the semiotics of reading, designated an 'open work': that is, a text '*in movement* … characterized by the invitation to *make the work* together with the author', causing it to be 'susceptible to a whole range of integrations'.[162] The next chapter considers several specific categories of interpretative movement to which *BD* has given rise in modern criticism, offering further evidence of its openness, as a work preoccupied with its own textuality, to readerly intervention and completion.

READING THE *BOOK* (II)

Themes, Problems, Interpretations

Now that the general landscape of critical opinion on *BD* over time has been established and its generic affiliations mapped, we may turn to key interpretative issues that emerge in scholarship on the poem as viewed synchronically. All of the 'nodes' of interpretative discussion presented here – communication, consolation and Boethianism, gender, sickness and health, and interlingualism – represent defining issues in the history of scholarship on the poem, and continue to resonate with critics to this day. While other thematic focal points could no doubt be isolated, these have been selected as the most richly productive, and often controversial, areas of scholarly discourse for a modern reader seeking an entrée to the vast critical history of *BD*. In practice, of course, these interpretative issues rarely appear in isolation: a great many fruitful analyses of *BD* incorporate one or more of these critical areas in the course of their readings. Finally, these coordinates of interpretation prepare us for the more focused appraisal of *BD*'s textuality and reception that follows in the remaining chapters. By recognizing the primary critical elements of the poem as materialized for a twenty-first-century audience, and by considering how unsettled they remain, we are in a position to appreciate – as the previous chapter illustrated from a diachronic perspective – how 'constructed' our experience of *BD* is. Only once we confront the poem's critical overdetermination for readers today can we re-enter it from the perspective of its own creative moment, as the next chapter will attempt to do, to inquire into how such a diverse range of interpretative possibilities issues from the poem's own performance of its textuality.

(Mis)communication: Speaking and Listening

It should not surprise us that a poem of such generic multivalence, one that critically scrutinizes the limitations of the genres it employs, fore-grounds problems of communication as a theme in its own right.[1] These problems in *BD* are pervasive and all-encompassing: it has been justly observed that the whole of the poem 'exist[s] simply in order to prevent [the] direct statement [that White is dead] from having been made earlier'.[2] Deferral and concealment constitute the poem's chief rhetorical strategies, and the poetry of *BD* is animated entirely by 'the need for avoidance of literal truth'.[3] Even the lengthy opening sequence, before the dream begins, reads as a chatty divagation from the real subject awaiting treatment: the dream itself, or perhaps the 'absent narrative' about the one physician who can heal the narrator, a story he does not wish to tell.[4] In these respects, *BD* communicates poetically in the very act of thwarting communication. Furthermore, it is everywhere alive to the ways in which both oral communication (conversation) and written text convey meaning, and all too often fall short. It is unusually conscious of its audience(s), with the narrator conversationally address-ing the imagined reader as early as line 16 ('And wel ye woot') and surmising onlookers' curiosity regarding his sleepless state and 'what me is' at lines 30–1.[5] Implicating us immediately in difficulties of inter-pretation, then showing these difficulties to redouble upon the dreamer in his encounter with the Man in Black, *BD* is a poem about trying to understand. It takes as its central subject – death – something that is finally beyond the limits of human comprehension, yet is mediated and countered, as the genre of elegy epitomizes, by the recuperative efforts of language.

When the Man in Black finally admits, in plain English, that 'She ys ded!' (1309), both dream and poem quickly disintegrate, as if nothing more can be said. True, unimpeded communication at last occurs between dreamer and knight, whose disproportionate speeches and testy exchanges up to this point are supplanted by the perfect symmetry of their final, shared couplet:

> 'She ys ded!' 'Nay!' 'Yis, be my trouthe!'
> 'Is that youre los? Be God, hyt ys routhe!' (1309–10)

The dreamer, who at the beginning of the poem had 'felynge in nothyng' (11), now feels, and the seeming antinomy of 'Nay'/'Yis' suggests a wholeness of experience that is rounded by the reciprocity of 'trouthe' and 'routhe'.[6] Especially in the manuscript presentation of these lines, lacking modern punctuation and inverted commas, the two men seem to speak the unthinkable in a single voice. This final exchange has been understood as unpoetic and anti-rhetorical, a harsh corrective to the figurative devices and loquacious circumlocution that characterize the Man in Black's attempts to explain White's loss up to this point, and a signal of the ultimate inefficacy of poetic speech.[7] Critical opinion has been more or less evenly divided between regarding this final exchange as inadequate or as generally appropriate. Furnivall, as noted earlier, declared this climactic sequence caneworthy. A. J. Minnis, also uncomfortable with these lines, finds them bathetic, and the effect of the rhyme 'inappropriately pat and curt'.[8] To D. W. Robertson, Jr, however, the dreamer's words to the knight strike the right note in their understatement, positioning a voice of reason against lugubrious despair.[9] Others have discerned a poignant simplicity and a human honesty in the dreamer's hushed reaction.[10] In any event, communication and understanding do occur here, and the register of the poem shifts irrevocably. This communicative revelation must be considered in the light of the initial breach of communication that induced the searching dialogue that constitutes the bulk of the poem: namely, the Man in Black's first lyric, overheard by the dreamer.

As noted in the previous chapter's discussion of genre, the apparent enigma of this first lyric – or at least its imperfection as a communicative act – is glossed and dilated upon for the entirety of the remaining narrative. Yet, despite its formative significance for the plot, it is never actually mentioned again. Instead, it is replaced in structural importance by the Man in Black's informal refrain, 'Thou wost ful lytel what thou menest; / I have lost more than thow wenest' (743–4). This the Man in Black self-quotes at the point of revealing White's death at the end; he refers to it as the text 'seyde here-beforn' whose meaning will now be made clear (1304). Significantly, this refrain, even as it rests on the idea of imperfect understanding, is structured by a communicative relation-ship between 'I' and 'thou'. It is thus dialogic, and as such it supplies a foundation for the genuine, shared communication that occurs in the concatenating utterances of lines 1309–10.

By contrast, the Man in Black's first lyric is a one-sided conversa-tion between him and death; accusing rather than truly interrogating, it expects no answer to the question of why death took his 'lady bryght' instead of him (477, 481–3). Part of the reason for the lyric's subsequent invisibility in the narrative – and for what many critics argue is the nar-rator's failure fully to understand it – is that it does not truly *communi-cate*. In a work that constructs genuine communication as dialogic and reciprocal, as 'an open and unfinished interaction between speaker and listener', the Man in Black's lyric is 'a poem without an audience' in the same self-cancelling way that it is a 'song / ... withoute song' (471–2).[11] So solipsistic is the knight's discourse at this point that he does not see or hear the dreamer standing 'ryght at his fet' and greeting him at lines 502–3; instead of conversing, he 'argued with his owne thoght, / And in hys wyt disputed faste / Why and how hys lyf myght laste' (504–6). Only when this self-argumentation is turned outwards, into the exchange with the dreamer, can it grow towards mutually enriching dialogue. Ultimately, the Man in Black's solitary and totalizing identifica-tion with sorrow, which evacuates human community – 'y am sorwe, and sorwe ys y' (597) – is replaced by an experience of sorrow shared intimately by knight and dreamer, in the ennobling avowal of 'routhe' (1310). On the level of language, a motion from 'I' to 'our' over the course of the poem culminates in a delicate equilibrium of emotional states, as the 'Allas' of the knight's early harangue against death ('Allas, deth, what ayleth the' (481)) grows by the end into a double 'allas', first uttered by the knight ('God wot, allas! Ryght that was she!') and, immediately after, the dreamer ('Allas, sir, how?') (1307–8).[12]

Various theories have been advanced to account for the seeming inconsistency by which the dreamer appears ignorant of the fact of White's death, despite overhearing the Man in Black's early song, until the explicit revelation at the end. Most of these interpretations register on some level that *BD*, in highlighting problems of communication, addresses interpretation as a serious theme in its own right. Peter W. Travis, advancing a nuanced deconstructive approach to *BD*, asserts that *BD* animates a poetics of 'aporia', in which central linguistic signs – 'I', 'fers' and 'White' – are thoroughly destabilized. The dreamer's supposed confusion, consequently, epitomizes the '*méconnaissance*' deliberately constituting 'the heart of the elegy's strategies of consolation', which amount to an enactment of the impossibility of 'adequately represent-ing an absent or lost *object*' (Travis's emphasis).[13] As the first and most striking instantiation of that *aporia* brought to bear on the larger project of linguistic representation, the Man in Black's lyric on the loss of his lady to death has served, in critical tradition, mainly to characterize the narrator. The question of whether the eavesdropping narrator, who emphasizes his accuracy in recording the song (473–4), is dim-witted or suave in his handling of the situation has long divided critics.

For some readers, the dreamer's failure to understand the knight's song, and his shock at the death of White when later disclosed, are to be taken at face value as evidence of a 'nonpareil dullwittedness'; rooted in insomnia and abetted by the vagaries of dreaming, this is manifested in his 'vexing inability to make sense of the world around him'.[14] Slightly different is the possibility that the dreamer understands the song only partially, grasping the fact but not the nature of the Man in Black's grief,[15] or perhaps construing that grief through the distort-ing lens of his own humbler experience.[16] Thus the dreamer seeks 'more knowynge of hys thought' through conversation (538). A distinct alternative to these readings, propounded by several critics beginning with W. H. French in 1957, holds that the dreamer justly assumes that there *is* no meaning in the knight's song because it would strike any bystander as a formulaic, as opposed to personal, lyric utterance.[17]

The poem as a whole, in this view, turns the tables on our (and the dreamer's) literary expectations. Far from being 'extremely stupid' for not comprehending the knight's song as concerning the death of his lady,[18] the dreamer emerges as rather too smart for his own good: like any devotee of love poetry in the Machauldian school, according to Steven Davis, his habitually sophisticated reaction is to assume (and admire) the artificial nature of the song, rather than to consider its possible authenticity.[19] French went so far in his emphasis on ceremony, in fact, as to venture that in medieval narrative, 'a person who heard a man under forty reciting doleful verse took it as an almost inevitable pastime of the fashionable younger set'.[20]

It is difficult fully to square this view – that the dreamer interprets the knight's lyric as merely conventional, and therefore without personal meaning – with the congruence between the song's sorrowful content and the knight's melancholic appearance. The song is framed, first, by the dreamer's wonder over how any creature could suffer such sorrow while remaining alive (467–9) and, second, by his account of the knight's sickly disposition and 'sorwful hert' after rendering his complaint (488). While it is true that the alignment of speech and countenance was in ancient and medieval rhetorical theory a practical recommendation (see *CT* V 103–4 for an expression of this), this in no way precludes genuinely felt emotion, and at the beginning of *Troilus and Criseyde* Chaucer draws from the conjunction of 'a sorwful tale' and 'a sory chere' a position of humane authority (1.14). Following this line of thought, critics who hold that the dreamer does fully perceive the knight's problem from the beginning regard him either as a strategic consoler who intentionally withholds his understanding to effect a 'talking cure', or as a model of diplomacy, quick to conceal ill-gotten knowledge from a social superior. The former position, advanced seminally by Kittredge and reinforced importantly by Bronson, figures commonly in readings of the narrator as 'consistent, skillful, and mature'.[21] The latter emphasizes the awkward situation that must be negotiated by the dreamer, whose eavesdropping could be construed as impertinent and who is bound by a decorum of courtesy to respect the 'privacy of grief'.[22] Notably, such discretion has a precedent in Machaut's *Dit de la fonteinne amoureuse*, in which the eavesdropping dreamer elicits a direct account of the Duke's predicament from him before delicately revealing his earlier, secret transcript of the nobleman's complaint.[23]

All these readings, of course, assume an *a priori* consistency for the narrator, such that his experience at one point of the poem can be invoked as a measure of his reactions at another. Narrative uniformity of this sort, however, is not a given in medieval poetry, and it is possible to see the narrator's different reactions and levels of knowledge at various points in the poem as local effects with a rhetorical – rather than strictly logical – function: as our lens on the narrative, the narrator may well be moved at one moment by the Man in Black's emotional song and held in suspense at another by his searching recollections.[24] Whatever our stance on the narrator's degree of knowledge, however, the coherence of *BD* as a communicative act cannot be detached from its status as a consolation, a verbal reckoning and mediation of loss. The extent to which this conceptual rubric bears upon the narrator's efforts and the poem as a whole will be considered next.

Consolation and Boethianism

How and whether consolation is effected in *BD* is a question both of historical consequence – if the poem was directed towards Gaunt, surely consolation was appropriate – and of literary-interpretative priority. On this topic there has been little agreement.[25] Debate has centred upon, first, whether consolation of some sort is achieved within the poem or only left implicit for the audience; and second, whether the manner of consolation is Christian, Boethian or purely aesthetic. If the Man in Black is brought to a fullness of understanding, even a level of acceptance, by his conversation with the dreamer (in which the Man in Black himself has done most of the talking), this is not clearly disclosed in the poem. We know only that he finally acknowledges that his lady is dead, without poetic figments or the denials wrought by self-loathing. We know furthermore that, whether he is to be identified or merely associated with the 'kyng' riding home to the castle, movement in space rather than melancholic paralysis issues from his admission.

Does this amount to consolation, marked by emotional release, or does the dominant mood of the poem remain one of grief? The political and dynastic register of the allusions to Lancaster and Richmond seem to indicate a larger context into which the Man in Black's private experience may now be transfigured towards socially generative ends, as does the narrator's own redirection of the mournful story towards new poetic possibilities.

Yet the Man in Black's own experience seems to be one of redoubled loss, the painful outcry 'She ys ded!' following hard upon the tender reanimation of the couple's life together, brought up even to the wished-for happy ending ('And thus we lyved ful many a yere / So wel I kan nat telle how' (1296–7)). In bemoaning the fact that 'She ys ded!', the Man in Black is not yet able to say, echoing the revenant Seys, that she is 'but ded' (204). The reality of her death still appears all-consuming. In many ways, the poem dwells on the 'pathology of grief', refusing closure, as its alternative authorial title 'the Deeth of Blaunche the Duchesse' indicates (*LGW* F 418).[26] However, even if the Man in Black does not, in Freudian terms, move from self-destructive melancholia towards remedial mourning, the experience of consolation may yet be present. In the view of some critics, although the central characters fall short of the enlightenment towards which they struggle, a roadmap of consolation is laid out for the perceptive reader or listener, whose superior knowledge plays out against the limited perspectives on death voiced in the poem.[27] If the Man in Black and the narrator do not grasp the big picture, in other words, the audience – including Gaunt himself – can do so, following the poem's own prompts towards consolation.

Medieval Christianity supplied a rationale of consolation for the loss of a virtuous beloved. The design of *BD* is in several respects germane to a Christian prospect on death: its prefatory fable about pagan love, lacking an ethical system in which the finality of death is mitigated by spiritual reward, prepares for a counter-narrative, set in the Christian present (as multiple references to biblical history and Christian asseverations reveal), that celebrates the moral virtue of a noble lady. In this scheme, White's heavenly salvation is assured. The Man in Black, in his despair, must be moved, like the dreamer in *Pearl* and Dante in the *Commedia*, towards a broadened perspective that recognizes his lady's death as confirmation of spiritual benefit and allows him to return to participation in the social community. What is striking is that any such 'message' in *BD* is inexplicit at best, absent at worst.[28] Unlike *Pearl*, the narrative structure of which accommodates Christian dogma to the extent that it reads at times like a biblical paraphrase, *BD* – apart from a failed attempt by the dreamer to speak instructively (albeit secularly, lines 710–41) – gives voice simply to the beauty of memory. Heavenly reward, God's mercy, the priority of spiritual well-being over bodily pleasure: none of these cornerstones of Christian consolation is once mentioned in conventional religious terms. The notion of 'repentaunce', 'mercy', and most tellingly, the prospect of being '[r]eysed as fro deth to lyve' (1115, 1219, 1277–8) all take shape in *BD* within the shadow-theology of *fin' amors*, and both dreamer and knight (who think, in effect, like pagans) appear unaware of their relevance to the matter at hand as Christian concepts.

Only on a submerged level of dramatic irony is a trajectory of Christian consolation manifested, through biblical patterns of imagery that imply, if only faintly, a spiritual awakening. Critics have noticed, for example, subtly allusive incorporation of imagery from the Song of Songs in the wordplay of 'toun of Tewnes' (310), in the physical description of White (e.g. the comparison of her neck to a tower of ivory), and in the rhetoric of sleep and waking.[29] Figurally speaking, such allusions circulate around the well-established allegorical equation of the Bride of the Song of Songs with the Virgin Mary, whose superlative qualities supply a model – and an eschatological trajectory – for White as a paragon of 'godnesse', 'trouthe' and 'governaunce' (985, 999, 1008). Apocalyptic imagery similarly infuses the poem with Judaeo-Christian texture, particularly in the reference to 'Seynt Johan' and the return homeward of 'this kyng' at the end (1314, 1319).[30] Apocalypse in the sense of 'an unveiling, a disclosure of something that was withheld or kept secret' allows for a conflation of sacred historical patterns with private epiphany.[31] In Robertson and Huppé's view, the implications of a Christian consolatory subtext – namely, that the memory of White's virtue should lead not to grief but to love of God as source of virtue – are clear enough for direct moralizing statement to be unnecessary.[32] In contrast, many other critics who have discerned Christian allusion in *BD* have defended, instead of any allegorical key that tidily decodes the poem's mysteries, a delicate and hermeneutically challenging '*sotto voce* affirmation about the mystery of immortality'.[33] It has even been argued that the interplay of 'secular and spiritual referents', with their contrasting claims on readerly interpretation, is essential to the poem itself as 'one large enigma' – much as it is for the hermeneutically multivalent Song of Songs.[34] *BD*'s secular register should thus not be regarded – as in the Robertsonian interpretation – simply as detritus to be sloughed off, revealing a pellucid Christian lesson, but as an integral discursive contribution to what is at heart a dialogic poem in which Christian consolation is enriched by its friction with secular concerns.

Boethianism seems, at first glance, to offer a framework for a consolation that harmonizes the opposing registers of worldly and spiritual: as a philosophical text on which Chaucer characteristically draws in pre-Christian settings, the *Consolation of Philosophy* conveys a roadmap from sorrow to happiness that complements the insights of Christian thought while remaining secular and rationalistic in its commitments. In many respects, the plot of *BD* overlaps with the structure of the *Consolation*, with its despairing, lyric-composing knightly protagonist, its combative dialogue between two central figures, and its inclusion of such Boethian motifs as the prospect of therapy and cure (544–57) and the denunciation of Fortune (714–19).[35] That the dreamer-persona, whom we first encounter struggling with his own melancholy, cuts an odd figure as Lady Philosophy *rediviva* is not in itself an argument against a Boethian interpretation, for Chaucer shows himself quite capable elsewhere of appropriating the *Consolation* creatively (as in *Troilus*, where Lady Philosophy is parodied in the devious character of Pandarus), using it as a barometer of characters' flawed processes of reasoning and judging. If such is the case here, then we must assume a Boethian framework of values for the Man in Black's experience. By this reading, the sorrowing knight is incorrect to think himself the victim of Fortune's wiles; since Fortune's gifts are only on loan, the inferior forms of happiness in which she deals cannot properly be possessed. Rather than regarding White, purely in physical terms, as a prized object that has been captured by Fortune (in the chess analogy), the Man in Black must recognize that the immutable virtue she represented is eternally present, linked with his own superior capacity of reason and thus to the godhead.

The capacity of this philosophical insight to reinforce a Christian trajectory of consolation (by which White's heavenly resting place is implied) emerges fully in Robertson and Huppé's reading of *BD*, which essentially conflates Christian-allegorical and Boethian argument. Other Boethian readings, some with different emphases and methodological assumptions, have drawn attention to the implications of the dreamer's lack of authority as consoler and his increased sympathy in comparison with Lady Philosophy;[36] to the Man in Black's Boethian lethargy as a function of his courtly fashioning;[37] and – moving into somewhat different territory – to *BD*'s resistance to or ironization of Boethian expectations.[38] An important question that impinges on such readings is the extent to which Chaucer was actually familiar with the *Consolation of Philosophy* when writing *BD* sometime between 1368 and the mid-1370s. Chaucer's translation of Boethius is usually dated to the late 1370s or early 1380s; he shows specific knowledge of at least part of the *Consolation* in the *House of Fame* (the date of which is unresolved, but often located around 1379–80) and assimilates it ambitiously and creatively in his poetry of the 1380s. That it would have been possible for Chaucer to fashion so elaborate and inventive a Boethian structure for the early *BD* as certain critics have discerned has struck some as unlikely.

As we have seen, a powerful temptation exists to read *BD* through the lens of Chaucer's mature poetry, one that is coloured by the ingrained cultural associations of 'Chaucer the poet'. By this logic, since Chaucer, in works like *Troilus* and the *Knight's Tale*, distinguished himself as a Boethian poet *par excellence*, so must *BD* register the lineaments of Boethian thought in a strategic and deliberate manner. Unlike all of Chaucer's later Boethian productions, however, *BD* contains no direct echoes or quotations of the language of the *Consolation*, and resemblances to situational aspects of the text, while suggestive, remain vague and associational.[39] This fact can perhaps be attributed to Chaucer being familiar with the *Consolation* but not having a copy to hand as he composed. More probably, it can be explained by way of indirect influence: the French sources that supply many of the details and motifs, though not the overall design, of *BD* themselves rehearse Boethian formulae and narrative situations (Machaut's *Remede de Fortune* most prominently, but not uniquely).[40] While this does not negate the relevance of Boethian consolation entirely, it does qualify the view of *BD* as a programmatic, tactically engineered defence of Boethian values (reason, fortitude, self-mastery) over the wayward attachment to physical pleasure. Even among those critics committed to a Boethian interpretation, differences of opinion once again surround the question of whether this lesson is positively grasped by the Man in Black or simply activated for the audience. This interpretative uncertainty underscores just how implicit any Boethian process of enlightenment is in *BD*, and how far the dreamer's conversational and argumentative tactics depart from Lady Philosophy's didactic precedent. To confront this point fully, it is necessary to consider the role of artistic expression and the power of memory in those aspects of the consolatory design of *BD* that fall outside the parameters of Boethian illumination.

Arguing against a Boethian reading, Robert A. Watson outlines multiple departures from the consolatory trajectory of the philosophical master-text. Specifically, the Man in Black's grief is not categorically dismissed but sympathetically indulged; emotive poetry, under the jurisdiction of the demonized Muses in the *Consolation*, is in *BD* neither rejected nor purged of its hazards, but given scope to articulate loss; and the distraught subject is not clearly transformed by a rational argument that reshapes his perspective.[41] Instead, if Chaucer in *BD* does seriously take up the possibilities of Boethian consolation, he seems to do so in order to show its limitations concerning matters of the heart. To the extent that the dreamer attempts, at least initially, a Boethian style of consolation, offering therapy and discoursing against Fortune, his rational efforts prove futile against the profundity of the Man in Black's grief, and lead to the problems of communication already noted (which are not, unlike in the *Consolation*, incrementally resolved). Rejecting the 'obviously unsatisfactory forms of conventional consolation' through the dreamer's ineptitude, *BD* has instead been seen to endorse a wandering, heterodox method of consolation through trial and error.[42] This searching consolatory strategy, furthermore, adopts the resources of imaginative art, both through the Man in Black's rhetorical fashioning of White as an idealized fictional construct immortalized within the memory, and through the preservative capacities of the very 'book' – Chaucer's poem itself – that suspends the duchess warmly in life, not death.[43] In this view, consolation inheres simply in the solace afforded by memorial reconstruction, salvation in the afterlife of the work of art rather than in a spiritual domain. Unlike Boethius, who is urged not to dwell on his losses, and unlike a typical Christian who must regard death as an opportunity rather than an affront, the Man in Black profits in remembering his beloved and celebrating her life in both its courtly and ethical dimensions. This results in no easy answers, no clear mastery of grief. The lack of closure inherent in this consolatory irresolution ultimately serves to vindicate poetic art, within the resources of which lie the salving powers of memory and, as the last lines of *BD* suggest, a generative means of continued invention.

The Lady Vanishes? Gender and Grief

Whereas debate over the means of consolation in *BD* dates to an early period of its critical history, interest in the poem's complex evocation of gender is a more recent phenomenon. The essence of the issue, as it has preoccupied critics of the last thirty years, is a question of affinity: to what extent does *BD* actually celebrate womanhood by immortalizing the much-loved duchess? Can it instead be read as a poem that is predominantly concerned with male relations and their advancement, one in which the ostensible female subject, conveniently for the patriarchal project, is silenced through death? In short, is *BD* a book *about* the duchess or about the men who made it (through recollection and composition)?[44]

Most early scholarship assumed that the Man in Black's long and tender description of his beloved was basically a realistic reflection of the historical Blanche of Lancaster, a view epitomized by James R. Lowell's remark, in 1845, that *BD* supplies 'one of the most perfect portraits of a woman that was ever drawn'.[45] The attractiveness of this interpretation has endured, even in critical moments suspicious of the idea of literature as a one-way reflection of history: as Colin Wilcockson writes in his Explanatory Notes to *BD* in the *Riverside Chaucer*, 'it is hard to believe that the passage does not contain a real portrayal of the Duchess of Lancaster.'[46] Alternative early views emphasized the conventional aspects of White's description, which Chaucer drew liberally from Machaut's *Jugement dou roy de Behaingne* and related *dits*. First Robertson and subsequently Wimsatt, analysing White's portrait in terms of Christian symbolism, challenged the biographical view in the observation that the account 'contain[s] much more emphasis on *invisibilia* than on *visibilia*' – meaning inner virtues in contrast with physical attributes – and thus is 'not, in the modern sense, a "portrait" at all'.[47] Rather differently, personalizing touches, such as the Man in Black's struggles to remember and articulate the uniqueness of White, also complicate the conventional formulae on which the description is based.[48]

Despite their differences of perspective, these dominant lines of interpretation up to the 1980s assumed the priority of White as subject of *BD* – even if the poem centres just as importantly on her survivor's experience – and saw in its account of White reverent and heartfelt love, 'in preysinge of [the God of Love's] name' (as the Prologue of *Legend of Good Women* has it (F 416)). Beginning with Maud Ellmann's pioneering Lacanian reading of *BD* in 1984, however, feminist critics have been suspicious of the tidiness of such an assumption. For Ellmann, the whiteness of Blanche encodes not simply her purity but an erasure of her personhood. Her function in the poem is that of a 'whitened signature' or blank cheque, iconic of the Freudian idea of lost origins, from which emerges the letter-rich blackness of 'male discourse and its dream of meaning'.[49] Further developing this approach, Elaine Tuttle Hansen, Gayle Margherita and others concur that *BD* is in essence a poem about maleness, understood as a socially constructed rather than biologically fixed category 'defined and recuperated by its difference and separation from the feminine'.[50] Central to this reading is the assertion that the thwarted dynamic of heterosexual union (Seys and Alcione, White and Black) is supplanted by more profoundly generative homosocial bonds (Black and the dreamer, the narrator and a lineage of male poets beginning with Ovid).[51] The recuperative motion of the poem – towards male relations, social reintegration and dynastic continuity – develops in response to the threat of feminization inherent in courtly love, which demands surrender. This danger emerges in the emasculating intensity of the Man in Black's mourning, which involves melancholic identification with his lost lady such that their identities are intertwined; it further surfaces in the 'undead' demeanour by which the mourner yearns to absorb White's misfortune.[52]

Over the course of the dialogue, however, identification gives way to difference, and memorialization of the historical woman yields to mystification of her idealized counterpart. The 'whit wal' of Black's sensible being (780), so receptively affiliated with White's influence, shifts from a medium of erotic psychology to a tableau of history: the 'walles white' of the 'long castel' that evoke the House of Lancaster (1318). Inherent in this image is a tradition of dynastic succession that privileges the masculine and, in the present case, epitomizes the male absorption of wealth and titles through the female bloodline. What results is not only enhanced noble privilege but a newly potent 'image of manhood made visible through White's neutrally coloured image'.[53] The poem thus advances a sacrificial model of womanhood, both for the duchess and for grieving women such as Alcione, who succumbs to grief, demonstrating her love through a negation of identity.[54] In contrast, the Man in Black, representing a different gendered model of mourning, finally resists such a definitive renunciation, survives, and prospers.[55]

Some readers have been disturbed not only by *BD*'s obfuscation of Blanche's voice and identity to articulate masculinity, but by its particular orchestration of gender in relation to death. According to Ellmann, *BD* – 'the Deeth of Blaunche the Duchesse' – enacts a textual encrypting that 'frames a blank, entombs a silence' because 'a lover's discourse can only really flourish in the absence of the woman'.[56] The Man in Black's lengthy physical description of White, which lingers over her smooth neck, plump arms and round breasts (while decorously refusing to go further), seems peculiar for a funereal poem, and the passage in question – wholly conventional in a romance – has struck some as 'quasi-necrophiliac' and 'grotesque'.[57] Ultimately, this focus on the beauty of the body, and inevitably by contrast its current state of decay, seems designed to transmute the woman who once was Blanche, either recalibrating her as an object of desire within the spiritual and immutable (in philosophical terms) or removing her, in anthropological terms, 'from the community of the living and, after a threatening liminal stage ... integrat[ing her] into the community of the dead'.[58] Like proponents of the consolation reading, then, feminist critics have generally discerned a re-establishment of equilibrium in *BD*, one that brings the Man in Black back from the brink not only of short-sighted despair but of a failure of masculinity.

If the masculine imperative is finally affirmed, the attraction of the feminine – and the feminizing potential of courtly love – underscores, for some readers, 'the instability at the heart of a paternalist poetics'.[59] The gendered position of the narrator-dreamer, perhaps even more than the romanticized unit of the couple, contributes to this deconstruction. Recent critics have been struck less by the homosocial bond between dreamer and knight which gradually supplants the heterosexual structure of intimacy, than by the set-apartness of the dreamer's desire more generally. For example, reading the ambiguity of the narrator-dreamer's desires and responses in terms of 'queerness' – in the broad sense of being at odds with the normative – Susan Schibanoff suggests that his passivity and lovelessness render him both enigmatic and especially receptive to the central poetic experience of *BD*.[60] Like the whelp who temporarily befriends him, '[r]yght as hyt hadde me yknowe' (392), the narrator-dreamer is an outsider – a stray – whose desires seem errant, lacking clear orientation in his cryptic remarks to the reader (e.g. at lines 34–43) and his imbalanced responses to the Man in Black. Similarly, Steven Kruger identifies the narrator's 'initial (non-)sexual stance' as 'potentially "queer"', associating this with the 'agaynes kynde', or unnatural, affliction that besets him before the dream (16).[61] It is even possible to apprehend the narrator's displacement as an indication of the poem's linguistic queerness: necessarily marked by a sense of 'cultural alienation', this English entry within a French tradition inscribes Chaucer's outsider status as a poet working without the benefit of national models. Insomnia, as Deanne Williams has interestingly suggested, becomes in this sense an index of the narrator-poet's discomfort with the headily French genre of dream-vision, in which articulate sleep functions both as ticket of entry and common currency.[62] Although the poem folds these hints of queerness back into normalcy, by affirming the investments of courtliness and restoring the dreamer to health, it leaves us with a variegated picture of gender as it shapes discourse, power relations and the very communicative structures of the poem – in miniature, a range of concerns similar to those informing later masterpieces of Chaucerian gender study such as *Troilus and Criseyde* and the Wife of Bath's Prologue.

Writing Sickness

In other ways too, the marginalization of Blanche noted by feminist critics contrasts with a surfeit of masculine experience. One of the curiosities of *BD*, and an indication of its unusual literary structure, is the vehemence with which the narrator upstages the emotional focus of the poem – a noble lady who died in a gruesome pandemic – with complaint about his own, assuredly more minor physical ailments. This is no mere segue: talk of the narrator's sickness, evasive and solipsistic as it is, occupies the nearly three hundred lines of the poem leading up to the dream. Insomnia, faintness, melancholy thoughts, incurable suffering – these undifferentiated symptoms of 'feeling out of sorts', which may reflect anything from lovesickness to writer's block, frame the narrator's stance on a poem about the effects of plague. Within the dream, the Man in Black's reluctance to articulate the fact of White's death openly and the obfuscation of her historical personhood, noted above, combine to repress the trauma of plague, to render it strangely invisible, in a poem that is everywhere marked by the resulting upheaval. For this reason, *BD* aptly has been characterized as a record of forgetting as well as remembering, an attempt towards a poetics of grief that rests both on 'obliteration and commemoration'.[63] The very whiteness of the duchess suggests a wishful evacuation and displacement of the black, maculate spectre of the plague that claimed her life, a spectre which resurfaces only in the hue of her survivor's sorrow.[64]

The devastation of the Black Death, beginning in the mid-fourteenth century, coincided with the flourishing of various European vernacular literary traditions. Though the reasons behind this histori-cal correspondence are complex (relating, among other things, to the social and economic shifts caused by the mass reduction in popula-tion), there emerges a reciprocity between the depth of the pandemic's impact and the vigour of creative expression, particularly within the evolving category of literature. This is true even – perhaps especially – in England, where the obliquity of medieval poetic evocations of plague contrasts with the direct representations on the continent by poets such as Boccaccio and Machaut, whose accounts are sufficiently full to stand next to historical chronicles and medical treatises in mod-ern scholarly anthologies of plague-writing.[65] The entertainment value of literature, as Glending Olson has influentially demonstrated, regis-tered in new ways in plague time, on account of the 'hygienic justifica-tion of fiction' that informed medieval discussions of disease. Medical treatises and regimens of health affirmed that composing and read-ing stories for pleasure could function medically to restore *gaudium* (cheerfulness) and supply a prophylactic against plague by restoring to proper balance a disordered and fearful imagination.[66] What is more, ancient and medieval medicine invested words, associated both with verbal charms and written texts, with the physical capacity to heal; in this sense, the exercise of reading – whether the object at hand was a medical regimen or a work of literature – was 'intimately bound with bodily cure'.[67] Viewed in this context, *BD* can be interpreted as a sus-tained, and in many ways cohesive, exploration of illness and therapy in relation to literacy: reading, writing and productive communica-tion more generally all intersect here with somatic disorder. The fatal trauma that the poem contemplates, and represses, is poised on a spectrum of pathological experience, from the narrator's foggy, sleepless melancholy to the Man in Black's physically disruptive heart-suffering (described at lines 487–513).[68] *BD* suggests a totality of response to plague, not just as the end of one woman's life-story but as a fluid, ongoing, collective narrative to be negotiated by characters, author and audience alike.[69]

Among the direct literary ancestors of *BD*, as Ardis Butterfield has expertly highlighted in her article on the tradition of counter-pastoral, is Machaut's *Jugement dou roy de Navarre*, which frames a love-question against an ominous, vividly realized backdrop of plague as it sweeps the land and causes the narrator to retreat in fearful seclusion.[70] Although in Chaucer's poem, unlike Machaut's, the plague is never explicitly mentioned in relation to the narrator's unsettled state, his demeanour is consistent, Butterfield argues, with contemporary responses to the pandemic, and the dream thus 'functions not simply as a narrative device but as a means of enabling the sorrowing narrator to withdraw from the sights and sounds of the plague and its attendant afflictions'.[71] Like the book to which he turns for pleasant diversion (lines 48–51), the dream is prompted by a spirit of play ('in my game', the narrator requests it light-heartedly despite himself (238)), and its initial effect is refreshing and socially integrative (the outdoor air, the hunting party, the verdant forest). That death from plague re-emerges as the dream's central subject, and familiar problems of melancholy haunt its protagonist, hints at a trajectory of healing – through the action of the imagination, which governs the dreamwork – by which 'the narrator [moves] towards an understanding, and correction, of his illness' because 'the narrator now stands separate from himself as the subject of illness'.[72] Awakening from the dream with a newfound sense of active purpose, 'to put this sweven in ryme' (1332), the narrator attests to his bodily restoration in his very commitment to advancing others' well-being through the composition of poetry, the therapeutic benefits of which his own experience has proven. Implicated at first in disease, the imagination becomes not only, as we have seen, a salvific abode for White, but 'a source of restorative value' for the dreamer himself, reborn as an author capable of channelling 'the image-making power of the mind' towards the good.[73]

In what is implicitly a plague-time setting, the narrator suffers initially from melancholy, or a surfeit of 'sorwful ymagynacioun' (14), resulting in numbness, indifference, restless worries and insomnia. His affliction, which he describes in some detail but cagily refuses to pin down, declaring the question of cure immaterial (lines 38–40), has been critically diagnosed in various ways. Some critics, turning to the sources of the first section of the poem for guidance, argue for an understated reference to lovesickness here, although the obliquity is a departure from French tradition (particularly, Froissart's *Paradys d'Amours*) informing the motif.[74] Others have discerned a more purely psychological ailment such as 'head melancholy', to be healed by sleep, or an obstruction of normal brain function resulting in 'creative dryness', to be rectified by the production of the poem itself (as a result of sleep).[75] In a recent interpretation, the malady has been described in philosophical terms as 'the ethical anesthesia of the melancholic', entailing 'an inability to participate in ethical reasoning, to discriminate between bad and good, joy and sorrow'.[76] Perhaps most compelling are those analyses that regard the ambiguity of the illness as itself meaningful. Phillips, for example, finds the 'multiple potential meanings' of the eight-year sickness to circulate in an atmosphere of 'puzzlement' that is appropriate to the poem as a whole as 'a text that is open to disparate, even contradictory readings'.[77] Similarly, the most thorough study thus far of *BD* in the context of medieval medical discourse concludes that the narrator's illness 'cannot be identified as a clear-cut case of lovesickness as set forth in discussions by classical and medieval physicians' in light of the interpenetration in symptoms and treatment of melancholy, *amor hereos*, and mania.[78]

By elaborating on the narrator's symptoms while obscuring their cause, *BD* maximizes the literary potential of diagnosis and cure, folding the ambiguity of the narrator's ailment into his own problems of understanding the Man in Black's suffering. The discourse of physical illness, which foregrounds issues of subjectivity and diagnostic interpretation, becomes an appropriate framework for the troubled acts of communication – of genuinely entering into another person's experience – that structure the remainder of the poem. It is no surprise that the rhetoric of the confessional, associated both with medical metaphors (witness *Le Livre de seyntz medicines* by Henry of Lancaster, Blanche's father) and the story-of-the-self, supplies a framework for the therapeutic colloquy between narrator and knight.[79] When, in the dream, the narrative persona adopts the (initially Boethian) role of physician, intent upon making 'hool' the Man in Black, who 'semeth ful sek under [his] syde' (553, 557), the core trauma of the poem – White's physical corruption by a black death – circles outward to threaten all the subjectivities touched by her. The Man in Black, not White in her recollected immaculacy, bears the mark of sickness. The narrator's earlier malaise seems also to reflect this. The irreversible loss of White, for whom medicine failed, is qualified and nuanced by the prospect of her survivors' cure – from morbid sorrow rather than plague – and her own story, in its status as a literary text, can contribute to an ongoing process of healing.

By adding such multivalent medical resonances to the love poems out of which *BD* is constituted, Chaucer evades the conventions of plague-writing available to him at the same time that he explores many of the topics that circulated in historical and literary accounts of pestilence: bodily disorder, existential upheaval, pervasive vulnerability and failures of social community. In the broadest sense, *BD* capitalizes on the established conceptualization of disease in the Middle Ages as dysfunction and disequilibrium, rather than evoking the unique manifestation of a single expression of illness (plague).[80] In doing so, Chaucer contributes to the figurative shaping of illness as an 'embodied rhetoric', or a way of thinking about and through the *corpus* (physical and textual).[81] He thus positions illness, in its full range as a disposition of body and soul, as a medium of literary creativity and communication.

Interlingualism: *BD* between French and English

In one important matter of diagnosis – not medical but cultural – *BD* itself has proven to be an especially recalcitrant patient. Namely, is *BD* an English or a French poem? This may seem like a trick question, but critics have found it surprisingly difficult to answer; indeed, the current response is along the lines of 'neither and both'. Paradoxically, the poem by which 'Chaucer earned the right to be called the Father of English Poetry' – the first clear instance of 'courtly' literature in English – issued directly from French tradition and was aimed at what was still an officially francophone court.[82] That *BD* closely adapts a number of French love poems, and to a lesser extent classical Latin works, drawing from them details of language, aspects of style and specific motifs, has long been recognized. As early as 1775, Thomas Tyrwhitt's scholarly eye identified aspects of Chaucer's imitation of French materials in what had been supposed an 'original' production – observations that would go unplumbed by anglophone critics for more than a century.[83] Despite the fact that the overall plot of *BD* is not paralleled by any one source, as are Chaucer's later, free translations of Boccaccian works in *Troilus* and the *Knight's Tale*, the poem is fundamentally a mosaic or compilation of various fashionable, courtly French materials. The range and degree of *BD*'s literary appropriations have been well established, and the seminal studies of Kittredge and Wimsatt remain indispensable on this topic.[84] In Wimsatt's view, the chief importance of *BD* for English literary history lies neither in its originality of expression nor in any conscious expression of Englishness per se, but in its function as a conduit for 'the stream of love narratives which found its source in the work of Guillaume de Lorris' to flow into English literature.[85] In these ways, *BD* is not so much a visionary work, staking out a new territory and idiom for English letters, as it is a retrospective and reverent one, looking to French tradition for content and guidance.

It is curious that the charge of derivativeness has been much more commonly laid upon *BD*, which amalgamates a number of source materials, than it has upon Chaucer's actual 'translations' of single Italian sources in his later poetry (although, of course, those translations are far from homogeneous).[86] Whatever the reasons for this, the hegemony of French in Chaucer's England, and the particular cultural tensions between the two national traditions – in the fourteenth century as in the history of scholarship – make these issues of creative expression and poetic authority much more loaded than is the case with Chaucer's Italianate experiments. The long kerfuffle over the priority of *BD* with regard to certain French materials, and the implications of this for the poem's reception history, constitute perhaps the clearest example of *BD*'s competing claims to Frenchness and Englishness. The debate between the French scholar Étienne Gustave Sandras and the English Chaucerian Frederick J. Furnivall in the second half of the nineteenth century establishes the territory. Sandras, for his part, found little to praise in Chaucer's 'suite des réminiscences' of French poetry apart from whatever value inheres in the original material itself. Opining that Chaucer never applied his hand to a subject – the death of a beloved duchess – as poignant while displaying inspiration as impoverished, Sandras outlines the French origins of supposedly original passages that are often admired (by Englishmen, he hastens to add), and concludes, 'Ce poëme qui, dans son ensemble et souvent dans ses détails, n'offre qu'une imitation servile de Machault, est certainement une des plus faibles productions de Chaucer' (This poem which, on the whole and often in its details, offers nothing more than a servile imitation of Machaut, is certainly one of the most feeble of Chaucer's productions).[87] In a spirited rebuttal of these charges, Furnivall – who, we recall, was not unqualified in his regard for *BD* – reclaimed for English patrimony several of the passages that Sandras identified as derivative, declaring his logic 'gammon'.[88] What may look like imitation, in Furnivall's view, can be explained by the coincidence of great minds working alike: 'There is nothing new under the sun: and if one man describes his mistress, says she's like the sun above the stars, speaks most sweetly, is his life and bliss, is rightly called Lily, Rose, or what not; why, of course he copies it all from a Frenchman!'[89]

In this gentlemanly turf war over competing national traditions in the early stages of institutional formation, Furnivall's position ultimately lost out, although some of the questions raised by early scholars' discordant accounts of influence remain unresolved to this day. By the mid-twentieth century, rigorous philological excavations by Kittredge and others established the pervasive influence upon *BD* of a core group of French texts: the *Roman de la rose*, several of Machaut's *dits* and

Froissart's *Paradys d'Amours* (this last formerly supposed to have been influenced, instead, by *BD*). A tone of special pleading sometimes characterizes these early assessments, which typically insist that although *BD* 'reveals at every turn Chaucer's dependence on French models', it equally testifies to his 'independence of them'.[90] What 'emerges triumphantly' from a schematic overview of parallels such as that provided in Kittredge's 1915 article 'Guillaume de Machaut and *The Book of the Duchess*' is, *mutatis mutandis*, the 'essential originality of Chaucer's genius'.[91] The need to maintain *BD* as a seminally English work is powerful, and the notion of imitation, shading as it does into derivativeness, runs the risk of conveying a submissive or even sycophantic Chaucer.

The general view that *BD* collocated a number of source materials but was independent in overall conception did not go unquestioned. The uncertain dating of a small handful of poems that seem clearly related to *BD* in a larger structural or thematic sense led some critics to dial back even further the extent of Chaucer's originality. For example, the anonymous *Songe vert*, first posited by W. Owen Sypherd in 1909 as a source of *BD*, features a narrator-dreamer mourning the loss of his beloved to plague; renewed by a dream-encounter with the Queen of Love, the black-clad dreamer finds himself newly garbed in green, ready to seek love anew.[92] The conjunction of dream-vision and elegy, often assumed to be a Chaucerian innovation, may derive from Jehan de la Mote's *Regret Guillaume Comte de Hainault*, datable to 1339 and composed in memory of John of Gaunt's grandfather.[93] Two complaints by the Savoyard knight Oton de Granson, who was at one point a retainer of John of Gaunt and whose influence on Chaucer's *Complaint of Venus* was duly acknowledged, share a number of striking motifs with *BD* – most importantly, the device of overhearing a knight's complaint about lost love in a forest, and a narrator despairing on account of his lady's death.[94] Finally, the *Dit dou bleu chevalier* of Froissart, whose *Paradys d'Amours* significantly informs the beginning and end of *BD*, intriguingly overlaps with the general plan of Chaucer's poem in its use of colour symbolism for the purpose of characterization and its staging of an encounter between narrator and knight that involves overhearing, dialogue and attempted consolation.[95]

With the exception of Jehan de la Mote's contribution, the dating of all of these peripheral sources has occasioned debate, and arguments for their predating *BD* have often rested on internal evidence or hypotheses concerning canonical order.[96] Wimsatt has argued in considerable detail that measurable borrowing patterns establish *BD*'s precedence over all of these poems except the *Regret*, even suggesting that the *Songe vert*, the most closely affiliated of these, 'seems almost a sequel of the *Book of the Duchess*'.[97] Two distinct possibilities emerge from this controversy, each surprising in its own way: (1) that *BD* is much less 'independent' than has often been supposed, relying on French source materials not only eclectically but programmatically for its overall design, or (2) that *BD* itself influenced the very French tradition from which it drew inspiration, thus representing the earliest and perhaps even the most profound node of reception for all of Chaucer's poetry in his own lifetime. The implications of either option are considerable. Did Chaucer, as the francophone critic Normand Cartier claims, act out of deference to French tradition, demonstrating his competence in the fashionable crafting of prince-pleasing poems; or, as Wimsatt contends, did he engage in a two-way creative conversation with French poets on literary topics of common interest?[98] It runs against certain deeply ingrained convictions regarding patterns of reception and vernacular hierarchies in the Middle Ages to suppose that a humble English poem could influence the literary development of French love poetry, and that a contemporary record of reception – so evasive for most of Chaucer's corpus, yet notably linked to Froissart's contemporary Eustache Deschamps in his famous ballade to Chaucer – might lurk beneath a poem that today is rarely counted among Chaucer's greatest achievements. At the same time, as William Calin rightly points out, Chaucerians have a vested interest in Chaucer's masterful originality, however inappropriate this bias may be in a medieval context of literary production, and have consequently tended to oversimplify the French sources of *BD*, to reveal Chaucer breaking free of their constricting artifice, bringing nuance and ambiguity to a flat if accommodating palette.[99] The debate over the priority of *BD* vis-à-vis these proximate French materials reveals, if nothing else, how closely interlaced were

the creative discourses of Chaucer and his French contemporaries, so
that a model of collaboration rather than imitation seems potentially
more appropriate. This, indeed, characterizes the direction that the
study of *BD* in the light of French tradition would take in the later part
of the twentieth century, as the methodology of source study gave
way to newer ideas of intertextuality, and as the late medieval political
context of Anglo-French relations came increasingly to be heeded as a
force in literary production.

A significant transitional moment for these new directions of interpretation emerges from a late essay by Elizabeth Salter, 'Chaucer and
Internationalism' (1980). Resisting the strict demarcation of 'English' and
'French' traditions that informed earlier studies, itself shaped by divisions among modern academic disciplines and nationalistic ideologies,
Salter emphasizes the 'interlocking social and administrative contexts'
that defined French and English literary production in the English court
in Chaucer's time. In doing so, she indicates the plausibility of various kinds of literary exchange, including lines of influence from *BD*
to Froissart and other French poets.[100] Chaucer's English contributions,
Salter argues, participate in international European trends in the later
Middle Ages towards the ennoblement of vernacular languages. What
results is a 'provision of alternatives for the same wide range of public
which had hitherto been satisfied by courtly literature in French only'.[101]

This nuanced perspective on Anglo-French literary relations in terms
of a shared vocabulary of internationalism and vernacular ambition set
the tone for various exploratory sociolinguistic approaches to *BD*, and
Chaucer's construction as an English poet more generally, which emerged
in the 1980s. These fall into three to some extent overlapping models
of interpretation: (1) polyglossia, (2) subversion and (3) intertextuality.

(1) Polyglossia. It is no longer possible for scholars to take the
Englishness of *BD* for granted, as if it were a poem essentially French
in style and texture, that just happened to be written in English. Instead,
BD increasingly has been understood as a text that self-consciously
contemplates issues of language – not only the polite English distinc-
tions of 'ye' and 'thou' that establish a social hierarchy between characters, but matters of register and resonance that more generally evoke

different linguistic ideologies and cultural associations. As a polyvalent and hybrid language forged from multiple linguistic contributions, medieval English was especially amenable to this sort of cultural inquiry, particularly in a poem so centrally concerned with issues of communication and textuality.

Critics have been struck by the 'juxtaposition of linguistic-poetic registers' visible, for example, in the opening lines of *BD*, which marry French form and content (octosyllabic rhyming verse, a description of melancholy carried over from Froissart's *Paradys d'Amours*) with an almost entirely Germanic diction that strongly conveys an auditory sense of 'Englishness'.[102] The effect, in Steve Guthrie's view, is of 'an Englishman reworking French material' and emphasizing that fact programmatically; thus, *BD*, 'by advertizing itself as English ... calls attention to its Frenchness as well'.[103] Chaucer appears in the course of the poem to augment or diminish the intensity of French loan-words – as did other Ricardian writers, notably the *Gawain*-poet – to summon particular cultural associations, for instance, with the emotional sensibility of courtly love. Overall, those who have studied *BD* from a linguistic perspective have observed its merging of characteristically French literary forms – dream-vision, complaint, sentimental lyric – with a preponderance of Anglo-Saxon vocabulary and speech-patterns that is the legacy of English popular romance (a submerged, rather than openly avowed, influence on Chaucer's poetics). This English style, often described as plain, colloquial, or 'expletive' (due to a heavy use of intensifiers and asseverations), grounds what is typically the abstract or allegorical discourse of French love-vision in an earthier sense of practical reality and conversational immediacy.[104]

At the same time, the poem's polyglossia highlights a disconnect between the dreamer and the Man in Black, and in turn between the narrator and his subject matter (cf. Williams's comment above, p. 65, on insomnia as a mark of the narrator's alienation from French literary tradition). One of the problems inherent in the Man in Black's lyric utterances, it has been suggested, is that something gets 'lost in translation' – rather than distilling complex emotions through performative fluency, they fail to resonate because of their very plainness of expression.[105] It is especially interesting, then, that the Man in Black's two lyrics are heavily English in style and vocabulary[106] – a microcosm of sorts for the challenges facing Chaucer in his larger poetic project to develop a communicative idiom for European poetry within the compass of English verse. Yet, at other points, the Man in Black is a creature of French tradition, mastering a French romance idiom as he learns (and recounts) the fundamentals of love. Although it is possible, as Guthrie valuably demonstrates, to read *BD* as a vindication of plain, non-lyrical, English speech ('She ys ded!') over French 'idealism' – since it is in this arena solely that true communication occurs – the poem finally resists such a simplification of the complex linguistic back-and-forth it negotiates: 'The Duchess is in English, but English is part French. It ends in what it has characterized as the native register, but much of the knowledge it acquired along the way has come from the foreign one.'[107]

(2) Subversion. Readings such as these suggest the delicacy of interlingualism as a component of style and theme in *BD*, but others focus on a more resistant strain in the poem's treatment of French traditions, one through which Chaucer manoeuvres a distinct vision of English authorship – rather than, as some earlier critics implied, allowing French sources to manoeuvre him. For Barbara Nolan, by privileging Anglo-Saxon diction and showing his narrator to abjure amatory sentiment, Chaucer exposes the limited utility of French idiom, particularly as it relates to *fin'amors* and the 'subjective authority' assumed by love poets. In effect, Chaucer parodies 'the pretensions of literary endeavor', displacing these onto the Man in Black and revealing their inadequacies in articulating serious matters of life and death.[108] Parody re-emerges as a key element of Steven Davis's reading of *BD*, which shifts the focus to the narrator rather than the Man in Black as the one to betray flawed literary values. By subversively fashioning his narrator as a 'Machauldian reader', Davis argues, Chaucer underscores the superficiality of French poetic conventions in light of harsher existential realities (i.e. that the crux of the problem turns out to be death, rather than erotic disappointment). Perhaps most interestingly, Davis extends these insights to Chaucer's own construction of French tradition as itself shallow and in need of English amendment. This is a view that Chaucer

canonizes, so to speak, not only for English poetry but for disciplinary history. Taking these notions of competition and subversion to their political extreme, John M. Bowers frames *BD* as a polemical contribution: an 'antifrancophone' entry in the discursive politics surrounding the Hundred Years War. Provocatively if not entirely judiciously, he positions Chaucer's innovative English corpus, buoyed by *BD*, as 'a life-long project of resentment and retaliation against the French'.[109]

(3) Intertextuality. For all their insights, such readings are often reductive – as the stark equation of literary relations with military gamesmanship suggests. What has seemed most productive in the last twenty years, and going forward, is the application of newer theoretical models of intertextuality, more commonly encountered in fields outside medieval studies, to Anglo-French encounters in *BD*. The notion of intertextuality, first coined by Julia Kristeva in the 1960s and elaborated into various sub-models by Roland Barthes, Michael Riffaterre, Gérard Genette and others, recognizes collaboration as well as conflict as essential to the relations among texts. It emphasizes the dynamic, mutually enriching nature of literary influence: the notion that 'source' texts are not static or fixed, but part of a two-way negotiation of meaning that enhances both texts. 'Both these interpretations', according to the classicist Alessandro Barchiesi, 'are ever on trial, in process, and continually influencing one another. The new text rereads its model, while the model in turn influences the reading of the new text'.[110] Rather than fixating upon linguistic differences, intertextual readings of *BD* tend to understand Chaucer and his French contemporaries as engaging in a common poetic enterprise, one that centres upon shifts of perspective and formulae of civilized debate. Approaching *BD* as 'hypertext', R. Barton Palmer contends that it offers 'the double experience of reading and rereading' insofar as the French sources behind it leave their traces in the manner of a palimpsest.[111] Apprehended as such, *BD* stands as a fluid intervention in an ongoing poetic conversation, rather than a simple dismissal or correction of a closed tradition. Neither a reverent nor a parodic interpreter of the French *dits*, Chaucer exposes the 'indispensable inadequacy of these models for his project through a selective, unauthorized representation of some of their elements' (taking

the liberties available to all Bloomian 'misreaders').[112] In doing so, he engages a French trajectory of rewriting already evident, for example, in Machaut's own reopening of the amatory debate ostensibly resolved in his *Jugement dou roi de Behaigne* to reverse its thrust in the *Jugement dou roy de Navarre*.

While it may be true, as Davis contends, that Chaucer fashioned a biased reading of French tradition to enhance the value of English, dismissal pure and simple was not a likely aim. In an intertextual view of literary relations, talking back to prior texts necessitates their continued existence as interlocutors; their incomplete authority, within which the newer text inscribes itself as needful, becomes integral to the experience of *both* texts, the intelligibility of which is predicated on a model of symbiosis. If *BD* did attract French adaptations in turn, then the 'collaborative power' of late medieval vernacularity would be even more fully realized.[113]

Approaches such as these have the advantage of placing *BD* in a literary and cultural context that is neither deterministic nor ornamental, thus highlighting Chaucer's conscious intervention in – rather than mere inheritance of – a living mode of cultural expression. To the extent that English lacked the courtly prestige and currency of French, Chaucer engaged the sibling tongues through a 'symbolic confrontation', epitomized by the pivot from Blanche to White, that entails both intimacy and distancing, resulting in a 'counter-discourse that contests the dominant presence of French language and culture in England'.[114] The best and most recent work on Chaucer's place in Anglo-French literary relations echoes Salter in insisting that the poet is 'working *with* the grain of a larger vernacular poetic enterprise' rooted in the English court and reflecting the interpenetration of England's two vernaculars in this context.[115] Regarding *BD* as fundamentally multilingual, rather than adversarial, in its creative investments, and Chaucer as working in tandem with, rather than in reaction against, his francophone contemporaries, such scholarship asks newly suggestive questions of a poem that creatively interrogates cultural divisions while figuring integrally in the developing narrative of English authorship. It is to this narrative that the following chapter turns.

3

ALL THIS BLACK

Reading and Making

Such sorowe this lady to her tok
That trewly I, that made this book,
Had such pittee and such rowthe
To rede hir sorwe that, by my trowthe,
I ferde the worse al the morwe
Aftir to thenken on hir sorwe.

(*BD*, lines 95–100)

It is striking that a poem whose central subject is death, the supreme ending, should so abound in the power of beginnings. On one level, *BD* is suffused with the language of sequestration and termination: variations on the phrase 'that is don' allow the narrator to discard hope of recovery from his eight-year sickness (40), to mark the completion of the 'hert-huntyng' (1313) and, ultimately, to dispense with the poem itself (1334). Yet the last of these iterations – 'This was my sweven; now hit ys doon' (1334) – seems less a dismissal than an act of deliverance, a first rehearsal of a device that in a future poem would see another 'litel bok' confidently sent forth for enrolment in an Elysian library (*Tr* 5.1786). By virtue of *BD*'s first-person narrative framework, the loss of White is all but subsumed by the realization of a new poem: black letters crowding out a white page. Indeed, the 'open', transactional textuality of *BD* that so intrigues its modern critics and, as later chapters document, its early readers and editors, first issues from its narrator-author's evocation of his text's 'making'.

The present chapter considers Chaucer's representation of acts of writing in *BD*, and how this is linked to the physical object of the book that we (like the narrator in bed) are imagined to be holding in our hands. It argues that the 'bookishness' of *BD* is in no sense incidental to its meaning and that it deserves fuller integration with larger patterns of Chaucerian textuality, critical discussions of which too often elide this early poem. In fact, *BD* in many respects anticipates the bookish concerns and pseudo-autobiographical reflections that emerge in Chaucer's later poetry. Thus, this chapter's first section explores this artistic continuum in the light of what may be termed a 'compositional consciousness' – an attention to the construction of authorship and material textuality – in *BD*. The second section of the chapter then considers the imaginative contact between Chaucer's first true 'book' and other, similarly self-conscious texts. Adopting an intertextual methodology, this section selectively evaluates Chaucer's portrayal of the process of composition in comparison with similar (or provocatively different) moments in poems by which Chaucer was influenced in writing *BD* (Guillaume de Lorris and Jean de Meun's *Roman de la rose*, *dits amoreux* by Machaut and Froissart) as well as a cross-section of works by his English contemporaries that he may or may not have known (Gower's *Confessio amantis*, Langland's *Piers Plowman* and Julian of Norwich's *A Revelation of Love*). The chapter as a whole is concerned with the complex temporality activated when an author represents himself in the act of writing the very poem we are now reading, which must, of course, be finished yet is represented as if 'in process'. By elliptically yet decisively contemplating its own 'making', I suggest, *BD* models – and solicits – re-making.

Thinking Books: The Legibility of Authorship

In a *mise en abyme* that encrypts both Chaucer's authorship and this interpretative paradigm of 'making', *BD*'s narrator (or, if you wish, Chaucer) draws attention to himself not far along into the poem as 'I, that made this book' (96). This offhand remark, which forms part of this chapter's epigraph, is misleading – intentionally so – in a number of respects. First, there is no logical sense at this point in the narrative in which the book, i.e. the *Book of the Duchess*, is yet 'made'. There has thus far been no dream, no duchess and no resolve to compose a new poem. The closest analogue of this line in *BD*'s sources, near the beginning of Machaut's *Fonteinne amoureuse*, underscores by comparison the awkwardness of this moment. In a lengthy prologue to his *dit* in which he establishes his identity as a lover and a clerk, Machaut incorporates an anagram – as he does in most of his *dits* – that names both himself and his patron, Jean, duc de Berry. As the anagram is introduced, Jean is referred to as 'Celui pour qui je fais ce livre' (The man for whom I'm making this book) (32). Machaut's attestation here of his act of 'making', woven into a poetic device that links his own identity with that of his patron, is foundational for his construction of authority as a 'professional writer'. As Kevin Brownlee observes, the conjunction of poet and patron issuing from Machaut's expression of book-making grounds the poem's rationale of a 'poet-narrator [able] to sing the love experience of another in a first-person context'. At the same time, Machaut's emphasis on both the craft and the veracity of the anagram (45–54) certifies that 'Machaut's language functions successfully qua poetic discourse', so that 'Poetic activity becomes, in an important sense, self-authorizing (and self-sufficient).'[1] Articulated in the present tense ('je fais') near the beginning of the *dit*, and linking the composition of the 'livre' clearly enough to a particular courtly setting and occasion, Machaut's 'Celui pour qui je fais ce livre' functions programmatically to bear an authorial signature and to frame the ensuing narrative as trustworthy and purposefully presented (as the attention paid to *dispositio* at lines 55–60 confirms).

By comparison, Chaucer's 'I, that made this book' only obfuscates. Rather than contributing to a logical narrative scheme, it interposes what seems a gratuitous digression in what is already a meandering, evasive (e.g. 39–43) opening section of the poem. Whereas Machaut's line is consistent with the temporal fabric of the poem – at the beginning of the *dit*, with other parts to follow, the act of making is naturally expressed in the present indicative – Chaucer's refers, in the past tense, to the 'book' as finished. Furthermore, unlike Machaut's line, Chaucer's says nothing about for whom the book is made or why; only much later in the poem, outside of any context of authorship or patronage, is there a hint that Chaucer recoups Machaut's anagrammatic strategies in his coded identification of Gaunt and Blanche through puns.[2] Lastly, Chaucer's 'book-making' assertion, unlike Machaut's, does not inscribe an authorial signature, despite broadcasting an instrumental 'I' and intimating veracity ('trewly' (96)). Indeed, even the 'book' in question is subject to disorientation.

Here arises a second respect in which 'I, that made this book' proves misleading. Chaucer's narrator mentions his book-making strictly in the context of a response to *another* 'bok', one that is repeatedly designated as such in passages surrounding this line (the term appears at lines 47, 52, 57 and 274). That 'bok', of course, is the volume containing the story of Seys and Alcione. The narrator's unexpected interruption of the story to record his reaction, in the manner of an oath on the authority of 'I, that made this book', comes dangerously close to the fraudulent marketing strategy of bait-and-switch: in a momentary misreading that seems deliberately staged, we are encouraged to confuse Chaucer's book with Ovid's.[3]

Intriguingly, this sets the stage for a similar conflation, one replete with significance for the compositional history of *BD*, in the account of Chaucer's corpus advanced in the Introduction of the *Man of Law's Tale* in the *Canterbury Tales*. There, Chaucer is said to have in his youth 'made of Ceys and Alcione' (II 57). While this may, as noted earlier, refer to an originally free-standing Ovidian adaptation, it appears by synecdoche to stand for *BD* as a whole. If the anachronistic self-reference in line 96 of *BD* highlights problems of 'making' in blurring the line between the end of one author's work and the beginning of another's, might its appeal to a yet notional 'book' also hint at the significance of books *qua* books to the inscription of Chaucerian authorship in *BD*?

In the two fifteenth-century MSS in which *BD* is scribally entitled (Oxford, Bodleian Library MSS Fairfax 16 and Bodley 638), it is designated as 'The bo[o]ke of the Duchesse';[4] this is also the title given it by Chaucer in the *Retraction*. In what respect is the label of 'book' appropriate? At a mere 1334 lines, *BD* hardly qualifies as a book in the modern sense, i.e. 'a portable volume consisting of a series of written, printed, or illustrated pages bound together for ease of reading' (*OED* s.v. 'book' 1(a)), or 'a written composition long enough to fill one or more such volumes' (*OED* s.v. 'book' 1(b)). Medieval definitions of 'bok' are only slightly more relevant: 'any collection of sheets or leaves, bound or unbound, making up a volume of writings; a book as a material object' (*MED* s.v. 'bok' n. 1(a)), or 'a written composition or compilation (in prose or verse), occupying one or more volumes; a book as an authoritative source' (*MED* s.v. 'bok' n. 2(a)).

In the catalogue of writings supplied in the Prologue of the *Legend of Good Women*, where *BD* is entitled 'the Deeth of Blaunche the Duchesse' (F 418), the term 'book' appears only in reference to the *House of Fame*, although not strictly as part of its title ('the book that hight the Hous of Fame' (F 417)). The application of official-sounding titles in this list (e.g. the 'Parlement of Foules' (F 419)) is interspersed with breezy nomenclature ('many a lay and many a thing' (F 430)), making it difficult to parse Chaucer's descriptive vocabulary for his own writings. The Introduction of the *Man of Law's Tale* muddies the waters further, both in its shorthand reference to 'Ceys and Alcione' and its concern with the actualization of *books*. If in the *Legend of Good Women* Chaucer's works existed virtually, in the confessional realm of intention, here they take on a more material reality, as a 'large volume' (referring to the *Legend of Good Women* itself) and 'o book ... [or] another' annoyingly scattered around space (II 52, 60). The diction of the Introduction cuts puzzlingly across orality and textuality, showing Chaucer to have 'seyd' and 'toold' stories in the form of written books, and to have 'spoken' of good women in his 'large volume', but to have 'made of Ceys and Alcione' (a verb specific to written composition; see *MED* s.v. 'maken' v. 5(a–e)) and to have chosen not to 'write' of other subjects (*CT* II 51–3, 57–8, 87; cf. 77). By contrast, Chaucer's *Retraction* evokes an almost claustrophobic bookishness, as texts that elsewhere floated freely as open discourse – quarrelled over in *LGW*, annotated and emended in the Introduction of the *Man of Law's Tale* – achieve the terrifying closure of 'publication'. In the *Retraction*, the term 'book' is applied to nearly every work listed, good and bad, long and short: the 'book of Troilus', the 'book ... of Fame', 'the book of the XXV. Ladies', the 'book of the Duchesse', the 'book of Seint Valentynes day of the Parlement of Briddes', the 'book of the Leoun', 'bookes of legendes of seintes, and omelies, and moralitee, and devocioun', and even forgotten compositions ('many another book, if they were in my remembrance') (X 1086–8). Not designated as a 'book' are 'the tales of Caunterbury' (although the absence of the singular 'book' in this case may serve to distinguish individual stories 'that sownen into synne' from a larger anthology),[5] the 'translacion of Boece de Consolacione', and 'many a song and many a leccherous lay'.

This last item in the *Retraction* highlights the only point of consistency across Chaucer's three catalogues with respect to the vocabulary of his compositions: in all of these, the term 'book' is contrasted with lyrical forms. It may thus be said in general that Chaucer uses the word 'book' loosely and without technical exactitude to refer to any predominantly narrative, non-lyrical written text (which may contain a residue of orality in its discursive constitution, as the Man of Law implies). Some suggestion exists that a pure translation – *Boece* in the *Retraction* – does not qualify as a 'book', which would instead be an autonomous production credited to the author.[6] A 'book' can be a collection of stories, such as 'bookes of legendes of seintes', but not exclusively so. Differently, a 'book' can be a formal subdivision of a larger work (*OED* s.v. 'book' 4), as occurs, upon Chaucer's own testimony, in the *House of Fame* and *Troilus and Criseyde*. Finally, a 'book' is not an inflexible or absolute construct: even a long work as polished as *Troilus* can be marked casually as 'Creseyde' in the *Legend of Good Women* (F 441) and, with greater formality, as 'the book of Troilus' in the *Retraction*; in this case especially, the two titles imply very different interpretations of the poem. In the same vein, we can wonder if *BD* is to be understood as a narrative about an individual's death, as the *Legend of Good Women* assumes ('the Deeth of Blaunche the Duchesse'), or as the textual reification of a noblewoman, as per the *Retraction* ('book of the Duchesse').

To be sure, a 'book' sounds more impressive than a 'thing' (although the two are not entirely distinct, as *BD* 219 implies), and it seems likely that Chaucer's designation in the *Retraction* of so many of his writings as 'books' functions in part to establish his authorial *bona fides*: even as he ostensibly 'takes back' these works, he broadcasts and preserves them for posterity, endowing them with the dignity of physical tomes. Indeed, as Stephen Partridge has recently suggested, Chaucer's emphasis on 'books' in the *Retraction*, reinforced by the surrounding rubrics, associates him with a clerkly model of authorship in which '"making" is inextricable from book-making' and – as Chaucer's collaboration with his scribe Adam Pinkhurst now indicates – whereby authors take an active part in the design and production of their works as physical books.[7]

Interestingly, the malleability of 'book' in Chaucer's usage is reminiscent of the similar character of the French term *dit*, which features in the title of several works associated with *BD*, such as the *Dit de la fonteinne amoureuse* and *Dit dou bleu chevalier*, and also supplies a likely precedent for Chaucer's 'book of the Leoun' (i.e. Machaut's *Dit dou lyon*). As a story or 'saying', however, the French *dit* is somewhat more closely associated with speech as opposed to writing, and it typically encompasses lyric: *dits amoreux* are characterized by an amalgamation of lyric and narrative, an allegorical dimension, and dialogue or debate on love problems. Even as, in medieval French literature, *dit* becomes a catch-all term for 'la notion moderne et neutre de poème, pour laquelle le Moyen Âge n'a pas d'équivalent exact' (the modern, neutral notion of a 'poem', for which the Middle Ages lacked an exact equivalent),[8] the English 'book' did not possess even this degree of generic specificity: the term was not exclusive to poetry, for example, and unlike *dit* it carried no formal expectations as a genre. Instead, a 'book', at least in Chaucer's usage, seems to constitute a mechanism for evincing the authority of a piece of writing (cf. *OED* s.v. 'book' 6(a), 'something considered as worthy of study, a source of instruction, or an example from which to learn') and suggesting its material coherence.

Further complicating *BD*'s preoccupation with books, and with itself as a book, is the fact that units of textual production in Chaucer's period do not align neatly with our modern sense of the book, nor was there available to Chaucer an exacting vocabulary for the cultural forms of textual representation with which he engaged. Scholars of late medieval manuscript culture have pointed increasingly to the 'booklet' or fascicle, as opposed to the 'book', as 'the primary unit of production and reception'.[9] As will be discussed more fully in the following chapters, *BD*'s representation in the fifteenth-century MSS that preserve it is structured upon the 'booklet' as a cluster of texts transmitted as a unit which could be combined variously with other textual units into marketable anthologies. If, as Joseph A. Dane observes, 'the physical book' is then 'necessarily more editorial than authorial', it follows that medieval authors could well have used the term 'book' in a sense that is closer to what we now call a 'booklet', for which no distinct word existed in English. In MS Tanner 346, which is probably the earliest and least editorialized of the three related MSS containing *BD*, the poem occupies a booklet of its own, rendering it a literal 'book' of the Duchess (although, somewhat ironically, this is the MS for which a scribal title of *BD* is lacking). In Tanner's sibling MSS, *BD* is gathered with other poems on courtly subjects to form a larger booklet. It is instructive, then, that the looseness of Middle English 'book' as a technical label, lacking fixed properties and reflecting varying motivations, is also informed by a material reality in which what constitutes a 'book', or booklet, is more provisional and contextual than our modern sensibilities readily allow. In the period before the printing press, a 'book', in short, was not so much a secure receptacle of literary intention as it was a vehicle of significance *in potentia*, a way of making meaning out of a text.

The 'book' acquired this type of significance in a cultural setting in which it also functioned as an 'episteme' to cohere various forms of meaning.[10] Common tropes in the Middle Ages included the 'book of nature (or the world)', the 'book of history', and the 'book of memory', among others. In all of these instances, the 'book' is a paradigm that facilitates the 'signifying, organizing, and remembering' of abstract experience and meaning.[11] The 'book of the self' is a particularly interesting coordinate for the bibliophilic engineering of *BD*, a poem that begins with an inchoate 'I' and navigates various bookish encounters to end in a completed 'hit' – the textual incarnation of a subjectivity ('my sweven') (1, 1334). As Eric Jager has insightfully demonstrated, the 'textual metaphorics of the self' and the 'inner self as textual space' were increasingly popular medieval constructs for representing individual experience in spiritual and amatory contexts. Rhetorics of disclosure and revelation, erotic inscription and self-examination all attended the codicological figuring of selfhood, naturalizing the idea that experience can be inhabited as if within the pages of a book.[12] This metaphor is in part a reflex of the fact that, on the one hand, books were ubiquitous – the dominant technology for conveying authoritative knowledge – and on the other, precious – costly, fleshly objects comprised of material resources (animal skin) and hard labour (scribal work). Like human beings, medieval books were compound substances, amalgamating letter and spirit, collective wisdom and idiosyncratic expression, sharing a common form yet each unique unto itself (particularly in the manuscript era, before the regularity made possible by mass production). The title 'speculum' or 'mirour', attached to many a medieval book, gives further evidence that books were seen to guide readers' conduct by bringing them face to face with themselves, revealing their present, flawed state as well as the ideal towards which they should strive.[13] In this setting, as readers in their encounters with books engaged in self-reflection, new kinds of agency inhered in the reading process, which became a forum 'for imagining structures of ethical action and selfhood that establish a relationship to spiritual meaning or inner truth'.[14]

Medieval arts of memory in particular rely upon the construct of a bookish self. As Mary J. Carruthers has influentially demonstrated, the work of *memoria* was fundamental to literary composition, or *inventio*, which is the 'finding' and subsequent arrangement of mental images deriving from personal and collective experience.[15] It has recently been argued that books were more than just a by-product of memory work: they were also an instrument of it, offering a conceptual medium – the codex – in which memories and experiences could be visually arranged as if in a 'virtual cell of the imagination'.[16] The manuscript book, in other words, appealed to the bibliophilic Middle Ages as an analogue for cognitive storage and disposition much as the twentieth-century US pop-cultural commonplace of the 'mental Rolodex' – or, more recently and globally, the computer as metaphor for cognitive processing – offers an intuitive shorthand for memory selection by virtue of its functional associations. Martha Dana Rust takes this point still further, arguing that the medieval book constituted a 'threshold' across which readers were encouraged to enter into an imaginative space, interacting with the physical and representational medium of the codex (words, images, script, mise-en-page) as it conditions an interior cognitive world marked by transformative encounters.[17] In these various associations between books and interiority, between textual form and personal narrative, books in the late-medieval period offered a way of thinking the self.

In this light, both Carruthers and Rust have read *BD* as staging a provocative immersion in a bookish space. By one reading, *BD* is 'a memory poem requiring memory-work on the part of all its partici-pants': the chamber painted with images of the story of Troy and the *Roman de la rose*, in which the dreamer 'awakens', evokes the writer's mental scaffolding in the process of *inventio*, and the story he in turn composes in memory of Blanche heals his earlier malaise by engaging him in communal discourse.[18] Somewhat differently, books as signifying entities in their own right may be understood to frame *BD*, a poem in which the narrator 'falls asleep on his book and seems to "wake up" inside one', thus 'absor[bed] in and into a book'.[19] For Rust, the nar-rator's reflexive identification as 'I, that made this book' (96) activates what she calls the 'manuscript matrix' – a 'virtual dimension' in which books, as forums of signification analogous to the imaginative faculty of the brain, can be freely interacted with and inhabited. The narrator, after all, does not only compose a story with the aid of bookish memo-rial images: he participates in that story and assimilates it to his own, 'finding' it, as it were, inside the book of the self.[20] Similarly attuned to the transformative properties of the Ovidian book of fables is the analysis of Martine Gamaury, who approaches the 'I, that made this book' passage as a 'vector' that activates a fluidity of creative modes by inserting anachronism in the narrative, exposing a rupture among thinking, reading and writing that is both traumatic and enabling. In this reading, the narrator's initial vacuum of inspiration, established in his insomniac struggle with mental focus, becomes a creative space that is filled by his bedtime reading and, subsequently, by his dream, culminating in the creation of a new text.[21]

It is suggestive, as I have argued elsewhere, that the bookish concerns of *BD* issue from an imaginative encounter with an Ovidian story.[22] In the Introduction of the *Man of Law's Tale* as well, Chaucer's résumé as a prolific, if undisciplined, architect of books – 'o book ... [or] another' – is cast in terms of a signature Ovidianism: he has told more love stories than 'Ovide' who, unlike Chaucer, is credited with only one volume (the 'Episteles') (*CT* II 52, 54–5). As observed earlier, the Man of Law collapses Chaucer's poetic output into Ovid's by referring to *BD*, so it seems, as 'Ceys and Alcione'. This might be compared to a moment of mischievous phrasal slippage in the *House of Fame*, when the eagle refers to the very source of the poem's titular image in Chaucer's 'oune bok' – by which he means Ovid's *Metamorphoses* – once again conflating Chaucer's *own* book (most immediately, the present poem, labelled the 'book ... of Fame' in the *Retraction*) with Chaucer's *favourite* book, Ovid's collection of fables (*HF* 712). 'I, that made this book', we have observed, evokes in *BD* precisely this creative ellipsis. Returning to the Man of Law's representation of an Ovidian Chaucer, the two love poets are further subtly associated insofar as they are both yoked to a concept of bookish antiquity. To the Man of Law, Ovid's 'Episteles' are 'ful olde', just as Chaucer's literary efforts have the air of *longue durée*, having been discharged 'in swich Englissh as he kan / Of *olde tyme*' – a phrase that also, significantly, is attached to the Ovidian book in *BD* ('in this bok were written fables / That clerkes had in *olde tyme*, / And other poetes, put in rime') (*CT* II 49–50, *BD* 52–4; emphases added). While this collocation of Chaucer's and Ovid's respective affinities with 'oldness' may be understood as an oblique, self-referential harnessing of ancient authority for a vernacular poet, what is important for our purpose is that the presence of Ovid in Chaucer's works, beginning with *BD*, often intersects with a preoccupation with the physical status of books and an image of the poet as a maker of books.

This is hardly coincidental: Ovid has been viewed as 'the most daring of ancient poets in personifying texts and animating books'

– books whose obligations include 'communicating *with other texts*'.[23] Ovid revelled in the metamorphosis of human forms into written texts: Daphne and Hyacinthus, for example, in their new forms as laurel tree (associated with poetic creation) and prophetic flower (the petals of which bear a future hero's name), become media for literate inscription. Furthermore, Ovid famously wished at the end of the *Metamorphoses* to achieve immortality by 'becoming' his own literary corpus, and subsequently bemoaned his exile as a severance from, and victimization by, the very books he authored. Chaucer, to be sure, endows books with similar agency in mid-career works such as *Troilus* and *Legend of Good Women*. These poems, which (respectively) send off books for posterity and are haunted by their misreading, draw heavily on Ovidian tropes of canonical formation, textual mobility and bookish subjection. In doing so, they show how erratic power relations between books and their creators come to destabilize the autonomy proper to authorship – issues that resurface in the book-laden *Retraction*. Viewing *BD* in light of these bookish coordinates of Chaucer's later works as well as the allure of Ovid as a paradigm for 'thinking books', we find value added to Martin Irvine's contention, remarked upon in the first chapter, that *BD* functions generically as a kind of commentary on Ovid's *Metamorphoses*. Irvine's discussion of manuscript textuality suggests that Chaucer's vernacular poem about love and loss can be imagined to 'surround' the core Latin text of Ovid's 'Ceyx and Alcyone' as if on a manuscript folio, glossing and dilating upon it not in the manner of the grammarian or allegorist but through the lens of a dream – a dream which, in the poem's final lines, is positioned as a satellite of the book still in the narrator's grip.[24]

In other respects as well, *BD* is a text comprised of other texts. Its assembly of written media is not confined to the physical codex; several kinds of figurative books also proliferate and demand scrutiny. The walls of the dream bedroom, as we have noted, materialize around the dreamer as if a projection of his own mental repository as a potential writer, or a larger-than-life manuscript page in which he finds his own emerging story inscribed. In addition, the two lyrical interludes within the narrative ascribed to the Man in Black (lines 475–86, 1175–80) cast the knightly protagonist as an aspiring poet as well as a lover, and his testing of various poetic registers in an attempt to articulate his loss, we have also seen, renders the larger poem a kind of anthology of poetic forms. In one sense, the Man in Black occupies the position of author – his is the central story, he possesses the secrets – and the narrator that of scribe: a dynamic that has been taken to indicate Chaucer's diplomacy towards John of Gaunt on a delicate subject.[25] And yet the Man in Black is also figured as a text: in his formative years, he was 'a whit wal or a table' that received the impressions of '[a]l that men wil theryn make, / Whethir so men wil portreye or peynte' (780, 782–3). This representation of the *tabula rasa* motif has often been considered in the light of its epistemological implications and its derivation from the courtly rhetoric of the *dits amoreux*,[26] but it is equally noteworthy for its foregrounding of writing imagery, as if the knight is a blank tablet receptively awaiting the etchings of a 'maker'.[27]

The one true blank slate of the poem, however, is – logically – not Black but White. Feminist and psychoanalytic readings, we have noted, have frequently remarked upon the poem's displacement (or erasure) of White and her own discourse: its treatment of her as a gap, or 'whitened signature', to be filled in by a masculine poetic cementing a homosocial fellowship.[28] By this reading, the pallor that evokes both purity and death ensures White's silence and thus sanctions her appropriation by male discourse, reorienting the potentially disruptive dynamics of heterosexual love towards a paternalist hegemony.[29] This gendered aspect of *BD*, which to some extent works against its ostensible purpose as an elegiac tribute, hints at an allegorical signification of Black and White other than that evoked in the chess analogy: namely, the inscription of black words on a white page. Maud Ellmann aptly isolates the coordinates of this compositional allegory: Blanche, as White, incarnates 'the unconquerable whiteness of the page', and the Man in Black 'represents the ink with which it is deflowered'.[30] Productive as this insight is for feminist analyses of *BD*'s gendered politics, it can also deepen our apprehension of the poem's textual self-consciousness and its contemplation of the lives of books, as we shall now consider.

The blackness of *BD*'s knightly protagonist and its imagistic connection to textuality may profitably be placed in dialogue with a comparable phenomenon in *Troilus and Criseyde*, from which the first
part of this chapter's title derives. When, in Book 2, Pandarus delivers
Criseyde's first letter to Troilus, he exclaims, 'Parde, God hath holpen
us! / Have here a light, and loke on al this blake' (2.1319–20). Criseyde
herself, of course, is a veritable Lady in Black for much of the poem,
her dark mourning garb so sharply expressing the iconographic properties of medieval widowhood – bereavement, prosperity, vulnerability
and sexual availability – that, like the Man in Black, her personhood
is evoked synecdochally by the hue of her garments: 'She, this in
blak' (1.309); 'she ... / That stood in blak' (2.533–4); and figuratively,
the 'bright ... sterre' under 'cloude blak' (1.175).[31] The image of the
black-clad Criseyde (reluctantly) penning what Pandarus heralds as
'al this blake' becomes linked with the poem's many representations
of Criseyde as an inscrutable 'text' in her own right (for example, at
3.1357). As Rust observes, Pandarus' tactical representation of what is
actually a rather cautious letter by Criseyde as 'al this blak' suggests
that 'in the form of her epistle Pandarus has brought a small patch of
Criseyde's robe into the room or, better yet, that the inky characters
on this missive are so many tiny embodiments of their author'.[32] That
this begins a male practice of imputing meaning to Criseyde's words
which will continue throughout the poem and permeate the 'future' of
her character reinforces the relevance of this imagery to *BD*, where a
similar inscription of the female protagonist has been thought to occur.

The notion of embodying a text through association with an individual's clothing – and of textualizing the body – has precedent elsewhere in Chaucer's works, which include representations of book
bindings as figurative clothing and written words as garbed in the
colour of their ink. Specifically, the *General Prologue* relates that the
Clerk's books of philosophy are 'clad in blak or reed', and the *House
of Fame* describes the celestial journey of words 'clothed red or blak'
(*CT* I 294, *HF* 1078). The correspondence between *Troilus* and *BD* in
the textual associations of blackness, furthermore, testifies to the intuitive connection for Chaucer between novel texts and mourning bodies,

both made legible by black markings (letters and garments). If death posits a lack – a page scraped clean – what exists to fill it, to substitute for the form now absent, are words of mourning and remembrance: black letters.

Returning to this chapter's consideration of the multiple textualities of *BD* with this in mind, one can argue that the Man in Black, set against an idealized (lost) White-ness and the narrator's yet barren imaginative landscape, is on one level a figure of *writing*: an image, like a black letter on a blank folio, of the very process of composition transpiring inside the narrator's head as a result of his dream. The lexical resonances of 'blak' in Middle English suggest the appeal of this symbolic reading. It was not uncommon for the noun 'blak' to function as a shorthand for black ink or black written characters (*MED* s.v. 'blak' n. 3(b), *OED* s.v. 'black' n. 1(a)), just as it could for black cloth or garments (*MED* s.v. 'blak' n. 3(c), *OED* s.v. 'black' n. 2(a)). To find something 'in blak' or 'in the blak', according to the range of Middle English sources cited in these entries, is to find it 'in writing' or 'in the book'. The emphasis in *BD* on the knight's being 'al in blak' (457) – this feature supplanting a personal name as a marker of identity – thus intensifies his associations with writing, the formation of letters, in a material sense. So pervasively does the knight's blackness define his subject – his perfect union with White and the extremity of his mourning – and, so to speak, colour the poem as a whole, that it is not unfitting to view it as a chronicle of 'al this blake'.

This label is appropriate, on one level, as an epitome of the dreamer's fascination with the Man in Black – in humoural terms, a personification of the melancholy, produced by black bile, that oppresses the narrator in waking life. At the same time, 'al this blake', read through the intertext of *Troilus*, captures the sheer excitement – exemplified by Pandarus – of unfurling a brand-new, hard-bought text for an eager reader. Applied retrospectively to *BD*, the phrase elicits the poem's concern with moving past the writerly stasis associated with melancholy and towards the production of 'al this blake': a new book. In this latter sense, dreaming the dream *is* synonymous and concomitant with writing the poem, as the final lines of *BD* imply: black letters inscribed on the white slate of the mind are replicated as words on the page. The compression of temporality and of media ('sweven' and 'ryme') evoked in the final line of *BD* – 'This was my sweven; now hit ys doon' – thus becomes coherent if we understand the Man in Black not only as the subject of the poem, but its substance as well. 'The dream imaging the Black Knight's grief', as Martine Yvernault proposes, 'may express the poet's dream of his own creation'.[33] As a dream about the writing of a book about a dream, *BD* prepares in provocative ways for later Chaucerian explorations of the subjectivities and afterlives of books.

Writing Books: The Author in the Text

The genealogical proximity of *BD* to the *dit amoreux* tradition associates Chaucer's first poem with a form that is thoroughly invested in the discourse of authorship, as Machaut's fondness for anagrammatic self-authorization, considered earlier in the light of Chaucer's remark on book-making, reminds us. Although Chaucer's reflections on writing and his responsibilities as a 'maker' are in *BD* more oblique than the confident, polished and public displays of clerkly achievement in the *dits* of Machaut and Froissart, they partake of a common tradition that finds in the matter of love a mirror of the art of composition itself. By framing his poem as a dream-vision – a narrative pattern generally incidental to, rather than synonymous with, the French *dits*, which sometimes feature inset dreams within a larger plot – Chaucer formally extended *BD*'s self-conscious engagement with textuality, for dreams are personally 'authored' texts that demand narrative ordering, enunciation and interpretation: as we have seen, the dream in *BD* becomes, quite literally, the material of a book.

    BD's relation to both the *dit amoreux* and the dream-vision traditions informs its complex staging of temporality, which figures in our present concern with the rhetoric of authorship – the moment (or moments) at which an author separates himself from a text, rendering it 'bookish' and opening it to potentially limitless transactions with readers. 'I, that made this book' is one such moment in *BD*; 'This was my sweven; now hit ys doon' is another. The shifting time frames of the poem – not only within the dream (e.g. the passage of Octovyen through a fourteenth-century forest), where this is to be expected, but outside it as well – have presented a challenge for critics seeking narrative unity and linear character development. Beginning in the present tense by relating an ongoing insomnia ('for day ne nyght / I may nat slepe wel nygh noght' (2–3)), the poem shifts to a time 'this other night' when bedtime reading led to sleep. Then, after a dream that dwells on its protagonist's past experience and features a return to the present ('where is she now?' (1298)) that proves cataclysmic, *BD* collapses the recent past (the 'other night' of the dream) into future resolve ('I wol, be processe of tyme, / Fonde to put this sweven in ryme' (1331–2)), only to derange any potential sense of 'processe of tyme' with the impatient 'anoon' and the peremptory 'now hit ys doon' (1333–4). The problem of logical coherence arising here is well captured by Ardis Butterfield, who correlates it with French love poets' play with 'the boundaries of life and art'; she notes that Chaucer's narrator 'says he cannot feel or write; yet if we re-read the poem, we find that these opening lines are the result of his decision at the end to put his dream in writing'.[34] In other words, if the poem itself is evidence of the narrator's progression past debilitating insomnia, or creative obstruction, to achieve 'poetic initiation' as an emotionally sensible writer, how are we to apprehend the present tense of the opening section?[35] The problem is especially acute because of the reminder of the narrator's presence *as author* at line 96, which wedges the finite, physical character of the 'book' which 'ys doon' against the indefinite present of 'sorwful ymagynacioun / Ys alway hooly in my mynde' (14–15, 96, 1334).

Critics have brought various hermeneutic constructs to bear upon this difficulty, citing an 'aesthetic of permeability' that incites motion across 'origins, chronology, and spatiality';[36] a dialogic activation of different cultural perspectives (past and future, French tradition and English literary possibilities);[37] and a resistance to linearity that encourages, via 'a present reading of a past condition', a sense of 'middle-ness'.[38] Perhaps more apt than these modern terms of convenience is an analogy from medieval music: 'the impression produced is of a contrapuntal composition built on a polyphony of voices superposing past and present, inverting and playing with tenses to lead from life to death and back to life'.[39] We may compare the problematic temporality of *BD*'s frame with that of Froissart's *Le Paradys d'Amours*, which as the most immediate source of these sections and the only precedent among the *dits* for an overarching dream-vision form, seems at first glance to create a similar effect. The narrator of *Paradys* begins with a present-tense expression of amazement that he can still be alive after enduring so long without sleep, in a state of unremitting melancholy. Unlike Chaucer's narrator, Froissart's explicitly attributes his sleeplessness to lovesickness and suggests that it is half intentional, owing to his devotion to his lady (lines 1–12).[40] He recounts a time 'n'a pas lonc terme' (not long ago) (line 13) that he was able to fall asleep after praying to Morpheus, leading to a dream of Love's fulfilment, heavily imbued by the allegorical structures of the *Roman de la rose*, from which he wakes suddenly. As at the end of *BD*, Froissart's narrator finds himself in his own bed, reflects on his dream and its cause, and takes comfort in it. Unlike Chaucer, Froissart does not project the writing of the poem itself, although in a fashion typical of French *dits* the body of the dream has included experimentation in various lyrical forms (which he recounts here) and has thus engendered poetic invention.[41]

In comparison to *BD*, the trajectory of *Paradys* is simply expressed: a disconsolate lover-poet experiences a dream that may bode well for success in his love affair, or at least serve the basic palliative function of wish-fulfilment (Macrobius, it should be noted, singles out lovers' dreams of possessing their sweethearts as a paradigm of the *insomnium*, a type of unprophetic dream[42]). In the final account, however, the dream is a temporary measure: 'Ensi fui je ravis *jadis* / Dedens l'amourous paradys' (Thus was I *once* ravished into the Paradise of Love) (1722–3; emphasis added). No real inconsistency inheres in the same narrator who utters this last line returning the next evening to the sleepless, melancholy state of the opening passage, wishing again for the remedial measure of slumber and finding in dreams a surrogate for action. This is not the case in *BD*, in which the newly invigorated narrator awakens at the end a writer rather than a reader, so alacritous in his determination to put his dream in rhyme that, by the final line, the writing has occurred as if by a magic act. Surely this is not the same narrator who before the dream could not control his 'ydel thoght[s]' (4), resolve on any course of action (29), or keep his 'first mater' straight (43).[43] In sum, Chaucer retains the temporal scheme of Froissart's *dit* – moving from present to past – but adds to it a future dimension, connected to the act of writing, which compresses and complicates the disclosure of time, and he capitalizes on the extratemporal properties of the dream to do so. In this, Chaucer is somewhat closer in spirit to one of the anterior literary structures in *Paradys*, namely the *Roman de la rose*.

As the archetypal medieval love-vision, Guillaume de Lorris and Jean de Meun's *Roman de la rose* (written between 1225–30 and 1269–78) establishes the coordinates of the play with temporality and author-ship that marks *BD* and other later medieval dream-visions. This was to some extent inevitable in light of the dual structure of the work: purporting to relate a dream experienced by a first-person narrator in youth, one that has since 'come true, exactly as the dream told it' ('tretot avenu ... / si con li songes recensoit'),[44] the *Roman* is narrated by two authors who lived more than a generation apart, sustaining the illusion that they are one and the same dreaming narrator. Putting aside the vexed questions of whether Guillaume's poem is genuinely unfinished and the extent to which the two authors' perspectives on amatory discourse cohere, both of which are beyond the scope of the present discussion, we may consider the God of Love's proph-ecy in Jean's continuation (lines 10465–650), near the midpoint of the *Roman* taken as a whole, as an indirect precedent for the 'com-positional consciousness' with which we are concerned in *BD*. This much-analysed prophecy is nothing less than a meta-literary *coup* by which Jean inscribes himself into his predecessor's dream and renders his poetic execution of it necessary. For Lori Walters, this section of the poem epitomizes how '[t]he *Roman de la Rose*, which deals simultan-eously with the experience of falling in love and the composition of a narrative about that very experience, is a text that metaphorizes its own processes of reading and writing'.[45] In his prophecy, the God of Love 'predicts' the death of Guillaume de Lorris, as the most recent love poet in a distinguished series, followed by the birth of Jean de Meun, his succession in Guillaume's literary task, and even the very line at which he will begin his continuation (which at this point is some six thousand lines back). In Macrobian terms, the God of Love's prophecy transforms Guillaume's dream from an untrustworthy *insomnium* – a lover's fantasy – into a reliable *oraculum*, in which a god or authority figure reveals the future, thus certifying beyond question Jean's authorship and his uncanny access to the same dream, long after the illusion of continuity has been foisted upon us. The fact that Jean is already writing this section of the work that predicts his own birth as a future event presents a creative ellipsis that is not entirely unlike the rupture in temporality that emerges from Chaucer's self-reference as 'I, that made this book' before the book, logically speaking, has been made. In both cases, prolepsis dramatically marks authorship: for Jean, it facilitates his self-naming as Guillaume's successor and also endows the poem with an official title (the 'Mirror of Lovers', according to the God of Love himself); for Chaucer, it formalizes his status as a maker of a 'book' whose responsive reading is modelled for us in this scene. Just as, in the prophecy, Jean harnesses Guillaume's authority as a love poet (who in turn is placed in a long tradition of love poets), so does Chaucer appropriate Ovid's currency as a poet of 'wonder thing[s]' (61).

The *dit amoreux* vogue inspired by the *Roman de la rose* was, as already noted, highly attentive to literary craft, even if this was typically detached from a dream frame. *Dits* such as Froissart's *Le Paradys d'Amours* and Machaut's closely related *Remede de Fortune* chronicle their narrators' mastery of the lyrical *formes fixes*, conflating poetic accomplishment and courtly finesse with successful education in love service. These *dits* supply rich territory for the assertion of vernacular authorship, which typically occurs through self-naming, anagrammatic inscription and emphasis on the poet–patron relationship. Often, as in Machaut's *Le Jugement dou roy de Behaigne* and *Le Jugement dou roy de Navarre*, they conclude with missives to the poet's lady that reflect on the completion of the work and project other kinds of poetic activity. An even more pertinent precedent for the 'compositional consciousness' of *BD* is Machaut's *Le Livre dou voir dit*, composed in 1363–5, at least a few years before Chaucer's poem, although it has rarely been considered as among *BD*'s direct sources (Chaucer was arguably to use a section of it later for his *Manciple's Tale*). As one of the most virtuosically metanarrative medieval poems, the *Voir dit* is quite literally a poem that takes as its subject its own composition: consisting of an exchange of letters and love lyrics between the aged author and a young female admirer, it documents the unfolding of a love affair, the authenticity of that affair in textual form, and the circulation and interpretation of this textualized romance as 'a material artefact that resists public performance at every turn'.[46] It is significant that the one point of contact between *Voir dit* and *BD* that has been proposed, by James Wimsatt, centres upon the most fully 'metanarrative' section of Chaucer's poem: the reading of the book of fables. Near the end of *Voir dit*, the narrator takes up an ancient book (Livy on Fortune) to relieve his boredom; after relating the content of the story, he connects the ways of Fortune with the changeability of his lady. Under similar circumstances, Chaucer's narrator reads, and recounts at length, a classical story to assuage his *ennui*.[47] It is attractive to consider that the metafictional frame of the larger *Voir dit*, with its elliptical reflections on its own construction as a book and its critique of the authenticity of personal experience, on some level prepared for *BD*'s own experimentation with these issues.

Other coordinates for *BD*'s 'compositional consciousness' can be located in Middle English visionary narratives by Chaucer's Ricardian contemporaries. The final section of this chapter considers a selection of these in an exploratory vein, not seeking direct influence – all of the Middle English works considered here postdate the probable period of *BD*'s composition, and only one (Gower's *Confessio amantis*, discussed further in chapter 5) may partly be indebted to Chaucer's poem – but instead sketching some forms, both analogous and distinct, taken by English authors' reflections on their own books in the making. Following the lead of the 1999 anthology *The Idea of the Vernacular*, the present analysis centres upon vernacular writers' own remarks on the writing process, often but not exclusively in the prologues and framing materials of their texts – remarks that frequently assimilate Latin academic discursive mechanisms for the study of *auctores*, but which are 'situated' in a cultural context of Englishness.[48] All of the works considered here formally inscribe authorial self-reflection insofar as they exist in multiple recensions, as products of authorial revision over time. The broadly intertextual, inevitably selective map of English authorship drawn here is a first step towards establishing a discursive field in which *BD* participated in a native register, preparing for the remaining chapters' examination of the material transmission and literary afterlives of Chaucer's *Book* in early modern England.

One would be hard pressed to identify a Middle English dream-vision more starkly different from *BD* than William Langland's *Piers Plowman*, the A-text of which is roughly contemporaneous with *BD* and the C-text of which coincides with Chaucer's mature literary efforts in the mid-1380s. Langland's and Chaucer's poems both contribute to a mythic construction of authorship, but in very different ways: the one is continuous with and inextricable from its author's life – a single, all-encompassing life-work existing in multiple stages of invention – while the other is a launching point and itinerary for a poetic career. They are similar, however, in evincing their narrators' interpretative and temporal perspective on the action narrated, their dreams and their involvement in writing. As Míċeál F. Vaughan contends in his reading of *Piers Plowman*, Will's representation of his journey of education is shaped by (what we presume to be) his achievement of enlightenment over the course of the dream series, and most pivotally between the ending of the final dream and the writing of the poem.[49] By the end of the narrative as it stands in the B- and C-texts, the search for Piers Plowman continues, but the cycle of dreaming ends – and the last associations carried by dreaming, in the abusive enchantment of Conscience, are negative (see B.20.378).[50] Vaughan draws attention to the abrupt disintegration of Will's final dream with the temporally curious phrase 'til I gan awake' (B.20.387), which may literally be translated as 'until I began to wake up' or, more loosely, 'at which point I did wake up', highlighting various potential temporalities at this important moment, which seems to linger between past and future. Preparing for this, it seems, is a new emphasis on *writing* in the waking scenes of the later *passūs*. Whereas at earlier points in the poem, Will awoke from dreams, reflected on their content to varying degrees, wandered through the world and again fell asleep, beginning in *passus* 19 Will 'awaked and wroot what I hadde ydremed' (B.19.1; cf. 19.485), thus staking out a position of testimonial visionary authority with biblical precedent (see Rev. 2:11). The presence of Will as writer in the later *passūs* hints at an ongoing act of textual construction that is confirmed by the implications of 'til I gan awake'. This offers a very different kind of closure from the similarly abrupt 'This was my sweven; now hit ys doon' of *BD*, but in both cases the conditions of authorship – of converting a dream into a book – have attached themselves to the narrators' dreaming experience in a way that intrudes on temporal consistency.

If Langland encourages a sense of immediacy, of a continuous present, in dreaming and writing, despite his poem's intimations of the course of a life passing, Julian of Norwich in the short and long versions of her visionary work entitled *A Vision Showed to a Devout Woman* (1373) and *A Revelation of Love* (1393), sought a model of authorship informed by distance, reflection and collaboration. The form of Julian's 'shewings' is presented resolutely in the past tense, as an exceptional event now over, but their content – Christ's words to her, in direct discourse – unfolds on the plane of present- and future-tense expression (epitomized by the refrain 'Alle maner thing shall be welle').[51] Julian's book, more explicitly than Langland's, is a cumulative composition: not only does the long text expand upon the short by amplifying detail; it functions as an express commentary on it, interpolating points of reflection that emerged only with the passage of years.[52] Like Chaucer, Julian reflects in her frame on the 'making' of her book, bringing to bear on this a complex tissue of causation that seems to register medieval academic prologues' identification of the 'twofold efficient cause' (*duplex causa efficiens*) in the production of texts, which distributes agency between God and the human author.[53] In the first chapter of *A Revelation*, Julian credits the work to Christ as maker: 'This is a revelation of love that Jhesu Christ, our endles blisse, made in sixteen shewinges' (1.1–2). What follows is a list of these 'shewinges' that at first seems a conventional enumeration of chapter headings at the beginning of a work but in fact denotes the structure of the revelations themselves, which is not coterminous with chapter structure. Julian's visionary experience is thus structured like a book, of which Christ is the 'maker'. At the same time, however, Julian develops her own textual structure for the representation of these visions, rendering her more than simply an amanuensis of Christ, for these visions, in the long version, take shape not only in the immediacy of the moment but also in the crucible of her understanding, resulting in a book of *her* making as well.

This point becomes explicit in the final chapter of *A Revelation*, which applies the vocabulary of 'making' this time to the 'boke' as a whole. Like Langland – and unlike Chaucer, who claims his work 'ys doon' – Julian projects the completion, or execution, of the book beyond the threshold of its final lines. She asserts that '[t]his booke is begonne by Goddes gifte and his grace, but it is not yet performed' (86.1–2). As Watson and Jenkins comment, 'The work's imperfection is linked to the conditions of worldly living, as responsibility shifts from writer to readers to continue to "perform" *A Revelation* until it is done.'[54] Julian thus registers the power of readers to shape meaning – a power that, if abused, can result in the distortion of a text, as the closing warning against heretical application confirms[55] – but she also claims her own place, as a creature, among God's 'making'. Just as Christ's having 'made' the sixteen 'shewings' now emerges as only the beginning of a book that we must complete, so, Julian writes, in 'oure making' as God's creatures 'we had beginning' (86.20–1). In other words, although God's love, out of which he 'made' us, is 'without beginning', that love, for us as temporal beings, is 'oure beginning' (86.21–2). By virtue of this rhetoric of initiation and subjection, Julian in fact opens the 'performance' of her text, to adopt her phrasing, for personal reclamation: framed here as a beginning, the text asks yet to be written, encouraging a creative act. Although her stance on authorship is different, Julian, like Chaucer, carves a space for her own role as maker – assembler and expositor of her visions – within a larger, authoritative discourse of 'making', and in doing so, she authorizes her book's re-making, much as Chaucer ends by placing his book in our unpredictable hands.

Our final example of 'compositional consciousness' is the frame of John Gower's *Confessio amantis*, which, as the latest of the works considered, was first released in 1390 and issued in distinct recensions up to 1393. This most 'bookish' of all the books considered here, with its authorial Latin apparatus and its classical structure, reinforces on several occasions its construction as a book (even using 'booke' as a verb signifying 'to compose'),[56] its circumstances of commission and its author's intention; its Latin *explicit* in the Lancastrian recension, moreover, designates it a *liber* and, following a venerable topos, sends it off to its intended recipient. The much more natural suitability of the label 'bok' for the *Confessio* casts into relief, first of all, the optative force of Chaucer's claiming of that label for his slender, less formally structured *BD*. Like Chaucer with his book preserving 'olde tyme' (*BD* 53), Gower begins by connecting books with 'olde wyse' (*CA* Prologue, line 7), and expresses his own purpose in 'wryt[ing] a bok' to portray 'the world that whilom tok / Long tyme in olde daies passed' (Prologue, lines 54–5). In the first recension of the poem, Gower dedicates the work to Richard II, emphasizing his 'making' of it: 'Whan I this book began to maake'; 'And eek somdel for lust and game / I have it mad'; 'That I this book have mad and write' (8.*3055, *3061–2, *3073). The third recension includes a 'Farewell to the Book' that recollects his intention '[i]n Englesch for to make a book' and comments further on his reasons for having 'maad' it (8.3108, 3110). In these framing passages, Gower speaks strategically as an author, displacing the vulnerable lover-persona he inhabits for the bulk of the *Confessio*. The fact that, in the first recension, this concluding section also features a playful communication to Chaucer by Venus, which encodes an ongoing literary exchange between the two English poets regarding the composition of love poetry (8.*2947–70), suggests the relevance of Chaucer's own bookish experimentations here in Gower's assertion of authorship. Gower, claiming a civic function and a scholastic integrity for his great love poem, accomplishes something that Chaucer did not in *BD*: the polished completion of a literate undertaking, the fulfilment of a bookish purpose made formal from the start. By contrast, Chaucer, with his closing remark, 'now hit ys doon', attempts to slip the composition of his poem by us, leaving us to weigh the authority of the proto-Gowerian 'I, that made this book' against an encounter with 'olde tyme' that also incorporates a lover's discourse in a durable textual edifice.

From the vantage point of these contemporary English explorations of 'making' in relation to first-person visionary experience, as well as the self-reflexive dimensions of authorship summoned in French tradition, *BD* appears less of an isolated or fledgling vernacular attempt to position the author in the text. It is clear that Chaucer took advantage of the opportunities afforded by a narrative about isolation, loss and the difficulties of communication to reflect on 'the book' as a subject in its own right. In doing so, he laid the groundwork for a series of future literary efforts that would engage books, in their status as material objects and forums of interpretative transaction, as a mechanism for reflecting on selfhood, literate creation and the responsibilities of authorship. The attention we have paid to moments of 'compositional consciousness' in *BD*, particularly as they expose problems of temporality and the curious momentum of the ending, prepares us to consider the early modern reception of Chaucer's poem, to which the final two chapters of this book are devoted. Moving from Chaucer's own contemplation of his poem as a 'book' to its actual construction as such in manuscripts and early printed editions, we will find *BD*'s fascination with book-making to prompt a striking range of re-makings that in various ways resist – and sometimes co-opt – Chaucer's insistence that his poem 'ys doon'.

4

REREADING THE *BOOK* (I)

The Materials of Transmission

The early transmission of *BD* is marked by several obscurities as well as some resonant patterns of response. As is the case with Chaucer's other 'minor' poems, no evidence survives of dissemination in the poet's own lifetime; the earliest MSS preserving *BD* are quite late (*c*.1440–50), a half-century after Chaucer's death and well after the production of important MSS of *Canterbury Tales* and *Troilus*. *BD* survives in only three MSS – the so-called Oxford group, consisting of Oxford, Bodleian Library MSS Tanner 346, Fairfax 16, and Bodley 638 – and is independently witnessed in William Thynne's 1532 edition of Chaucer's *Works*. The latter is especially important for supplying various lines missing from all the MSS, most notably lines 31–96, which include the narrator's eight-year sickness and the first part of the Alcione story. Among Chaucer's other dream-visions, by comparison, *House of Fame* is also represented poorly in the MSS, while *Parliament of Foules* and *Legend of Good Women* weigh in a good deal more favourably. The textual traditions on which our understanding of *BD* is based are frustratingly corrupt insofar as they derive from a flawed archetype missing a significant portion of text and issue from MSS at several removes from Chaucer's own language and metre. Hence the state of the text in the surviving MSS and Thynne's edition necessitates the existence of lost exemplars. Further complicating matters is the lack of certainty over Thynne's editorial procedures: did he have access to a superior

MS tradition, or did he take editorial liberties with the puzzles of the text?[1] What is clear is that in the earlier part of the fifteenth century *BD* circulated in material forms that were lost to posterity, leaving its initial circulation and readership largely in obscurity.

Several scholars, beginning with Aage Brusendorff and including the editors of the facsimiles of the Oxford group MSS, have argued that poems such as *BD* initially circulated in independent booklets, their patterns of transmission shaped by booksellers' needs and customers' individual preferences. By a process of accretion, these booklets 'could become associated with other texts and be incorporated into a larger exemplar', resulting eventually in the fifteenth-century Chaucerian anthologies of vernacular courtly verse – the closely related collections in the Oxford group, which appeal fashionably to a readership within the landed gentry – that give us our earliest surviving instances of the poem.[2] Alternative possibilities based on stemmatic reconstruction are that the Oxford group MSS derive from Chaucer's own rough working papers, passed down in no good order and further mutilated over time, or from a lost compilation.[3] It is unclear, on balance, whether a clean and complete iteration of *BD* did at one time exist, circulating in Chaucer's lifetime or soon thereafter and informing the tradition represented by Thynne's text; or, quite differently, whether the survival and transmission of *BD* were precarious from the start, with editorial remediations over time further distorting the poem as Chaucer wrote it.

The present chapter does not newly engage this debate, the dimensions of which are well established in various resources and cannot be dealt with briefly. Instead, it aims to document how the material circumstances of *BD*'s preservation, such as we know them, affected its scope and meaning for early readers. It considers, in other words, how the MSS and early printed editions of *BD* positioned the work in relation to Chaucer's canon and related texts, and how such textual settings contributed to notions of the 'Chaucerian' that influenced early readers' apprehension of the poem. We will discover, in particular, that the urge to integrate *BD* interpretatively with Chaucer's mature poetry, discussed in chapter 1, is by no means exclusive to modern criticism; indeed, this trend had a dramatic beginning in pre-modern presentations of the poem. The following chapter enriches this study of material transmission, and the textual dilemmas that underlie it, with literary evidence of early responses to *BD* which indicate its accessibility to certain readerships. Several of the poetic responses considered there predate the earliest MSS, and some – such as John Lydgate's *Complaint of a Loveres Lyfe* and the anonymous *Isle of Ladies* – were drawn into the orbit of *BD* in courtly anthologies and early printed editions, becoming an integral part of the very patterns of transmission to which their composition serves as witness.

BD from Manuscript to Print

It is surprising that so little is known of *BD*'s early circulation when one considers its topical currency and potential political value in the first part of the fifteenth century. Submerged as its references to John of Gaunt and his lineage may be, *BD* is a poem that puns on the House of Lancaster, and the probability of its earliest reception within the English royal family – buttressed by Chaucer's own reference to the poem as 'the Deeth of Blaunche the Duchesse' in the Prologue of the *Legend of Good Women* – renders it distinctive within Chaucer's corpus. One could easily imagine such a poem being fastened upon in the years after Chaucer's death, as Henry IV, son of Gaunt and Blanche, consolidated his power and Henry V encouraged literary production and the copying of MSS in the native vernacular to advance the cultural prestige of English – a climate from which much of the poetry of Chaucer and his successors benefited.[4] As we have seen, however, *BD* cuts a rather odd figure as a prince-pleasing poem – hence the sharp divisions among modern critics regarding its topical purpose – and its political resonances do not appear to be registered in the century after Chaucer's death. In the MSS, *BD* is grouped among other dream-visions and love poems (including some by Lydgate and Sir John Clanvowe) and is not explicitly ascribed to Chaucer, although Chaucer's own references to *BD* verify its authenticity. As we will see, probable literary appropriations of *BD* from the fifteenth century also treat it as a love-vision pure and simple, eliding its topical associations and even, in most cases, ignoring its concern with death and mourning. Instead it becomes a template for examining courtly aspirations and the frustrations of noble love more generally.

Not until the second half of the sixteenth century was the poem's original occasion articulated, according to extant records. A notation in the margin of MS Fairfax 16, fol. 130r, probably in the hand of John Stow, the Tudor antiquary and editor of Chaucer's works, indicated that *BD* was 'made by Geffrey Chawcyer at ye request of ye duke of Lancastar: pitiously complaynynge the deathe of ye sayd dutchesse/ blanche'. As if to cement this point, Stow also wrote three times in the margins the name 'blanche' next to appearances of the word 'white' (at *BD* 905, 942, 948). It is not impossible that this historical understanding existed in the century prior – some have hypothesized that Stow's notation derives from a lost rubric by the fifteenth-century scribe and compiler John Shirley, known for this sort of 'gossipy' commentary in MSS to which he was connected – but if it did, it left no other trace, in no way enhancing the cultural capital of *BD* as a poem worthy of preservation.[5] As Kathleen Forni observes, the fact that William Caxton, Richard Pynson and Wynken de Worde – all of whom printed works by Chaucer in the decades before Thynne's 1532 edition – failed to print *BD* suggests that, lacking MS attribution, the poem may not even have been commonly perceived as Chaucer's work.[6]

Beginning with Thomas Speght's 1598 edition, however, the political connection highlighted in passing by Stow came to dominate the textual presentation of *BD*, which in turn helped to anchor Chaucer's biography in the monarchical power structure of the late fourteenth century. Speght sought to present Chaucer as an 'Antient and Learned English Poet', as the volume's title has it, positioning him among the great authors of antiquity as an ennobler of his native tongue. To convey Chaucer's poetic dignity, Speght in his 1598 edition and, with some differences in arrangement, in his corrected 1602 edition, embellished Chaucer's works with copious supplementary matter including a portrait illustrating the poet's heraldic associations and family tree, an account of his biography, a selection of poetic tributes, a glossary of unfamiliar words, a list of authors cited and other types of editorial apparatus befitting a classic. Speght's 'Life' of Chaucer, based on records gathered by Stow but not represented in his own edition, passes quickly over Chaucer's mercantile family background to establish the social respectability he swiftly attained as a man of the court and an intimate of such powerful nobles as John of Gaunt. The genealogical illustration entitled 'The Progenie of Geffrey Chaucer' in Speght's 1598 edition encapsulates this rationale by showing Chaucer's family line to unfold illustriously in tandem with John of Gaunt's, by virtue of Philippa Chaucer's kinship with Katherine Swynford, Gaunt's third wife, and, further along, Alice Chaucer's marriage, in 1430, to William de la Pole, Duke of Suffolk. Chaucer's status as a vintner's son is thus wholly displaced by his new-found gentility as brother-in-law of John of Gaunt and grandfather of a duchess.

With this genealogical context as setting, Speght's presentation of *BD* affirms Chaucer's royalist *bona fides*, defining for the poem a central and confident position in the poet's output quite apart from its modern critical understanding as an oblique and even tentative appeal for a superior's favour. The argument to *BD* in Speght's 1598 edition states unequivocally, 'By the person of a mourning knight sitting vnder an Oke, is ment Iohn of Gaunt, Duke of Lancaster, greatly lamenting the death of Blaunch the Duchesse, who was his first wife.'[7] Supplementing Speght's interpretation of *BD*'s royal allegory is the apocryphal poem now known as the *Isle of Ladies*, introduced to Chaucer's canon in the same edition under the title *Chaucers dreame* (confusingly similar to the title typically used for *BD* in early printed editions, as the next chapter will detail). Speght presents this courtly dream-vision, which culminates in a double wedding, as an account both of Gaunt's marriage to Blanche and Chaucer's marriage to Philippa.[8] The section of Speght's 'Life' devoted to Chaucer's marriage reinforces this: referring to Philippa, Speght writes, 'This gentlewoman, whome hee married ... as it may be gathered by Chaucers owne wordes in his dreame, was attendant on Blanch the Duchesse in the Duke of Lancasters house, as also her sister Katherine was.'[9] (In fact, Philippa served Constance of Castile, Gaunt's second wife, not Blanche.) Speght's rather convenient historical interpretation of these two dreams of Chaucer – one genuine, one apocryphal – thus interlaces Chaucer's own romantic life with that of Gaunt, making him an integral part of almost Gaunt's entire history with Blanche, from nuptials to death, and accomplishing with literary evidence what the genealogical chart achieved decoratively.

The intimacy of Chaucer's involvement with the House of Lancaster is also stressed in Speght's argument to *An ABC*, printed for the first time in his 1602 edition, which states that the poem was composed 'as some say, at the request of Blanch, Duchesse of Lancaster, as a praier for her priuat vse, being a woman in her religion very deuout'.[10] This attestation by Speght has occasioned scepticism on the basis of its 'suspiciously' clean fit with Speght's portrayal of Chaucer's 'aristo-cratic connections'; furthermore, what can be extrapolated of Chaucer's compositional development points towards a stanzaic, decasyllabic poem such as *An ABC* postdating the 1360s (Blanche died in 1368).[11] Nevertheless, it is possible that the authority of a subsequently lost or damaged MS stands behind this statement, and Blanche's special devotion to the Virgin Mary and her involvement with a programme of translation from French to English (*An ABC* derives from a prayer in Guillaume de Deguileville's *Le Pèlerinage de la vie humaine*) affirms the appropriateness of *BD*'s adoption of Marian imagery in its tribute to White as well as its creative motion between French and English.[12] The next major edition of Chaucer's works, by John Urry in 1721, retains these Lancastrian interpretations of *BD*, *Isle of Ladies* and *An ABC*. This volume's 'Life of Geoffrey Chaucer', for which Urry's asso-ciates John Dart and William Thomas were responsible, consolidates these topical claims, reinforces the 'singular value' in which Gaunt and Blanche placed Chaucer, and adds yet more evidence of their close association by suggesting that the *Complaint of the Black Knight* (i.e. Lydgate's *Complaint of a Loveres Lyfe*, long held to be Chaucer's work) was composed 'during *John of Gaunt's* Courtship with *Blaunch*', thus forming a preface to the account of their marriage in *Chaucers dreame* (i.e. *Isle of Ladies*).[13]

The political interpretations that encrusted *BD* are important indi-ces of early editors' commercial and cultural agendas in marketing Chaucer – often against the grain of his own poetic personality – as a respectable, well-connected sire of English letters. In singling out *BD* as proof of Chaucer's noble affiliations not only in headings and lists of contents but in the poet's own biography, editors from Speght onward crafted a readerly experience of *BD* as a politically meaningful poem that testifies to the established nature of Chaucer's relationship with Gaunt and Blanche and even, through its twinning with *Isle* and the connection with Chaucer's marriage, to Chaucer's own absorption into a noble genealogy. This poetic and biographical narrative achieved impressive longevity, appearing in similar form as late as Godwin's 1803 *Life of Geoffrey Chaucer*.[14] Despite its inauspicious textual pres- ervation in the fifteenth century, over the course of time *BD* and its poetic satellites played no small part in establishing Chaucer's virility as a socially ascendant *paterfamilias* of lords and dukes who was at the same time responsible for ennobling – rendering more 'noble' – the English tongue, the humble origins of which, in early modern accounts, mirror Chaucer's own. The heraldic and titular allusions near the end of *BD* that function to reintegrate the Man in Black into the imperative of a noble lineage yet intact, in this sense, embrace Chaucer too: the poem itself becomes a key chapter in the story of his own destined bloodline.

Endings and Envoys

Equally noteworthy in *BD*'s early modern transmission history is the trend of supplementation and enlargement witnessed by its (in some ways unlikely) affinities with *An ABC*, *Isle* and Lydgate's *Complaint of a Loveres Lyfe*. The latter two poems, written by fifteenth-century poets, became associated with *BD* partly because they engaged in dialogue with it, attempting to fill its gaps or to 'complete' it. Indeed, the coy declaration 'now hit ys doon' with which *BD* closes (1334) seems to have been received by early readers as a kind of tease – or perhaps a dare – that instigated its potential for undoing and redoing. The tidy, aseptic text of *BD* presented by modern editions and assumed by most literary criticism is a far cry from the ambulatory material life of the poem in MSS and editions up to the nineteenth century. In these earlier textual settings, *BD* was part of a larger story, and although the evidence is less complete than one would wish, it appears to have elicited a variety of responses. What follows is an overview of the textual filters through which *BD* was represented and viewed across its pre-modern transmission history. The next chapter will then fill out the picture of literary responses by later authors whose works circulate in some cases separately, in some cases in tandem with *BD*.

Of the three extant fifteenth-century MSS in which *BD* was anthologized, one – Fairfax 16 – contains occasional glosses generally agreed to be in the hand of John Stow, as acknowledged earlier. We have already observed the political cast of these notations, which describe the poem's occasion and decode references to 'white' as 'blanche'. Stow's final marginal intervention at line 1298, where the dreamer asks 'where is she now?', is different in character. The answer to this question in *BD*, which of course has hovered over the whole poem, takes eleven lines to unfold in this final scene: the Man in Black's physical transformation ('he wax as ded as stoon' [1300]), his repetition of the I-have-lost-more-than-you-know refrain, and further befuddlement from the dreamer all stand between the question of White's whereabouts and her survivor's admission of her death. Interestingly, next to the inquiry at line 1298, Stow's gloss provides the answer: 'she ys dede'. This seems more than a simple redundancy, and various interpretations suggest themselves. Does this sixteenth-century reader's anticipatory notation here register an impatience with the poem (or its narrator) often experienced by modern readers on account of the suspense surrounding a fact – she is dead! – that was clearly stated from the start? Might it suggest that even early readers sensed something out of sync in the final exchange between dreamer and mourner, which critics have repeatedly viewed as awkward or anticlimactic?

Or, rather differently, is it possible to detect a more subtle interplay between reader and text here, one that gains further suggestiveness if we accept that this gloss is in the hand of Stow, who as an editor, book collector and expander of Chaucer's canon would contribute much – for better and worse – to the early modern understanding of Chaucer. In giving away the 'secret' before its rightful moment, the glossator inhabits the position of eavesdropper himself, redoubling the schema deployed throughout the poem, in which the dreamer – whose narrative existence began, of course, as a *reader* – overhears the Man in Black and thereafter conceals or mislays his knowledge. In this most dialogic passage of the poem, the reader of the manuscript enters into dialogue with the narrative, interposing a third voice with the power to anticipate and clarify. Much as the poem's narrator gamely obtrudes upon fiction in his earlier prayer to Morpheus, a mythic character whose arm can be twisted, so does the glossator step in, as it were, to the fictional scene at hand in an attempt to repair a gap in understanding. The power of the reader here, both intimate and intrusive, effectively captures the imaginative agency attributed to the reading process in the poem itself, which links engagement with books to other acts of communication and miscommunication. A poem that ends, quite literally, by placing itself as text into the hands of readers thus invites – and affirms – this early reader's appropriation of textual authority vis-à-vis the possibilities of dialogue at a pivotal moment in the narrative.[15]

A more far-reaching challenge to the closural moves of *BD* came in the form of annexation. In Fairfax 16, as in Bodley 638 and Tanner 346, *BD* is grouped with kindred Chaucerian love-visions, but in the case of Fairfax an envoy follows the *explicit* of Chaucer's poem. This envoy is given no title either in the body of the MS or in the table on folio 2. It begins 'O lewde boke with thy foole rudenesse' and elsewhere (in Tanner 346 and Thynne's 1532 edition) is appended to Clanvowe's *Boke of Cupide*. The four-stanza, rhyme royal poem's Lydgatean aureation marks it as a fifteenth-century composition; it is now known as the 'Envoy to Alison', after an acrostic in its final stanza.[16] Given the unknowns surrounding the early textual descent of *BD*, it is impossible to identify the circumstances in which this envoy merged with *BD* (or with the *Boke of Cupide*, for that matter), and the association is not perpetuated elsewhere, as far as surviving texts indicate. The pairing of *Envoy to Alison* with *BD* is not without a certain logic, however, and it could be argued that it helps homogenize *BD* into the fabric of the surrounding courtly love-visions and complaints that constitute this MS's first booklet: although these present a variety of perspectives on amatory ethics, they generally feature narrators implicated directly in love. The *Envoy to Alison* is a conventional literary send-off, indebted to similar pieces by Lydgate and Hoccleve, that deploys the humility topos fulsomely to recommend an undeserving poem to a lady's attention, and to sue for her mercy despite such a poor effort. Placed at the end of *BD*, to which it appears seamlessly attached without an independent title, the envoy compensates for the diffidence of Chaucer's narrator in refusing to identify his eight-year sickness, in a breach of literary expectations as shaped by the *dits amoreux*. From the perspective of a reader of this MS, the matter would seem to be righted by the poet's missive to his lady at the end. By this conjectural reading, the whole work, with its portrayal of love's powers of ennoblement and its subtle message that lovers should enjoy happiness before time runs out, was for the poet's lady, none other than the one physician who can heal him.

The effect of this annexation is to reintegrate *BD* with the narrative pattern of Machaut's *Remede de Fortune* as well as many of Boccaccio's poems, which feature a lover-narrator who directs the work to his lady. In so doing, it suggests a reciprocity of experience between dreamer and Man in Black and leaves the impression that the overarching amatory predicament is the poet's own. The address to the book that rhetorically forms the premise of the *Envoy to Alison* – itself distantly modelled on the 'Go, litel bok' topos at the end of *Troilus* – also carries a fibre of logic from *BD* insofar as it follows upon the narrator's closing reflection on the book still in his hands, and his own intention to make a new book out of the dream. With the book having been made – 'now hit ys doon' – the envoy then sends it off as a material object to the lady whose lack of favour thus far incited the circumstances that brought about the dream in the first place.

It is deliciously apropos, in the odd constellation of literary circumstances that joined *BD* with this envoy in Fairfax 16, that the lady's name is Alison, for beginning with Thynne's 1532 edition a *different* envoy is annexed to *BD*, where it remained all the way up to Pickering's Aldine Poets edition of Chaucer's works in 1845. The envoy in question – *Lenvoy de Chaucer a Bukton* – although genuinely Chaucerian, makes for a much more curious fit with *BD* than did its apocryphal manuscript predecessor. As was the case with *Envoy to Alison* in Fairfax 16, *Lenvoy de Chaucer a Bukton* does not merely succeed *BD* in early printed editions, it follows it continuously (after the *explicit*), without a title of its own, thus logically appearing to be an envoy to *BD* itself. In Thynne's edition, furthermore, *Bukton* is not given a title or presented as an autonomous poem in the table of contents at the beginning of the volume; *BD* is entered there as 'The dreame of Chaucer / with a balade'. Presented in the table of contents as a nameless pendant to *BD* rather than a free-standing poem, and only minimally demarcated in the text itself, *Bukton* was treated uniquely in Thynne's edition, which otherwise formalizes the presentation even of short poems. With only one exception, discussed below, *Bukton* rode the tide of titular invisibility, annexed to *BD*, until the nineteenth century, and this inevitably affected the reception of Chaucer's dream-vision.

The connection between these two poems – in all likelihood Chaucer's earliest narrative poem and a piece of light verse written in the last years of his life – is in many ways surprising. *Bukton* is a verse epistle in quasi-ballade form directed either to Sir Peter Bukton of Holdernesse, Yorkshire, or Sir Robert Bukton of Goosewold, Suffolk, both of whom were connected to the royal court; based on the poem's allusion to imprisonment in Frisia, it is usually dated to 1396, when an expedition there took place. Its playful reference to the Wife of Bath – another Alison – in the final stanza and, by way of echo, at line 6, further situates *Bukton* in the period of Chaucer's artistic maturity. Importantly, in all printed editions up to the 1822 Chiswick edition, Bukton's name in the first line of the poem (intact in the MSS and the one printed edition before Thynne's in which *Bukton* was preserved) was replaced by '&c.' – this despite Thomas Tyrwhitt's restoration of the correct reading in the 'Account of the Works of Chaucer' appended to the glossary in his 1775–8 edition of *Canterbury Tales*.[17] Lacking a title and named recipient, therefore, the poem thus printed allowed for multiple interpretations regarding its addressee, which theoretically could even be the same individual to whom *BD* was directed.

The conjunction of *BD* and *Bukton* has largely escaped scholarly consideration; for the purpose of the present study, two questions present themselves. What is a poem that begins by cynically entertaining the possibility, attributed to Christ himself (!), that '"No man is al trewe," I gesse', doing entangled with an idealizing love-vision that celebrates a woman in whom 'Trouthe hymself' chose 'his resting place' (*Buk* 4; *BD* 1003, 1005)? And, more challengingly, how does *Bukton's* (at least somewhat tongue-in-cheek) warning against remarriage relate to *BD* as a poem of consolation for John of Gaunt upon the death of his first wife?

In pursuit of answers, we must first look to Thynne, his editorial procedures, and the texts with which he was working. As is the case with *BD*, relatively little is known of *Bukton's* early transmission history, and Thynne's MS source for this poem is unknown. *Bukton* survives in only two MSS – Fairfax 16 and Coventry, Corporation Record Office MS – and one earlier print, Julian Notary's edition of the *Complaint of Mars* and *Complaint of Venus* (1499–1501). Fairfax 16, we have seen, also contains *BD*, but unlike Thynne's edition, it does not present the two poems in conjunction: they appear in separate booklets suggesting independent patterns of descent, with *BD* grouped largely among love-visions and *Bukton* among short verse epistles and complaints. The best reconstructions of *Bukton's* stemma based on the slim surviving evidence place Thynne's edition of the poem 'in a line all its own'[18] – coincidentally, the same circumstance as with Thynne's version of *BD*, which contains passages missing in all the MSS. Thynne is known to have worked from multiple MS sources and earlier blackletter editions in executing his volume of *Works*, a practice for which we have the authority of Thynne's own assertions in his 1532 Preface, corroborated by general scholarly opinion, as well as Francis Thynne's defence of his father's editing in the *Animadversions*. Five extant MSS and 'at least four hypothetical manuscripts' are believed to have been used by Thynne.[19] In attempting to gather and publish neglected works of Chaucer's – *BD* among them – Thynne gravitated towards poems containing echoes of Chaucer's material, discerning authenticity in what is often simply literary tribute. As a result, Thynne inaugurated a powerful trend of canonical expansion, bringing under the Chaucerian signature such spurious pieces as Clanvowe's *Boke of Cupide*, Usk's *Testament of*

Love, Henryson's *Testament of Cresseid* and other works that quoted or engaged in dialogue with Chaucer.[20] If Thynne's text of *Bukton* lacks an independent title because the MS source he used was similarly wanting, it is likely that the poem as he found it also lacked an attribution, since in Fairfax 16 and the Notary print Chaucer is named in the title (respectively, these are 'Lenvoy de Chaucer a Buktoun' and 'Here foloweth the counceyll of Chaucer touching Maryag &c. whiche was sen te te [= sente to] Bucketon &c.').[21] Thynne may have been drawn to the neglected *Bukton* because of its Chaucerian allusions, which for him (in this case correctly) marked it as genuine Chaucer: its explicit references to the Wife of Bath, after all, are among Chaucer's most self-referential in-jokes. Thynne's placement, rather than his selection, of *Bukton* is harder to understand.

Whether *Bukton* was juxtaposed with *BD* in Thynne's MS source, or whether this was Thynne's innovation, is impossible to say with certainty. The fact that both poems appear, albeit in separate booklets, in Fairfax 16 might hint at their association at an earlier stage, especially if, as has occasionally been thought, a lost compilation rather than independent booklets stands most immediately behind the Oxford group of MSS of which Fairfax 16 is a member – although, of course, Thynne's primary source for *BD*'s text must come from elsewhere, since the Oxford group archetype is flawed.[22] The odd coincidence by which *BD* travelled with a different 'envoy' in Fairfax 16, itself elsewhere attached to a poem by Clanvowe, may in some way relate to a lost tradition linking *BD* with *Bukton*. Clearly there are lost MSS intervening between the initial release of *Bukton* and its first documented appearance in Fairfax 16 in 1450, and there is good indication that Chaucer's lyrics, perhaps like *BD*, were 'apparently well-known and influential at an early date' despite the paucity of MSS. Circulating in ephemeral forms, the lyrics' material stability emerged only with 'the kinds of manuscript in which they might be carefully and lengthily preserved', i.e. courtly anthologies.[23]

It may be significant that the pairing of *Bukton* and *BD* is inconsistent with Thynne's usual practice of grouping disparate texts, for he typically links poems that are thematically related. Forni highlights, for example, the literary felicity of Thynne's pairing of the *Legend of Good Women* and the 'courly panegyric' *Mother of Nurture*; *Parliament of Foules* with another Valentine's Day poem, the *Floure of Curtesy*; *Complaint Unto Pity* with *La Belle Dame Sans Mercy*; and *Anelida and Arcite* with *Assembly of Ladies*, which also concerns female abandonment.[24] The narrative associations forged by Thynne could be far-reaching, as is the case with his placement of the *Testament of Cresseid* after *Troilus*. *Bukton* as a postscript to *BD* cannot be accounted for by means of thematic similarities of the rather obvious sort dovetailing these other poems. Furthermore, although *Bukton* does pass the test of Chaucerian allusiveness that dictated many of Thynne's additions to the poet's canon, it does not enhance the volume's overarching presentation of Chaucer as a love poet. It has been observed that virtually all of Thynne's apocryphal additions 'are either addressed to women or treat women sympathetically', rendering Chaucer an 'official panegyrist' of the female sex.[25] With its playful appeals to a well-worn tradition of anti-matrimonial rhetoric that portrays wives as diabolical slave-drivers, *Bukton* hardly qualifies for this poetic category.

So far there seems little explanation for the conjunction of *BD* and *Bukton*, if it was in fact Thynne's initiative rather than a relic of a lost MS tradition. It is surprising, having decided to include *Bukton*, that Thynne did not place it where it more logically fitted: in the mini-anthology of 'goodly balades' in the last gathering, the content of which reflects an arrangement of verse epistles and complaints, comparable to the second booklet of Fairfax 16 (where *Bukton* is included), with logic and currency. Several of Chaucer's Boethian ballades, the *Complaint of Chaucer to His Purse*, and *Lenvoy de Chaucer a Scogan* are all printed together among these 'goodly balades'; this last gathering thus rounds out Thynne's volume with an image of Chaucer as not only a love poet but a 'a reliable source of philosophical and practical wisdom, or what was generically known as "good counsel"'.[26]

It might be suspected that Thynne's placement of *Bukton* at the end of *BD* is due simply to the practical consideration of filling a gap or the like, but this does not account for the situation either. This is clear from the case of a ballade Thynne appends to the *Legend of*

Good Women (*LGW*), the presentation of which in the list of contents follows the same pattern as *BD*: 'The legend of good women / with a balade'. This Lydgatean triple ballade with envoy, known as *Mother of Norture* after its first line, appears for the first time in Thynne's edition; like *Bukton* to *BD*, it remains attached to *LGW* through subsequent blackletter editions. In other respects, the textual setting of *Mother of Norture* is distinct from the case with which we are concerned. Whereas *Bukton* merges almost seamlessly into the end of *BD*, separated only by a minimal *explicit*, the ending of *LGW* – following Thynne's usual practice – is marked more formally and the ballade positioned as a distinct piece: 'Thus endeth the legendes of good women / and here foloweth a balade of Chaucer' (fol. 234r). Unlike *Bukton*, this ballade is presented with its own title – 'A goodly balade of Chaucer' (fol. 234v) – and it appears on the verso of the folio. As Walter W. Skeat observed, Thynne's rationale in inserting this ballade here was utilitarian: something was needed to fill the 'blank page at the back of the concluding lines of The Legend of Good Women, so that the translation of Boethius might commence on a new leaf'.[27] *Bukton* performs no such function in respect to *BD*: its first stanza completes a verso and its next three begin a recto, after which *Parliament of Foules* begins two-thirds of the way down a column. (In Thynne's 1542 *Works*, *Bukton* does begin a verso leaf, where it fills a full column before the start of *Parliament of Foules* on the same page, but this has no bearing upon Thynne's reasoning for placing *Bukton* after *BD* in his first edition.) As already noted, *Mother of Norture* also differs from *Bukton* in complementing the thematic make-up of the preceding poem closely: as a courtly ballade in praise of a lady, after the fashion of marguerite poetry, it issues quite logically from *LGW*, offering a kind of closure lacking therein by returning to a poetic mode folded into the Prologue and reinforcing its themes. The speaker of *Mother of Norture* worries, for instance, that his lady will find 'in my wryting … som offence' owing to 'negligence / And not … malice', a sentiment having structural and verbal parallels in *LGW* (58, 61–2; cf. *LGW* F 362–72). For practical as well as thematic reasons, clear indications exist of Thynne's deliberate arrangement of *LGW* and *Mother of Norture* in sequence, and the clarity with which he relates them as kindred yet textually distinct pieces contrasts markedly with his approach to *BD/Bukton*.

On the whole, although the evidence is far from conclusive, the scale tips slightly towards Thynne as the inheritor rather than fashioner of *Bukton* as postscript to *BD*, with the point at which Bukton's name was replaced by '&c.' (because of an illegible exemplar, or to make the envoy's placement more flexible?) remaining an open question. More rewarding of interpretation is the fact that at whatever stage *BD* and *Bukton* did become textual partners, the conjunction proved attractive and enduring, for it remained all the way up to what is effectively the beginning of modern Chaucer scholarship in the mid-nineteenth century. It must be remembered that Thynne, and perhaps other early readers of *BD* as well, seems not to have been aware that *BD* was written for John of Gaunt (the scribes of Tanner 346, for example, left the poem untitled); to them, the poem was 'The dreame of Chaucer', and signals of its identification with the work that Chaucer elsewhere calls 'the Deth of Blaunche the Duchesse', the 'book of the Duchesse' and 'Ceys and Alcione' were at best mixed, possibly reflecting circulation of the poem in different forms or stages of revision.[28] The disorientation we feel when seeing an elegy produced for the Duke of Lancaster mingled with a ballade for Chaucer's colleague Bukton, therefore, would not have affected early readers, particularly given that Bukton's name was replaced with the open signature of '&c.', meaning potentially *anyone*.

An awareness of *BD*'s historical occasion, as noted above, crept back into the editing of Chaucer beginning with Stow's 1561 edition and, more prominently, in the 1598 Speght. By the time of Urry's edition in 1721, matters became more complicated, as John of Gaunt came to be explicitly identified as the recipient of *Bukton*. First, Stow, who as we recall had access to Fairfax 16 (containing both *BD* titled as such and *Bukton* with recipient's name intact) and had noted its topical significance there, covered all possible ground in his first table of contents, presenting *BD* as 'The dreame of Chaucer, otherwise called the boke of the Duches, or Seis and Alcione, with a balade to his master Bucton'. This departure from Thynne both in titling *BD* and naming Bukton does not extend to the body of Stow's edition, however, for there Stow

reverted to 'The dreame of Chaucer' as title for the poem itself and followed his predecessor in merging *Bukton* with *BD* after a diminutive
explicit, and printing '&c.' instead of Bukton's name in the first line.
Speght follows Stow in his 1598 list of contents, but in the 1602 and 1687
editions, the title of *BD* has been condensed and any mention of Bukton
has been dropped from the table. In all of these editions, the main body
of the text, with the '&c.', continued to follow the precedent established
by Thynne, while at the same time *BD* was framed with the Lancastrian
explication that bolstered royal connections in Chaucer's biography. It
was left to Urry in his 1721 edition to draw the conclusion – albeit not
without a note of hesitation – that inevitably issued from the history of
association between the two texts: presenting *Bukton* (with the '&c.')
after the *BD explicit*, Urry inserts, 'This seems an Envoy to the Duke of
Lancaster after his Loss of *Blanch*.'[29] Although Tyrwhitt impugned this
interpretation as 'most unaccountable', pointing to the name 'Bukton' in
Fairfax 16 and arguing quite logically that the 'familiar style' of *Bukton*
would be inappropriate for a poem directed to Gaunt,[30] Urry's heading was reproduced in John Bell's 1782 edition of Chaucer and Robert
Anderson's 1795 edition. It was dropped thereafter, but the suppression
of Bukton's name was to continue for another twenty-five years and the
annexation of *Bukton* to *BD* (with the singular exception of the 1843
Moxon edition, which incorporated Tyrwhitt) for another sixty.[31]

Odd as the conjunction of *BD* and *Bukton* thus modified may seem,
it is not entirely opaque, and it potentially opens new perspectives on
the reception of *BD* as well as Chaucer's poetics of address more generally. In his influential 1989 study of Chaucer's audience, Paul Strohm
singled out short poems like *Bukton* as indicative of Chaucer's horizontal associations – like-minded court bureaucrats as opposed to upper
nobility – and their receptivity to the 'multivoiced' design of poetry that
challenges by 'shifting rapidly among different perspectives'.[32] Other
critics have emphasized how the rhetorical strategies and pervasive
irony of *Bukton* in fact inscribe – even conjure – an expanded sense
of an audience-in-the-know that is camouflaged by the poem's seemingly 'occasional' nature.[33] The roots of this argument about a larger
audience extend back to Kittredge's suggestion that the poem may have

been intended as a benign joke on the follies of marriage akin to the humour associated with 'pre-nuptial "stag dinners" now-a-days'.[34] For Richard P. Horvath, *Bukton* assumes a kind of double audience: the first consisting of a private sphere occupied by an epistolary recipient, the second evoking an expansive, undetermined, public readership that must engage virtually with the construction of Chaucer's corpus by puzzling through the ironic, self-referential layers of the poem. Reception, in this light, is an essential medium of the epistolary dynamic: the envoy invites readers to 'receive, interpret, and complete [its] address', to endow it with new meaning.[35] This textual amicability even extends, in Stephanie Trigg's view, to the shaping of modern readers' responses to Chaucer, who 'are keen to wind themselves into the same environment [of the Chaucerian envoy], identifying themselves with Bukton and Scogan, as Chaucer's best readers'.[36] With this construct in play, the erasure and alternative inscription of addressee in *Bukton* over time makes a certain degree of sense: the poem itself activates multiple potential audiences and does not weld itself to an occasion. It is in a way fitting that a poem whose humour rests on saying one thing and meaning another – the entire injunction against marriage rests confusingly on *praeteritio* – ends up meaning something in the black-letter editions so different than its compositional scenario originally dictated. More importantly, the intertextual dynamic prompted within *Bukton* through allusion to the Wife of Bath's Prologue (itself a text that explores the shifting possibilities of discourse), which the poem directs us to read at line 29, paves the way for other affiliations with Chaucer's works, *BD* included. The fact that *Bukton* was already in dialogue with one Chaucerian text, in effect, may have encouraged its repurposing as the closing gambit of another.

At this point, *Bukton*'s status not only as a ballade but an 'envoy', as it is labelled in Fairfax 16 and the Notary print, becomes significant. Properly speaking, *Bukton*, like *Scogan*, is 'a verse letter ending with an envoy to the addressee'.[37] Furthermore,

> the *envoy* in the ballade is a brief stanza, usually differing in form
> from the main body of the poem, which addresses the recipient

directly ... it is not necessarily the logical conclusion to the poem but often is rather a means of connecting the action to actual life, by establishing a realistic context for the abstract ideas of the poem.[38]

The *Clerk's Tale* supplies a Chaucerian precedent for the annexation of an 'envoy', itself a ballade, to a narrative poem that is distinct in perspective and tone. Intriguingly, the *Lenvoy de Chaucer*,[39] which is attached to the *Clerk's Tale* in all but three MSS, also explicitly mentions the Wife of Bath, and its engagement with anti-matrimonial tradition – here directed at wives rather than husbands-to-be, but employing similar stereotypes about female tyranny and marital woe – turns the tables much as *Bukton* does to *BD* on a foregoing narrative that por-trayed something quite different. As is the case with *BD/Bukton* from Thynne's edition onwards, *Lenvoy de Chaucer* is presented in several important MSS, including the Hengwrt MS, as both of and apart from the *Clerk's Tale*: introduced after an *explicit* to the tale in some cases, it follows a tale lacking formal containment in others, rendering ambigu-ous whether it is part of an ongoing tale, a postscript, or a distinct text in a different voice.[40] Similarly, as we have seen, *Bukton* always fol-lows an *explicit* to *BD*, but this is a flimsier signpost of an ending than most narrative poems receive in the blackletter editions, and the lack of a title for *Bukton* suggests its continuity with the preceding work. The performance of voice also aligns *Bukton* with *Lenvoy de Chaucer*, as it is designated (whether rightly or wrongly – its appropriateness to the Clerk as narrator remains a vexed issue) in about half the MSS. For *Lenvoy de Chaucer* too conveys at least the illusion of authorial intimacy and a recognizably streetwise tone, so that Chaucer's 'personal opinions' on marriage might be seen by early readers as consistent across these two envoys.

In these ways, it is possible to see how the narrative positioning and editorial treatment of *Lenvoy de Chaucer* could form a template for the similar application of *Bukton* to another narrative poem cel-ebrating a woman of idealized virtue. Read as an appendage to *BD*, as early readers would necessarily have done, *Bukton* similarly reverses the message of what preceded – avoid rather than strive for a perfect love culminating in marriage – and it employs irony, cued in part by reference to the Wife of Bath, to suggest that its instruction not be taken at face value. The shift in tone in each case comes as something of a relief: from earnest to game in the *Clerk's Tale*; and from 'ye' to 'thou' in *BD* – from a one-sided, hierarchical discourse to the familiarity of horizontal address. In a fashion similar to the transformation of register at the end of *BD*, where poetic evasion gives way to blunt, monosyllabic utterance and monologue to dialogue, *Bukton* bursts the bubble of aristocratic enchantment. If the *Envoy to Alison* in Fairfax 16 supplied closure to *BD* in the form of the narrator's own designs upon his beloved, *Bukton* in the printed editions restores to the narrator his misplaced role as adviser and healer of a man whose experience on some level he shares.

Reading *BD* and *Bukton* as a continuous sequence, we can see that the narrator, mocked or stunned into relative silence for most of *BD* and unable to say much of anything right, recovers his composure in *Bukton* and offers the ultimate consolation by turning to the big picture: why marriage brings less happiness than it would seem. Whatever weight we may want to give such hypothetical readings, they do render these interlocking texts legible, and though they do not resolve the issue of by whom and at what point these poems first became connected, they may well recover some of the logic behind that connection. Perhaps the largest point to be taken is that the curious textual history of *BD* evinced by these alternative endings participates in a trend that can also be discerned in literary appropriations of *BD* in the fifteenth and sixteenth centuries, namely defiance of its own attempts at closure in favour of integration with larger dramas of courtship or marriage.

Despite its obscure prehistory, the melding of *BD* and *Bukton* did not occur in a vacuum. The logic by which the poems were paired as idealistic and ironic reflections on conjugal bliss was reinforced elsewhere in Thynne's edition and further extended in Stow's, then remained more or less entrenched through the Speghts and Urry. The sole exception, besides *Bukton*, to Thynne's selection of works portraying Chaucer as an advocate of women is an anonymous sixteenth-century poem of meagre quality first attested in this edition, the *Remedy of Loue*, aptly characterized by Forni as 'an interesting potpourri of late medieval misogyny'.[41] Pedantic and long-winded, *Remedy of Loue* is formally unlike the pithily ironic *Bukton*, but it displays certain thematic affinities: opining that the remedy for love is to reflect on the perfidy of women, the poet raises the topic of married men, with whose pain he sympathizes ('with hym complayne / ... as partener of hys great payne').[42] He warns single men to beware of matrimony, for chastity is best – yet he will not assert that marriage is to be avoided, quoting St Paul, 'melius est nubere quam uri' (it is better to wed than to burn; 1 Cor. 7:9). The poem is mainly addressed to unwedded men since, he says, the plight of married men is beyond cure, although some practical advice may be of use, such as controlling one's wife. Despite its rehearsal of similar motifs, particularly the twisting of St Paul's advice (cf. *Bukton* 17–18), *Remedy of Loue* is not directly related to *Bukton*: they owe mutually to a common tradition of anti-feminist advice literature. What is suggestive is that in the context of Thynne's volume the *Remedy of Loue* corroborates the expanded reading of *BD* by which the Man in Black, in the aftermath of White's death, is – ironically or not – dissuaded from remarrying. In light of recent scholars' interpretations of *BD* as a literary encouragement, or even justification, of Gaunt's second marriage (to Constance of Castile) or compensation for a budding liaison – rather than being a simple elegy for a recently deceased Blanche – this is a rich historical irony.[43] At the least it bespeaks the longevity of readers' suspicions that *BD* is more than a quaint poem about a perfect romantic relationship: that life goes on past and beyond it, and that its hushed evocation of married life – passed over in one blissful yet nondescript passage in which the Man in Black never explicitly mentions marriage (1287–97) – demands reparation, much as the idealized balance of courtly and matrimonial gender relations at the beginning of the *Franklin's Tale* invites deconstruction. In terms of literary transmission, the shared concerns of *BD/ Bukton* and *Remedy of Loue* helped define a sub-current to Thynne's courtly Chaucer that issued in a 'misogynist definition of Chaucer's canon' that would be further enriched by Stow.[44]

Stow's 1561 edition expands upon the kind of material represented by *Remedy of Loue*, shaping an acerbic, anti-feminist voice with a 'light and self-deprecating' tone that in the sixteenth century 'may have been considered distinctly Chaucerian'.[45] Although Forni acknowledges that Stow's contributions to Chaucer's canon in this vein derive from the 'clerical' as opposed to courtly understanding of women in works such as the Wife of Bath's Prologue, the envoy of the *Clerk's Tale*, *Bukton* and others, she does not consider how the transmission patterns of such materials – our present concern – relate to the textual conditions of this development.[46] Stow rather infamously added a number of poems, almost all apocryphal, to those printed by Thynne; these he grouped together as 'certaine woorkes of Geffray Chauser, whiche hath not here tofore been printed'.[47] Two of these bear a particular relevance to *BD/ Bukton*. The first follows, and is thematically related to, *Against Women Unconstant*, which may be a genuine work of Chaucer's. Introduced by Stow as 'a balade whiche Chaucer made in þe praise, or rather dispraise, of women for their doublenes', this spurious piece is now known as *Beware of Doublenesse* and generally attributed to Lydgate; it survives in numerous MSS including Fairfax 16 (Booklet 2, which also contains *Bukton*).[48] This poem is a dilation upon the tradition represented by *Bukton*, and it deploys irony to similarly clever effect. The speaker of *Bukton*, after suggesting that 'No man is al trewe' (4) – including himself – protests against the notion of speaking ill of marriage, then proceeds to do just that hypothetically before alluding cryptically to Paul's guarded approval of marriage and the Wife of Bath's example. The double-speak of *Beware of Doubleness* is comparable in orchestration: its refrain professes that doubleness exists everywhere except the hearts of women, yet this claim is juxtaposed with abundant highly conventional evidence to the contrary, such as the example of Delilah, the wisdom of Solomon, and the changing of the seasons. If the joke were not apparent enough, the context supplied by the surrounding apocryphal poems clinches it, for these draw on the same kinds of examples to certify that doubleness *is* a key trait of women.

Beware of Doubleness closes with a highly tongue-in-cheek envoy directed at women who wish, 'by influence of [their] nature', to maintain

a reputation for 'trouth' (98, 100). They are advised to arm themselves
with a 'mighty sheld of doubleness' against men who would test their
fidelity (102, 104). Interestingly, these rhetorical moves in the envoy
are reminiscent of *Lenvoy de Chaucer* after the *Clerk's Tale*: here too an
address to a female audience highlights an ironic message latent in a
poem that brings idealization of women to impossible extremes. Once
again, an Amazonian image of female dominance in a militarized battle
of the sexes (cf. *Lenvoy de Chaucer's* portrayal of the arrows of wives'
'crabbed eloquence' piercing their husbands' armour (*CT* IV 1203))
conveys a transparently anti-feminist message. If Thynne's *Bukton* can
be taken even indirectly as the impetus of this tradition of an ironically misogynist Chaucer, via the *Remedy of Loue* and Stow's additions,
then the echoes in *Beware of Doubleness* of *Lenvoy de Chaucer* further
corroborate the relevance of the *Clerk's Tale* paratext to the literary
evolution of *BD/Bukton*.

A second short poem, which like *Beware of Doubleness* was printed
in this section for the first time by Stow, illuminates *BD*'s relationship
to *Bukton* from a different angle. This four-stanza, rhyme royal poem
of the fifteenth century, entitled *Of Theyre Nature* after its first line, is
itself part of a family of related proverbial pieces concerning marriage
and women, and it is more explicitly concerned with the perils of wedded life than the work just examined.[49] Like *Bukton*, it is an advice
poem warning men against marriage; it claims that maidens' humility
disappears as soon as they become wives, at which point their energies centre upon out-mastering their husbands. Rather than expanding
on this claim, as poems of this type usually do not hesitate to do, *Of
Theyre Nature* shifts into *abbreviatio*. The speaker does not 'dar' speak
more of this matter because he is overcome by weariness; excessive
study has resulted in 'defaute of slepe' and his 'spyrytes wexen feynt'
(15–16; cf. *BD* 25–6: 'Defaute of slep and hevynesse / Hath sleyn my
spirit of quyknesse').[50] It is difficult to fathom why the speaker is so
exhausted after a mere two stanzas, and it quickly emerges that the
actual reason he wishes to 'make an ende and ley me downe to rest'
(22) is fear of retribution (by women) or poetic justice (by falling into
the trap of marriage himself) by speaking ill of wedded life. Having

warned 'yong men' to beware since 'the blynde eteth many a fly', he now prays that 'God kepe the fly out of my dyssh!' (14, 21).

Brushing shoulders thus, in the vocabulary of insomnia, with *BD*, the poet then engages in rhetoric that is notably reminiscent of *Bukton*, where the joke – a much more successful one, admittedly – also rests on the speaker's fear of falling 'in the trappe' he warns against, so that he refuses to do so in so many words (*Bukton* 24). Even the diction is similar: 'I dar not writen of [marriage] no wikkednesse' in *Bukton* (7), and 'Of thys matyer I dar make no lengor relacion' in *Of Theyre Nature* (15). Finally, both poems appeal to 'experience' to prove their points. In the last stanza of *Of Theyre Nature*, the speaker claims to 'know by experience verament' that he would be 'shent' if women discovered who wrote this poem (23, 25), as if rounding out his allusion to book-learning in the previous stanza – the long 'study' that so exhausts him (17) – with empirical evidence. *Bukton* concludes its counsel against marriage similarly, complementing the authority of 'hooly writ' with the proof of 'Experience', in yet another nod to the Wife of Bath (21–2).

In many respects, *Of Theyre Nature* confirms Stow's taste for lit-erary 'patchworks or pastiches', that is, poems consisting of extracts from other poems.[51] Here we can see, apart from its areas of overlap with related (non-Chaucerian) anti-feminist poems, what may just be early traces of the cross-pollination of *BD* and *Bukton*. Both seem to be echoed here, and the gratuitous nature of the *BD* allusion – there is no logical reason for the speaker to suffer from 'defaute of slepe' in such a context – accentuates the possibility that our fifteenth-century poet encountered *Bukton* either attached to or associated with *BD*. As we will see in the next chapter, insomnia does on occasion become a touchstone for poets' encounters with the framework of *BD* in their own love-visions; its placement in *Of Theyre Nature* is so incongruous with the usual associations with lovesickness that it suggests a distinct reading of *BD*, about which more will be said in closing.

Apart from Stow's edition, *Of Theyre Nature* appears in one MS: Cambridge, Trinity College MS R.3.19, from the third quarter of the fif-teenth century, a mostly non-Chaucerian miscellany of Middle English verse that formed the basis of a great many of Stow's additions to

Chaucer's canon. *Of Theyre Nature* thus certainly predates by a number of years Thynne's 1532 edition, the first known volume in which *Bukton* is appended to *BD*, and what appears to be its interlacing of the two poems increases the likelihood that an earlier textual tradition linked them. Evidence from elsewhere of the creative attraction of the *Clerk's Tale*-plus-*Lenvoy* for poems that idealize love helps fill in the blanks of how such a literary conjunction could take place. What is clear is the solidity of the conjunction and its surrounding associations in the materials that do survive. If *Of Theyre Nature* helps establish the convergence of *BD* with *Bukton* before Thynne's edition, its main literary value is as a witness and conduit of that convergence. Recalibrated in Stow's edition as a poem *by* Chaucer – rather than the clumsy imitation of *Bukton* that it is – it helps advance, along with its neighbouring poems, a corrective to the courtly Chaucer. This is a Chaucer whose youthful experiment, in *BD*, with French fashions in courtly poetry is enveloped by the confidence and cynicism of a mature poetic counsellor.

Such a poet, who in Urry's reckoning could be thought to advise John of Gaunt himself against remarriage, could not really be thought to languish in lovesickness for eight years over a cruel mistress, as the earlier hybrid text of *BD* and *Envoy to Alison* imagined. Instead, his insomniac fatigue must be positioned with the type of restless study pursued by *Of Theyre Nature*'s narrator, who is ostensibly preoccupied by an abundance of books documenting the horrors of marriage. Or perhaps it is married life itself that torments Chaucer and keeps him from sleep, as the linking of *Bukton* with *BD* implies. The theory of a marital context for the frame narrative of *BD*, advanced by Frederick Gard Fleay in 1877, aligns neatly with the composite text familiar up to a quarter-century before his time of writing. Refuting the view that the eight-year sickness encodes unrequited love, Fleay argued: 'The sickness is married life which was, as we shall see in the *Canterbury Tales*, anything but satisfactory to Chaucer; he had been married eight years and a bit. The physician is death.' Fleay supports this interpretation with reference to lines 560–2 of the *House of Fame*, in which the eagle cries 'Awak' in a suggestively familiar voice, a passage that is often read as a quip at Philippa Chaucer's expense.[52] With a daily diet of such abuse, he concludes, it is small wonder that Chaucer had trouble sleeping year in and year out!

Despite its dubious biographical (and mathematical) auditing, Fleay's theory foreshadows a twentieth-century critical view of Chaucer that still to some extent proves attractive: Chaucer as a poet of marriage who views 'courtly love' with cynical detachment. The creator of the Wife of Bath is still reckoned as more essentially 'Chaucerian' than the commemorator of Blanche, and some of the best recent readers of Chaucer have argued appealingly that Chaucer's virtuosic construction of the Wife of Bath cuts to the heart of his poetics, whether by exemplifying newly sophisticated notions of 'impersonatory realism' and textual performance,[53] exposing the makings of authority in an era of contestation,[54] or enacting a multidimensional rhetoric that 'opens up a space in which what we have come to call literature can find its home'.[55] One of the most extensive recent considerations of the *dit amoreux* tradition as appropriated by Chaucer in fact devotes significantly more attention to its culmination in the autographic mode of the Wife of Bath's Prologue than its permeation of *BD*, which is treated only incidentally.[56] Even if modern critics disdain such textual contaminations as formerly yoked *Bukton* to *BD*, they cannot claim to be wholly innocent of perpetuating a mode of reading that regards an early, experimental work like *BD* through the lens of Chaucer's mature accomplishments, or elides it altogether in considerations of the 'Chaucerian'. The textual history of *BD/Bukton* offers, among other things, a corrective to our own assumptions in the interpretation of Chaucer as a canonical author, reminding us of the ease with which the cult of Chaucer's personality and the filter of his corpus can overdetermine an engagement with his first major poem.

5

REREADING THE *BOOK* (II)

Literary Reception up to the Sixteenth Century

A s the previous chapter demonstrated, the early textual transmission of *BD* reveals a powerful trend of completion and supplementation. Although the poem was not literally 'continued' by early editors, as was the unfinished *House of Fame*, it was liberally contextualized and re-integrated into larger narratives such as Chaucer's biography and popular discourses of marriage and misogyny. The early literary responses examined in the present chapter, spanning the late fourteenth to the sixteenth century, evoke a complementary pattern; at the same time, they underscore an early familiarity with *BD* of considerable creative reach, contrasting markedly with the underwhelming representation of the poem in MSS. It is certain from the literary appropriations datable to the earlier part of the fifteenth century that *BD* was well known to at least some readers before the production of the MS anthologies – the earliest surviving witnesses of the poem – in the middle of the century. The range of early poetic responses outlined here is impressive both in variety and depth; indeed, the first two hundred years of *BD*'s afterlife emerge as a period of efflorescence without parallel until the resurgence of critical interest in the poem in the twentieth century, when similar levels of richness were discovered in it.

Early poetic appropriators of *BD* engage its cruxes to varying degrees, but they are all attuned to the 'openness' of its textuality, its various prompts and solicitations for rewriting. In the examples given

here, *BD* functions as a point of departure for the development of prequels and sequels; it invites correction, interpolation and reversal; and
it contributes to an incipient discourse of vernacular authority. What
connects most of these disparate literary re-creations, apart from their
common inspiration, is their tendency to respond to the poem that *BD*
was *not* – be it a 'traditional' elegy or a straightforward love-vision.
Frequently, these adaptations plug gaps and smooth over inconsistencies, repairing the *aporia* that creates in *BD* a sense of both uneven-
ness and profundity. In these ways, early poets think their poems into
Chaucer's, collaborating in the production of their own 'Chaucerian'
texts: indeed, several of the works under consideration were absorbed
into Chaucer's canon through the early modern period.

While it is impossible in the space available to detail every instance
of literary response to *BD*, rewarding a project as that would be, the
following case studies are advanced as representative of the chief literary coordinates in play up to the sixteenth century. For practical
reasons, the examples offered here are confined to English-language
appropriations; the still inconclusive state of opinion on the priority of
BD over certain related French-language *dits*, discussed earlier in this
book, makes non-anglophone patterns of response hazardous to venture. Quite possibly, new paths of research on the multilingual aspects
of literary and cultural exchange in the English court (see chapter 2 for
an overview) will clarify the issue so that a fuller picture of the earliest
literary conversations with *BD* can one day be drawn.

Correcting Chaucer: Sleep and Love in Gower's *Confessio amantis*

In the *Confessio amantis* (*c*.1386–90; rev. 1393), John Gower inevitably engaged in dialogue with Chaucer, his friend and poetic sparring
partner, to whom Venus herself famously directs a missive at the end of
the first redaction of the poem. Working from a familiarly Chaucerian
palette of literary influences – the medievalized Ovid, Boethius, the
Roman de la rose and the *dit amoreux* tradition – Gower thought
through, and with, Chaucer as he shaped his own essentially ethical

perspective on love.[1] The relevance of the *Confessio* to Chaucer's *oeuvre* is not confined to the various narrative exempla having counterparts in the *Canterbury Tales*, or to the schema of the story collection more generally: Chaucer's earlier love poetry, including *BD*, set a precedent for English amatory fiction with which Gower also consciously worked. Indeed, the tradition of vernacular love poetry marked for English culture by *BD* is canonized by Gower's Venus, who identifies Chaucer as 'mi disciple and mi poete' and attributes to him '[d]itees and ... songes glade' composed 'in the floures of his youthe' (*CA* 8.*2942–3, 2945). Reading the *Confessio* in conjunction with *BD* offers an intriguing glimpse of an axis of early reception defined by a contestation of literary visions. *BD* emerges here less as a 'precedent' to which Gower 'responds' than an alternative set of possibilities – yet in flux – for a nascent English representation of love.

The story of Ceix and Alceone, narrated in Book 4 of the *Confessio* in connection to the vice of Somnolence and again evoked in Book 8, where Alceone appears among the faithful wives in Love's company, supplies a point of intersection between Gower's poem and *BD*. Chaucer's and Gower's respective versions of the Ovidian narrative have often been compared, with Gower's version being generally admired for its greater faithfulness to classical precedent – it retains and elaborates the couple's metamorphosis, for example – and its more balanced portrayal of conjugal love.[2] It is tempting to surmise that Gower had Chaucer's much earlier *BD* to hand while translating from his Ovidian source: a not insignificant amount of verbal overlap exists between the two versions, although, as Helen Phillips acknowledges, 'Given identical situations, and the obviousness of certain rhymes, the similarities may be fortuitous.'[3]

Two similarities are especially interesting. All but two MSS of the *Confessio* designate Juno's messenger Iris as 'he' in line 2973, despite the feminine pronouns that are used in the remainder of the passage. This may owe to a false (authorial) cue taken from Chaucer's version, which presents the (unnamed) messenger as male (*BD* 134–5, 154–5, etc.), perhaps under the influence of a corruption in one MS family of Pierre Bersuire's *Ovidius moralizatus*.[4] Another potentially Chaucerian touch in Gower's version is the presence, in the god of sleep's dream-strewn chamber, of a 'fethrebed ... al blak' and 'many a pilwe of doun' (4.3020–1, 3025).[5] By comparison, Ovid's Somnus slumbers on an ebony *torus*, or couch, that is *plumeus* (down-filled), with a dark coverlet but (apparently) no pillows (*Met.* 11.610–11).[6] Machaut, trans-lating this passage in his *Dit de la fonteinne amoureuse*, adds a touch of refinement to Ovid's rather morbid image: the god's place of repose is 'un lit trop riche et une couche' (a bed, a quite elegant couch) (604). To improve on this further, Machaut's lovestruck duke, petitioning Morpheus to send a dream-message to his lady, promises the god a 'mol lit de plume de gerfaut' (a soft bed filled with feathers) (809). Chaucer goes one better than his French forebear, bribing Morpheus or any of his ilk with a 'fether-bed' covered with imported black satin and 'many a pilowe ... to slepe softe' (*BD* 251, 254–5). Gower has, in effect, fleshed out the core Ovidian image of Sleep's abode with the vocabulary of Chaucer's solicitation (featherbed and pillows) – as if, a recent editor of the *Confessio* remarks, 'Gower's Iris made her journey after Chaucer's narrator fulfilled his pledge'.[7] Gower has inherited a dreamscape that has become richer through successive acts of literary propitiation (in a macrocosmic image of Gower's own *oeuvre*, from Latin to French to English). If in these small details, Gower does intend a nod at Chaucer – who has, of course, recently nodded at him in the dedication of *Troilus and Criseyde* – then there is reason to consider a broader affiliation with *BD* in the matter of dreams that frames this section of the *Confessio* and prompts the familiar Ceix story.

Like Chaucer, and like Froissart and Machaut before him, Gower appropriates the story of Ceix and Alceone selectively to exemplify the power of dreams within a charged reflection on the values, impera-tives and communicative properties of erotic love, particularly as these pertain to sleep and sleeplessness. In so doing, Gower participates in a tradition that more than usually strongarms the Ovidian narra-tive – which would seem more appropriate as an exemplum of fidel-ity, for example – to fit an agenda, specifically, the self-actualization of the love poet within the circuit of literary sensibilities proper to the *dit amoreux* tradition. By the time Gower was writing, the Ceix story had achieved currency in several prominent moments of literary torch-passing. Indeed, it had become a kind of signature by which love poets marked adherence to, and shifts within, an ongoing textual conversation. The conversation was inaugurated by Machaut's *Dit de la fonteinne amoureuse*, in which the melancholy duke relates the Ceix story seemingly as a digression in his complaint about his captivity and frustrated love. His interpretation of the Ovidian narrative is both illogical and ingenious, relating it to the insomnia from which he suffers as a lovesick man. Miserable, unable to sleep and on the verge of madness, he considers begging the God of Sleep to send Morpheus not to him – as we would expect, and as later writers will insist – but to his lady. He asks Morpheus to transmit a dream-message, as he did for Alceone; furthermore, he commissions his own impersonation by Morpheus, on account of his being 'moitié morte' (half dead) (717) – thus not so different from the drowned Ceix. Far from being spun as an amusing diversion, the Ovidian story thus interpreted emerges as a powerful template for the remainder of the *dit*, in which Machaut's persona will absorb Morpheus' role as intermediary to the duke's lady. Likewise, the dream shared by the two men at the fountain, in which the duke's lady reciprocates his love, will vindicate the communicative potential of oneiric experience, affirming the success of the narrator's Morpheus-like poetic mission.

Froissart registers the thematic priority of Machaut's Ceix story by revisiting it in the opening lines of his *Paradys d'Amours*, in one of many intertextual motions that affiliate this work with that of his predecessor. This time, it is the narrator himself who is lovesick and sleepless; he prays to Morpheus for sleep, and through the aid of Juno, Iris and others, falls asleep and has an amorous dream that fills the remainder of the poem. Upon waking, he is both comforted in love and newly versatile as a poet, thanks to the variety of lyrics he composed within the courtly paradise of his dream. Chaucer, combining the opening rhetoric of Froissart's insomniac narrator with Machaut's lengthier, embedded version of the Ceix story, then marks his participation in a continuous tradition that interrelates love, dreams and literate communication. Like Froissart's narrator, Chaucer's wakes up a writer; like Machaut's, he has been transported by the Ceix story – albeit more indirectly, in this case – into the sphere of noble sentiment.

Entering into this richly overdetermined literary conversation, Gower's Genius tells the story of Ceix and Alceone in the course of an examination of Somnolence, a species of Sloth. Gower also advanced this classification in his earlier *Mirour de l'omme* (lines 5180–96), where it contributed to a critique of dream exposition and the discourse of dream-visions more generally.[8] In the fourth book of the *Confessio*, in a section that includes definite Chaucerian allusions, Genius contrasts the imperatives of sleep and love, averring that a good lover will never indulge in sloth or behave lazily. A man who goes to bed 'unkist', hoping to fulfil his desire through dreams rather than action, deserves no reward (4.2712, 2734–45). Amans needs no convincing of this: he despises sleep, cousin of death and impediment to love's fulfilment (see esp. 2863–74). His lady is 'wakere of mi thoght' (4.3162); every conscious moment is devoted to her service, be it dancing, playing dice, debating love questions, or indulging her desire (as if a latter-day version of Dante's Francesca da Rimini, with her amorous bookish appetites) '[t]o rede and here of Troilus' (2795). However, these feints at romance – the prospect of a storybook union like that imagined by the narrator of *Troilus and Criseyde* for his audience of lovers, who 'bathen in gladnesse' (*Tr* 1.22) – are dissolved by the arousal of '[h]ire daunger, which seith evere "nay"' (*CA* 4.2813). Waking life turns out to be a literary nightmare: instead of Criseyde's voluptuous 'Welcome' (*Tr* 3.1309) or Francesca's fateful assent to read no more that day, Amans receives only White's discouraging 'Nay' (*BD* 1243).

Going home reluctantly, he curses the necessity of sleep, which severs him from his lady, and endures further torment 'til that the dede slep me hente' (2890). Once again, Chaucer's *Troilus* presses against Gower's narrative: a virtually identical line introduces Criseyde's dream of the eagle in Book 2 of that poem, a turning point in her decision to love Troilus (*Tr* 2.924: 'Til at the laste the dede slep hire hente'). Amans, however, experiences the inverse of what Criseyde's enigmatic dream projects – appropriately enough, since his lady is no Criseyde. His pellucid dream – 'that I alone with hire mete / And that Danger is left behinde' (2902–3), no less than an epitome of the *Roman de la rose* and the *Paradys d'Amours* – appears, on waking, vain and illusory (2906–12). For this reason, Amans resists sleep, cursing the night's slowness to pass (in an anti-aubade), and wishes that, in his lady's service, 'I mihte dryhe / Withoute slep to waken evere' (2836–7). Genius, modifying his earlier position somewhat, responds by granting the veracity of some dreams, illustrating the point with the tale of Ceix and Alceone. Fantasies of love's fulfilment, Genius claims, can be comforting, and sleep 'helpeth kinde / Somtyme, in Phisique as I finde, / Whan it is take be mesure' (3303–5).[9]

The recurrent Chaucerian echoes and allusions that pepper Gower's treatment of Somnolence, coupled with the incorporation of the Ceix and Alceone story (with diction that may well echo *BD*), suggest that among Gower's aims here may be a critical rereading of *BD*. Amans' commitment 'withoute slep to waken evere', true to the spirit of the French *dits*, confirms his status as an active lover.[10] Militant in his resolve that he 'mai noght slepe, thogh I wolde' (3368), Amans casts into relief the aberration embodied by the narrator of *BD*, who wonders, despairingly, how much longer he can endure without sleep (*BD* 1–3, 18–21). For Amans, to be lovesick is to be wakeful, and dreams have value strictly as a conduit of love. Insofar as Amans' waking efforts mirror those of the youthful Man in Black, who serves his lady diligently at court and is similarly rebuffed, but ultimately achieves his reward, Chaucer's poem – placed alongside Gower's – offers a trajectory that complements the generally encouraging thrust of Genius's counsel in this section. That this trajectory is violated by death is not in the purview of Gower's concerns here, which are with courtship pure and simple – unless, of course, the full scope of the *Confessio*, in which the natural processes of ageing and decay displace the pleasures of Venus, is brought to bear on this section.

If Chaucer's poem offers something to Gower's, Gower's also talks back to Chaucer's. Within the framework of Genius' logic regarding Somnolence, Gower posits a discursive correction to *BD*: in retrospect, it appears that Chaucer's narrator, unlike Amans, does not grasp the conceptual value of insomnia, regarding it only as a hindrance rather than an opportunity and badge of honour. The vagueness in *BD* surrounding the cause of the insomnia – unlike all other poems employing this motif, Chaucer never specifies that it is rooted in lovesickness – suggests in a Gowerian reading that the narrator has not mastered the imperative of love on a rhetorical level, leading to the writerly impasse with which he struggles at the beginning of *BD* as a passive consumer of, rather than participant in, stories about love. Finally giving in to the brute demands of the body rather than the aspirations of love, Chaucer's narrator succumbs to the kind of sleep identified by Genius as slothful (rather than restorative or love-bringing – its depressive content being perhaps deserved). In these ways, Gower reads *BD* not primarily as an elegy but as an unfulfilled love poem: a *dit* that is not fluently *amoreux*, requiring the remediation both of Gower's *Confessio* itself and of a future Chaucerian 'testament of love' (*CA* 8.*2955).

Writing between the Lines in Lydgate's *Complaynt of a Loveres Lyfe*

If Gower echoed and emended *BD* in the *Confessio*, Lydgate inhabited it in *Complaynt of a Loveres Lyfe* (*CLL*) (*c.*1398–1412?), sometimes titled *Complaint of the Black Knight* on the precedent of early printed editions.[11] Both Gower's and Lydgate's works, which enjoyed widespread manuscript circulation, helped disseminate Chaucer's poem, even as their creative responses in many respects underscored the poem that *BD* was not. A kind of satellite of *BD*, *CLL* appears in all three MSS of Chaucer's poem as well as several other 'Chaucerian' miscellanies featuring dream-visions and complaints. In Oxford, Bodleian Library MS Arch. Selden B.24 and the 1508 Chepman and Myllar print of *CLL*, the poem was attributed to Chaucer; beginning with Thynne's 1532 Chaucer – which, we recall, is also an important witness of the text of *BD* – *CLL* was presented as part of Chaucer's canon, where it remained until it was expunged by Skeat in 1878.[12] Like much of Lydgate's work, *CLL* reads like a Chaucerian pastiche, melding the language and imagery of *BD*, *Troilus*, *Parliament of Foules* and *Complaint unto Pity* into a new poetic whole. Interestingly, Lydgate in *CLL* conjures up a specifically French Chaucer: his poem may well engage the *dit amoreux* tradition directly, possibly turning for narrative models to Froissart's *Dit dou bleu chevalier* as well as *BD* and favouring French over Chaucerian precedents for the vision frame.[13]

CLL is part of a cluster of fifteenth-century poems, popularized by their inclusion in Chaucerian miscellanies, that creatively expand formal precedents set by Chaucer. The poem's most recent editor, Dana M. Symons, identifies it with a broader experimental 'redeployment of the conventions of dream vision, complaint, and debate' in post-Chaucerian verse, one that frequently employs 'dream vision conventions in non-dream contexts'.[14] As a 'dreamless dream poem', she argues, *CLL* looks back towards the French *dits amoreux*, which only sporadically adopted an overarching dream frame, but it differs in the lack of intercourse between onlooking narrator and suffering protagonist, engendering an aesthetic of voyeurism that may encode Lydgate's monkish detachment from the courtly love tradition.[15]

The narrative situation of *CLL* unfolds in tandem with *BD*, like a running commentary or a parallel-text transliteration. Against Chaucer's persona, with his undifferentiated melancholy, Lydgate situates his own narrator more explicitly as a failed lover. Like Chaucer's narrator, Lydgate's is oppressed by 'sorow' and 'sekenes'; his emotional state affects him somatically, causing him to be 'sore ... in euery veyn' (17, 18, 21). The cause of his malaise is simple to diagnose, however: it is a 'brynnyng that sate so nygh my[n] hert', attributed to the effects of 'Daunger and Disdeyn' (106, 114; cf. 13, 18). Despite this, he does not suffer from insomnia, that occupational hazard of lovers, and later in the poem his instantaneous cure by the waters of a well said to be *unlike* the one that captured Narcissus suggests, as A. C. Spearing puts it, that in posing as a lover he was merely 'go[ing] through the motions' – an interpretation with which Gower's Genius, were he to apply his interpretation of Somnolence, would agree.[16] At the beginning of *CLL*, Lydgate's narrator, rather than struggling to fall asleep as does Chaucer's, awakens from 'slombre' to an enlivening springtime scene: a walled garden, vibrant with birdsong and vegetation, situated in a 'wode' (23). Lydgate's poem, reliving Chaucer's, thus collapses the opening scene of *BD* – the narrator's suffering and sorrow – into the beginning of the vision proper (the Chaucerian persona's 'waking up' inside his dream bedroom then wandering into the verdant forest), while eliding the dream state itself, as well as all that led up to it in *BD*. Avoiding the polarities of waking and sleeping, which Chaucer had played to such intricately paradoxical effect,[17] Lydgate literalizes the transformation of the outlook of Chaucer's narrator, who arises refreshed at the start of the vision, by depicting an easy cure – the healing water from the well – of a sort quite impossible in *BD*. By neutralizing his narrator's emotional investment, Lydgate shapes a context within which his Black Knight's ensuing sorrow can emerge as a non-threatening spectacle for the observer rather than a shared and reciprocal experience.

Next, the *CLL* narrator becomes attentive to his new environment, noticing the forlorn knight in language that closely evokes Chaucer's: 'As I was war, I saw [w]her lay a man / In blake and white' (compare 'so at the laste / I was war of a man in blak') (*CLL* 130–1; *BD* 444–5). Two differences here are immediately striking. First, as Raymond P. Tripp, Jr has observed, subtle semantic differences between Lydgate's and Chaucer's statements reveal a contrast between, on the one hand, 'an after-the-fact, even redundant observation' of a person's presence and, on the other, a sense of sudden, disorienting realization of existential scope.[18] Second, the addition of white to the colour palette associated with the garb of Chaucer's grieving knight reorients, indeed contests, the tenor of the earlier work. In *BD*, the knight's blackness marked his privation, his lack, of all that White embodied; it epitomized his view, allegorized in the chess metaphor, of life as an all-or-nothing contestation. By comparison, in *CLL* the associations of black and white are mapped onto the knight's own person, signifying the inner qualities of 'sorowe' and 'clennesse', as Lydgate glosses these colour associations in his courtly ballad *My Lady Dere*.[19] *CLL* is not a poem about mourning, and the knight's black sorrow, referring to his frustrated love, is one that is offset – and perhaps can be mitigated – by the strength of his chastity, the purity of his purpose. His problem, it emerges, is that his lady has rebuffed his love on account of false rumours; her mercy is imprisoned by Daunger and Dispite. Interestingly, the editorial title

Complaint of the Black Knight – a misnomer, strictly speaking – familiar from the early folio editions and still used by some critics, conflates these distinct models of the knightly protagonist by reading the later poem in the light of the earlier one.

As in *BD*, a detailed account of the knight's physical suffering immediately follows the narrator's first sight of him. Like Chaucer's knight, Lydgate's is handsome – 'to speke of manhood oon the best o[n] lyve' (158; cf. *BD* 452) – and appears grievously ill. His complexion is 'pale and wan' (131; cf. *BD* 470, 497–9), and he is overcome by 'sekenesse', 'malady' and 'hertly wo' (134, 138, 139; cf. *BD* 488–92). He suffers from a 'hote accesse', or love fever, and Lydgate's narrator, like Chaucer's, reacts with pity (at line 145; cf. *BD* 465), albeit in this case with a certain bathos that hints at the less consequential nature of the knight's predicament: 'Hyt was a deth for to [her] him grone' (136, 140). Significantly, nothing in this scene corresponds to the lyric rehearsed by Chaucer's Man in Black, which figures so problematically in the interpretative scheme of *BD*, centring as it does upon urgent issues of communication and understanding. Instead, Lydgate's narrator, observing the knight's visible suffering and solitude, simply wonders what is wrong with him and decides to 'espye' the cause (148).

Before recounting the knight's monologue – in this version, there is no dialogue between observer and protagonist – the narrator provides a lengthy disclaimer regarding his status as recorder of this material (155–217). In doing so, Lydgate merges the *BD* narrator's self-presentation just before the Man in Black's first lyric with the rhetorical position of Chaucer's narrator at the beginning of *Troilus*. Like the *BD* narrator, who insists on his close attention to the knight's lyric and his ability 'ful wel' to '[r]eherse hyt' (*BD* 473–4), Lydgate's narrator – speaking of the knight's whole performance rather than any distinct lyrical unit – promises, 'I wol to yow (so as I can) anone / Lych as he seyde reherse[n] euerychone' (174–5), and he reinforces the accuracy of his reportage at the end (596–609). Furthermore, he acknowledges the need to know the 'cause and rote' of the knight's malady in order to represent it properly (189), transmuting the *BD* narrator's offer to the knight of medical assistance (*BD* 544–57) into the framing of the material itself. Lydgate's narrator's lack of direct involvement with the knight's emotional experience is registered, in turn, by his identification with the reporter-stance of the *Troilus* narrator. Like him, Lydgate appeals to classical forces of inspiration to give feeling to his tragic subject matter – here, Niobe and Myrrha rather than the Furies (176–82) – and he further echoes his Chaucerian predecessor in remarking on the correspondence between subject matter and emotion (183–6; cf. *Tr* 1.13–14), defining his role as a 'skryuener' deprived of 'sentement' (194, 197; cf. *Tr* 1.10, 2.13), and addressing an audience of lovers who can appreciate the knight's pain (204–17; cf. *Tr* 1.22–56). Like the narrator of *Troilus*, and like the *BD* narrator eavesdropping on the Man in Black's first lyric before making his acquaintance, the rhetorical position of Lydgate's narrator for the remainder of the poem is that of voyeur. His own experiences as a frustrated lover, forgotten entirely since he took the well's healing waters, do not influence or complicate his perspective on the knight, as they do for the narrator of *BD*. Lydgate's narrator is merely an outsider looking in.

The knight of *CLL* then engages in a lengthy monologue thickly shaped by the language of *Roman de la rose* and *Troilus* to reveal the cause of his suffering, without ambiguity, as rebuffed love. Male-Bouche and his allegorical henchmen wage war on his Trouthe, causing him to be oppressed by Cruelte and Disdeyn (260–80). His fever and sickness are the effects of garden (of Deduit)-variety lovesickness, as a rather diffuse rendition of Chaucer's Petrarchan *Canticus Troili* makes clear (225–38; cf. *Tr* 1.400–20). Like Chaucer's Man in Black, Lydgate's knight invokes classical exempla to fortify his own drama – in this case, paradigms of famous lovers frustrated or destroyed by love despite their *trouthe*, as well as instances of false lovers undeservedly rewarded (323–99; cf. *BD* 1054–87). The sheer conventionality of the knight's idealistic pose as lover aligns him closely with the youthful Man in Black, whose plea for 'Mercy!' was similarly frustrated by his lady's disdain (*BD* 1219; cf. *CLL* 442–6). In this respect, one can recognize the appeal of John Urry's conjecture, in his 1721 edition of Chaucer's works, that *CLL* (which he believed to be canonical) may have been composed for John of Gaunt's courtship of Blanche of Lancaster.[20] The poem is a kind of interpolation in the middle of *BD*, and its rhetoric of suffering, accordingly, is squarely in the spirit of the Man in Black's conviction that '[a]nd but I telle hir, I nam but ded' (1188) rather than his painful articulation of real death – both White's and the one he quite seriously seeks. In *BD*, elusive death supplants the cruel mistress (583–97) and, perversely, offers the only avenue for communion (686–709); in *CLL*, death functions as emotional blackmail, pure and simple, in the knight's suit for mercy. Far from the swift and luminous paradoxes of the Man in Black's dance with death ('I wolde have hym, hyt nyl nat me' (586)), Lydgate's knight's less urgent suicide speech swells, like Dorigen's similarly anticlimactic deliberation in the *Franklin's Tale*, to more than sixty lines, reaching no conclusion other than that his life is in his lady's hands.

To be sure, the 'lake of pite' shown to Lydgate's knight is presented in more extreme terms than the corresponding phenomenon in *BD*: it is as though his lady is deliberately torturing rather than educating him, and he supposes that 'she hath ioy to laughen at my peyn' (448). Revisiting the Fortune motif in *BD*, Lydgate's knight maps his lady's 'cruelte', her readiness to believe the 'doublenesse' and 'fraude' of false gossip, onto the actions of Lady Fortune herself (422, 426, 446). *BD*'s chess analogy memorably represented the duplicitous Fortune, antithesis of White's singular purity, as the antagonist of Love and destroyer of the lovers' bliss. By comparison, *CLL* conflates Fortune with Love (and by extension, with the lady herself): both are irrational, cruel, changeable (456–62). As was the case with his treatment of suicide, Lydgate's discussion of Fortune here reopens the structuring ambiguities of *BD* in order to flatten them. In a sense, Lydgate takes up the role of Chaucer's naïve dreamer and validates his perspective: the horrible truth in *CLL* is simply what Chaucer's dreamer queries at *BD* 1140–2: 'Nyl she not love yow? ... Or have ye oght doon amys, / That she hath left yow? Ys hyt this?' Since the answer to these questions is clear from the start, the poetics of *aporia* are absent and the dawning of insight is attenuated. Confronting the intense emotionality and narrative structure of *BD* more directly than Gower did, Lydgate nonetheless intervenes in a similar spirit, transforming a poem about mortality and its effects on communication into an amatory tableau that safely rhetoricizes death.

When the knight ceases his complaint, its physical effects on him are detailed. He sighs as though his heart would break in two, and his 'woo and mortal peyn' cause the onlooking narrator to weep (578). Here Lydgate interestingly conflates two thematically related passages in *BD*: the detailed account of the Man in Black's physical suffering after his first lyric regarding White's death, and the rhetoric of his ultimate revelation that 'She ys ded!' What marks Lydgate's engagement with these two moments is a strategic use of the 'routhe'/'trouthe' end-rhyme, in the narrator's assertion that his tears fell 'for [v]erry inward routhe / That I hym saw so langwysshing for trouthe' (580–1). The same rhyme pair, we recall, surfaces in the communication that unites Chaucer's interlocutors so crucially at the end (*BD* 1309–10); it also, significantly, appears in the dreamer's introduction of Black's first lyric, which consists of '[t]he moste pitee, the moste rowthe, / That ever I herde; for, by my trowthe ...' (465–6). Lydgate's appropriation of this loaded rhyme pair, in a context that manifestly engages these two Chaucerian moments, reveals his sensitivity to the thematic coherence of *BD* around these key moments of communication and emotional expression. The shift of emphasis that occurs here in *CLL* is thus all the more striking. Rather than marking a genuine, if momentary, communion between strangers, or a hard-won integration of different sides of the self, the reciprocity of 'routhe' and 'trouthe' in Lydgate's poem intensifies division and displacement. The following lines return us to the narrator's position hiding in the bushes, as he takes care to remain concealed while the knight retreats to his lodge. The narrator's position actualizes that of Chaucer's dreamer, who similarly feels 'rowthe' in proximity to 'trowthe', had he never taken the emotional risk of introducing himself to the Man in Black.

It is hardly surprising, in this safer and finally less generative scenario, that no clear resolution occurs. The speechlessness and finality of the end of *BD* give way in *CLL* to something more akin to the ceremonial anticipation of the end of the *Parliament of Foules*. The knight, we discover, utters this complaint every May. Never achieving closure, his experience merges with the cycle of nature – his 'hurtes grene' (i.e. raw, fresh) coincide with the appearance of 'bowes grene' – because in the mythology of erotic love springtime arouses desire (133, 588). In a nod to the closing lines of *BD*, Lydgate recounts his own process of composition, writing down the knight's complaint verbatim while it was still fresh in his mind, under the beams of Venus (596–644). Eschewing the rich compression of temporality achieved in the last line of *BD*, Lydgate instead compresses his poem into Chaucer's, in a revealing twist: at the end, his narrator, thus far having avoided a dream-vision, finally falls asleep, but not by reading a book by Ovid, or even by Chaucer. It seems that it is the experience of writing his own book that leads him to feel 'that I ne may noo lenger wake' (652). Sleep – weary, rather than imaginatively restorative – overcomes him, and he ends where he began.

BD Otherwise: Charles of Orleans' *Fortunes Stabilnes*

The mixed-form collection of English verse preserved in British Library MS Harley 682 and attributed to Charles of Valois, Duke of Orleans, entitled *Fortunes Stabilnes* (*FS*) by its most recent editor, bespeaks a more 'intense and discriminating understanding of Chaucerian idiom' – and a more profound encounter with *BD* – than any work thus far considered.[21] This semi-autobiographical poetic collection, composed in the course of the duke's twenty-five-year imprisonment in England after being captured at the battle of Agincourt in 1415, overlaps in varying degrees with the corpus of French lyrics and narrative poetry contained in the duke's autograph manuscript (BnF MS. Fr. 25458). The English and French cycles are of uncertain chronological relationship; while some have thought the English poems the work of an anonymous trans-lator rather than Charles himself, recent scholars have tended to favour common authorship, and the present analysis follows suit. Variegated literary resonances at once affiliate *FS* with Chaucer's poetry and com-plicate a notion of linear influence on account of their common inspira-tion by a heterogeneous tradition: Boethius' *Consolation of Philosophy*, Alan of Lille's *De planctu Naturae*, the *Roman de la rose*, and a range of

French *dits amoreux* were well known to both poets. Charles may also have been acquainted with some of the works of Gower and Lydgate, the latter being a major conduit of Chaucerian style for fifteenth-century letters.[22] Nonetheless, direct dialogue with Chaucer's poetry unquestionably occurs through much of *FS*, and *BD* surfaces as an especially rich site of encounter, one that reveals Charles in many respects breaking with the traditions of response outlined above.

Charles's sprawling English love-narrative, rich with lyrical experiments and interludes, embedded dreams, and courtly topoi, can appropriately be considered an 'English *dit amoureux*',[23] and hence a benefactor of Chaucer's innovative merging in *BD* of French form with English register. As a widely read member of the French royal family who found himself exiled in England, writing French-inspired poetry, sometimes awkwardly, in his acquired language of English, Charles offers testimony of both the creative polyglossia and the cultural abjection that informs *BD* as the first English *dit amoreux* (discussed in chapter 2). Unlike Gower and Lydgate, Charles reads *BD* as a poem about mortality as well as the hardships of love. *FS* tells the story of the narrator's two loves: the first lost to death, the second frustrated by emotional turbulence. As Mary-Jo Arn suggests, *FS* may be understood structurally as a kind of *demande d'amours* stretched across 6,500 lines, the implicit question being, which of these amatory predicaments is worse?[24] As such, *FS* would seem creatively to re-envision Machaut's *Jugement dou roi de Behaigne*, which imposes a similar spectrum of possibility on the personal experiences of a lady and a knight debating the value of their respective misfortunes. However, *FS*'s compression of these experiences into the life of a single individual results less in a debate poem than an emotional autobiography, one that takes the Man in Black's experience in *BD* as a point of departure. Whereas for the Man in Black, the difficulties of courtship lead to a fulfilment thwarted by death, for Charles's persona, loss of his lady to death comes early, and the challenges of love service come after. The poetic significance of death – the crux of *BD*, a segue in *FS* – and the dynamic of mortality and erotic expression are two interpretative areas in which Charles's intricate response to *BD* may be apprehended in detail.

Viewed as a literary response to *BD*, *FS* rests on an aesthetic of reversal. If White's death, in *BD*, impels the Man in Black towards the past, where he can revisit his youthful frustrations and recover a sense of fulfilment, the death of Charles's lady points him toward the future, where frustrations abound. His self-actualization as a lover largely rests in that forward trajectory, not in the consummated past, which he does not resurrect in detail.[25] The first echoes of *BD* occur in Ballade 9, one of the wooing poems directed at his first lady with which the collection opens. Like the Man in Black, Charles celebrates the conjunction of his lady's 'Bewte' with 'trouthe' and other virtues ('Bounte, Honour, Astat, and Gentiles') (B9, 440, 458–66; cf. *BD* 999–1005). Charles insists that these superlatives do not rest on his unique perception: they are corroborated by 'alle hir seth with eye' (B9, 465). This recalls the Man in Black's somewhat defensive assertion, in response to an insensitive comment by the dreamer, that White's virtuous beauty was perceived not only by 'myn' eyes but by 'alle that hir seyen' – all '[s]eyde and sworen hyt was soo' (*BD* 1052–3). The implication levied by Chaucer's dreamer, that White's beauty resided in the eye of the smitten beholder ('Whoso had loked hir with your eyen' (*BD* 1051)), registers elsewhere in *FS* as well, surfacing playfully in a later roundel concerning the lover's life: 'Who so biholdeth wel *as with my eye* / Mi verry lady and my sul maystres, / In hir he shall se a gret and hvug [*sic*] larges' (R10, 3269–71; emphasis added). Like White – in a paradox we shall see extended – Charles's lady is unique: 'the sovl fenyx of Araby' (*FS* B9, 471; cf.'The soleyn fenix of Arabye' (*BD* 982)). These suggestive parallels of thought and phrasing reach their apex with the lady's sudden death, which occurs just 2,000 lines into the 6,531-line poetic series.

The ballade (no. 57) that announces the lady's death after an illness follows a recognizably Chaucerian pattern while engaging the broader medieval tradition of laments for the dead.[26] Like the Man in Black in his first complaint, Charles addresses his ballade to Death, bemoans the theft of such a treasured lady, and asks Death to take him as well. The ballade begins with phrasing very similar to that found in the second half of Chaucer's eleven-line complaint:

Allas, Deth, who made thee so hardy
To take awey the most nobill princesse ...
But syn thou hast biraft me my maystres,
Take me, poore wrecche, hir cely serviture[.] (*FS* B57, 1994–5, 1998–9)

Compare the Man in Black's lament:

Allas, deth, what ayleth the,
That thou noldest have taken me,
Whan thou toke my lady swete[.] (*BD* 481–3).

Continuing to build on the rhetorical framework of his Chaucerian predecessor, Charles in an ensuing series of ballades allegorizes his loss through a chess game with Fortune. Like the Man in Black, he situates the life-and-death stakes of chess within an economics of gambling, rather than a noble pursuit of honour, which defines felicity more generally.[27] Imagery of Fortune as gamester initially surfaces in Charles's account of the ups and downs of courtship, here imagined as a 'short game of tablis' in which his successful moves, encouraged by Love, are foiled by Fortune, who 'doth turne the dise so, welaway!', leaving him to ponder 'this iupart' (i.e. 'iupardy', a trick or stratagem in chess or tables) (B46, 1629, 1645, 1656). Chaucer's dreamer, by comparison, rejects the idle diversions of 'ches or tables' only to dream of a knight who obsesses over 'jeupardyes' he wishes he had mastered (*BD* 51, 666). When his lady becomes ill, the chess game Charles plays against Daungere and Fortune turns deadly:

O woo worthe she [i.e. Fortune] that my game ouyrthrew!
For tane she hath my lady, welaway!
That y am matt, this may y se and say,
Without so be y make a lady newe. (B61, 2115–8).

Checkmated, like the Man in Black, by 'seytfull Fortune, with hir dowbil chere' (B61, 2129), Charles similarly places exceptional emphasis on the importance of the queen, whose capture spells disaster in both

BD and *FS*. When the Man in Black's 'fers' (queen) is taken, he concludes, 'Allas, I kouthe no lenger playe' and is immediately mated; in the same way, the loss of Charles's 'lady', whose positioning on the chessboard always thwarted 'trobill or distres', kindles the perception that he has 'lost ... / ... all my good, god wot, that on hit lay' (B61, 2121, 2125–6). The resemblance between these statements stands out all the more – and argues against their dependence on any common repository of experience with the game and its literary iterations – insofar as they both, oddly, defy medieval rules of chess, in which the queen lacked her modern importance and her capture was not necessarily catastrophic.

Despite these similarities, the game is not quite over for Charles. Line 2118, the refrain of the ballade, conditionally depicts the prospect of checkmating against the alternative possibility of 'mak[ing] a lady newe' – that is, promoting a pawn to queen. A complex resistance to the precedent, and to some extent the overall rationale, of *BD* begins to operate here. In the long-standing critical puzzlement over the chess analogy in *BD* – the grounds of which are established by Chaucer's own dreamer, who expresses astonishment that anyone would 'for a fers make this woo!', deepening the crux with his enigmatic reference to 'the ferses twelve' (723, 741) – the apparently ahistorical importance placed on the queen has been the subject of numerous interpretations. Chaucer's shaky knowledge of the game, the availability of non-standard chessboards, the symbolic rather than strategic importance of the queen, and Chaucer's reliance on theoretical rather than practical understandings of chess have all been advanced as explanations.[28] Perhaps most artistically sound is the possibility that the Man in Black does not himself grasp the implications of his performance – that he has in fact made a strategic blunder in resigning himself to defeat pre-emptively, since the queen's loss need not have meant the end of the game.[29] The legibility of this subtext, brought out by the dreamer's confused reaction to the knight's account, has even been understood as a subtle encouragement to John of Gaunt to remarry, since practically speaking, a 'fers' is replaceable, 'for games are always replayed'.[30] In *FS*, Charles's rumination, in the negative, on 'mak[ing] a lady newe' to replace his lost queen registers this very possibility, finding new poetic direction in a fissure left unsealed in *BD*. In his poetic vision of love lost and renewed, Charles does not reject outright *BD*'s insistence on the beloved's singularity; instead, he boldly capitalizes on it to support a different trajectory.

The ballade immediately following exemplifies this intertextual strategy. Returning to the imagery of the 'sovl fenyx of Araby' that earlier denoted the lady's pre-eminence (B9, 471), Ballade 62 is structured on a refrain that links the absolute nature of her death with the parallel necessity that 'the fenyx lyveth withouten ayre' (B62, 2148). Charles's logic here is paradoxical and to some extent self-defeating. First, in appropriating the phoenix as a template for his lady's uniqueness – she is the '*sovl* fenyx of Araby', just as the Bestiary states the phoenix is unparalleled in the whole world – Charles quite blatantly imitates Chaucer's use of the same phrase, as we have seen, to insist upon another lady's uniqueness. The presence of the allusion militates against the validity of the claim in a way that discloses that the world has produced more than one superlatively virtuous lady – even, perhaps, implying that consummate beauty, as Chaucer's dreamer suggests and Charles himself later admits, is a matter of subjective judgement. Moreover, the example of the phoenix cannot help but put us in mind of new life rising from the ashes: the bird may be without heir, but its own form is renewable. The common medieval interpretation of the phoenix as an allegory of the Resurrection renders Charles's use of the image to certify the absolute nature of his lady's death doubly ironic. On the one hand, as was also true of the Man in Black's use of the phoenix image, this reminder of the soul's eternal reward ought to be comforting to the Christian mourner, but instead it functions only as an index of loss. But at the same time, the phoenix's associations with renewal shift the cast of Charles's refusal to 'make a lady newe' from defiance to ambivalence. Over the course of time, Charles does exactly this, and his new lady does, in a sense, rise from the old one's ashes when, in a dream-vision later in the poetic series, he falls in love with a woman whom he mistakes for his dead lady (*FS* 5051–5155). The new lady of the vision sits on Fortune's wheel, and the dreamer renews his hostility against Fortune, who 'stale with deth my lady' (5103), but subsequently reconciles with her (5174–81), recognizing her role in bringing future prosperity.

The phoenix ballade advances a final set of associations that link it with *BD*, further delineating the aesthetic of reversal we have been noting. In a curious *praeteritio* that evolves into what seems an *amplificatio* of the Man in Black's climactic admission at the end of *BD*, Charles bemoans his lady's death:

What nedith me, allas, hir to discryue?
Hir prays doth ay vnto eche ere repeyre.
She ded is (what need y more prays contryue?) ...
Lef of, my penne! she deyde, she deyde, more routhe! (B62, 2153–5, 2167)

In *BD*, as established earlier, the hard-bought confession that 'She ys ded!' – so obvious, and yet so unfathomable – is only voiced after several hundred lines of praise and description that function in part to forestall and qualify death, to sustain life through poetic memory. Read against this template, this ballade in *FS* makes the opposite point: *since* she is dead, praise and description are futile. There is no avoiding the subject here, no vicarious reliving of the past. Instead, Charles's ready acknowledgement of her death and his repeated insistence on it foreclose the possibility of living in the past, gradually opening the door to thoughts of renewing his love elsewhere – thoughts that first appear here, if only in the negative.

The poetic possibilities offered by *BD* on the subject of sorrow and mourning result in further intertextual colloquy throughout this section of *FS*. Unlike in *BD*, where the acknowledgement of White's death functions apocalyptically to end all discourse, the parallel announcement in *FS* opens the poetic floodgates, generating a series of funereal ballades (58–74) in which Charles ruminates on death and its rituals, the fragility of worldly happiness, and his desire to join his lady in death. The last of these ballades, of particular importance structurally insofar as it is followed by a dream-vision in which Age instructs Charles to abandon the pursuit of love, is a mourning poem thick with Chaucerian resonances. Ballade 74, unparalleled in the French redaction, reads as an extended suicide wish that stylistically coalesces the beginning of *Troilus and Criseyde* with the Man in Black's melancholy self-portrait in *BD*. Not even Tisiphone, '[w]hich clepid is the Goddes of Turment', writes Charles, can fathom the sorrow of his heart (B74, 2522–3; cf. *Tr* 1.8). Like the Man in Black, who avows 'y am sorwe, and sorwe ys y', and that all who encounter him can say they have met with sorrow itself (*BD* 595–7), Charles fashions himself as sorrow incarnate: 'Who so that lust aqueynt him silf with sorowe / As come to me and seche no ferthir wey' (B74, 2529–30). Begging Antropos and the other Fates, like Troilus (cf. *Tr* 4.1208), to bring him death, Charles imagines himself in a liminal death-world, 'ay diyng y lyue and neuyr deed', just as the Man in Black describes his condition as '[a]lway deynge and be not ded' (B74, 2536; *BD* 588).

In *BD*, the morbidity of the grieving knight's sentiments is lightened and offset by the memories of a joyful past that he proceeds to recount. Chaucer encourages us to weigh the angst of the young suitor the Man in Black once was against the much graver distress of the living corpse he has become. The hyperbole of the courtly lover, epitomized by the youth's certainty that 'I nam but ded' unless he gains an audience with his lady, casts into relief the literal reality of these words, first uttered by the drowned Seys (204). A deconstruction of *fin'amors* may well play out in this exposure of the rhetorical roots of courtly longing in the imaginative *terroir* of death – a poetic manoeuvre reminiscent of Petrarch's *Canzoniere*, in which Laura's transformation from a distant beloved to a dead beloved is rendered nearly invisible. If *BD* gently mocks the high drama of romance by revealing its appropriation of life-and-death registers, the resurgence of real death – when 'I nam but ded' becomes 'She ys ded!' – makes it impossible to ignore how finally trifling such frustrations are. Remembering them, in the face of greater sorrow, is a kind of comfort, especially as these setbacks were overcome in the achievement of a happy ending ('And thus we lyved ful many a yere / So wel I kan nat telle how' (*BD* 1296–7)) – if that had been the end of the story. At the same time, as Chaucer would go on to convey in *Troilus and Criseyde*, the sorrow involved in love's fulfilment demarcates the gravity of a later, more profound loss.

FS similarly deconstructs the morbid entanglements of courtly love by revealing their proximity to mortality writ large. The picture of emotional torment drawn here, however, does not serve to underscore the enormity of grieving, nor does it provide an imaginative respite in a simpler time when problems were more easily solved. It is, instead, the path of the future: the narrator, having rejected love and retreated to the Castle of No Care, displaces his unrelenting fixation on his dead lady into the continued production of love poetry and, eventually, devotion to a new lady who resembles the first. One of several roundels Charles produces for a courtly banquet in the mid-section of the work exemplifies a shift towards the amatory rhetoric of death that will surround his second love affair:

> Yowre departing
> Is, me felyng,
> the deth, <straynyng>
> Myn hert to die ...
> For deth y crie[.] (4537–40, 4545)

Revealingly, Charles at a later point appropriates language and imagery from the Man in Black's discourse on mourning – some of which *FS* had earlier used in number 74, the suicide ballade – placing it now in the context not of death but of love. In Ballade 99, Charles first details the physical ailments attendant upon his lovesickness (5840–7), then catalogues the inversions of experience that he suffers: 'Myn ese in harme, my wele in woo, / Mi hope in drede, in dowt my sikirnes, / And my delite in sorrow loo, / My hele seeknes' (5849–52). Conventional as this litany of amorous paradoxes may be – the motif derives from a passage in the *Roman de la rose* (lines 4293–334) and was rendered in Machaut's *Jugement du roy de Behaigne* (lines 177–87) – its immediate source is certainly *BD*, which shares nearly all of its elements ('my wele is woo', 603; 'My good ys harm', 604; 'my delyt into sorwynge', 606; 'Myn hele ... into seknesse', 607; 'In drede ys al my sykernesse', 608).[31]

In *BD*, the Man in Black delivers the corresponding speech immediately after his self-identification with sorrow and before the Fortune analogy. The third stanza of Ballade 99 makes explicit the connection with the Man in Black's melancholy state, employing phrasing familiar both from *BD*, whose presence here and throughout this ballade is especially visible in Charles's uncharacteristic use of octosyllabic metre, and from an earlier section of *FS*:

> For who with Sorowe list aqueyntid be,
> As come to me and spille no ferthir wey,
> For Sorow is y and y am he[.] (5856–8)

Rather than wishing for death as in Ballade 74, however, Charles ends this ballade by entreating his new lady, source of this suffering, to turn it into its 'amverse' (contrary) (5867).

In these respects, *FS*'s artistic relationship to *BD* runs deeper than that of the other early adaptations examined thus far. Alive to the deconstructive energies within *BD*'s portrayal of *fin'amors* in the context of mortality as well as the interlingual shading of the seminal English *dit amoreux*, Charles of Orleans presses his Chaucerian model to its breaking point. What results is a poetic narrative impelled by death in a different sense: rather than treating death as ineffable and supplanting it – finally unsuccessfully – with a living past, the lover-narrator of *FS* goes on living, only to find that the travails of courtship can be just as debilitating as the work of mourning. This yields, in the final account, a rather sour commentary on the ideology of noble love: it lacks the quiet dignity with which *BD* leaves the Man in Black as a lover, as well as the sense of detachment afforded by the narrator's separation from the grieving figure. *FS* may even be understood as a kind of sequel to *BD*, one that recreates the Man in Black's recollection of his courtship – the very material on which the other poets considered thus far focus in reading *BD* as a love poem pure and simple – as a new, troubled future for the lover. Such a continuation of the story intriguingly resembles early printed editions' annexation of *Bukton* to *BD*, discussed in the previous chapter: whether through the lens of courtship or marriage, both supplementations of *BD* concern the torments of a future relationship.

FS's strategy of revision, in a final twist, may also function by way of correction, enhancing the affiliation of *BD* with the *Songe vert*, an anonymous French *dit amoreux* that may well have been written in imitation of *BD* (on which see chapter 2).[32] In the *Songe vert*, we recall, a black-clad mourner eventually finds new love, changing his clothing to green. The hopeful future that lies beyond the last lines of *Songe vert* is, by implication, a remedy to the impasse faced by Chaucer's Man in Black – one that *FS* then explores as an alternative reality with its own disappointing twists and turns. For Charles to read *BD* through its colloquy with French courtly poetry, particularly a poem such as *Songe vert*, which confronts the problem of death and mourning in a way most other works in *BD*'s family tree do not, is a fitting tribute to the literary make-up of Chaucer's ambitious early poem. *FS*'s lack of reverence in intervening in the very rationale of *BD* – in exposing the problems it raises and taking their intractability to new lengths – shows Charles to have captured some of the spirit of Chaucer's own creative manipulation of his French sources.

Dreaming Chaucer: The *Isle of Ladies* as Serial Fiction

Although the plot of the late fifteenth-century love-vision now known as the *Isle of Ladies*, composed by an unknown north Midlands author, is farther afield from *BD* than those of the works thus far examined, it participates decisively in the network of literary relationships that structures the reading of *BD* in the first stages of its reception history. Like Gower's *CA*, *Isle* playfully stages the wish-fulfilment dreams of lovers against a backdrop of erotic vigilance. Like Charles of Orleans's *FS*, it confronts the tragedy of death within a larger romance framework. And like Lydgate's *CLL*, *Isle* was disseminated as part of Chaucer's canon until the late nineteenth century.[33] *Isle*'s connection to *BD* is in fact more intimate than that of other fifteenth-century poems inspired by Chaucer's work: not only was it attributed to Chaucer both in manuscript and print, but it masqueraded under a title also attached to *BD* (with certain variations), namely 'Chaucer's Dreame'. The confounding textual history of *Isle*, which survives in two sixteenth-century MSS and was first printed by Speght in 1598, finds it conflated variously with *BD* and with Lydgate's *Temple of Glass*, itself ascribed to Chaucer (the latter attribution in Longleat House, MS 256, and reaffirmed by Francis Thynne in his *Animadversions* (1599)). *Isle* was mistitled 'The death of Blaunche, the Dutchesse of Lancaster' (in British Library MS Additional 10303, and similarly in Speght's 1602 edition ('the death of Blanch')), as well as the more commonly encountered 'Chaucer's Dreame'. *BD*, for its part, was first designated 'The Dreame of Chaucer' in Thynne's 1532 edition, with variations including 'Chaucer's Dreame' – a title Speght, in the Arguments of his 1598 edition, presents only to reject in favour of 'The booke of the Duchess, or the death of Blanche' – although the title he uses in the body of his edition is 'The Dreame of Chaucer'. In his *Animadversions* on the errors in Speght's first edition, Francis Thynne insists upon 'The Dreame of Chaucer'; this title, accordingly, appears as the running title of *BD* in Speght's 1602 edition, although the title head of the poem itself reverts to the formerly rejected 'Chaucer's Dreame'.[34]

In this quagmire of misattributions and doppelgängers, a fibre of logic connecting *BD* and *Isle* does exist. In both his 1598 and 1602 editions, Speght prefaces *Isle*, presented as 'Chaucer's Dreame', with an argument that interprets it as 'a couert report of the mariage of Iohn of Gaunt the kings sonne, with Blanch the daughter of Henry Duke of Lancaster'.[35] The connection of *BD* to the same historical personages, obscured in the earliest stages of its reception history, was by this point well established: there is, as we have seen, Chaucer's own reference to the poem as 'the Deeth of Blaunche the Duchesse' in *LGW* F 418, Stow's marginal note in the Fairfax MS regarding the connection with Gaunt, and the argument supplied in Speght's own 1598 edition equating the Man in Black with Gaunt and White with Blanche.[36] Thus these two poems circulating under near-identical titles were marketed as companion pieces, with *Isle* achieving currency as a sort of prequel to *BD*.[37] This poetic affinity is also significant for the apocryphal poem's amalgamation with Chaucer's biography as represented by Speght both in the argument to *Isle* and in the Life of Chaucer prefixed to his volume, which emphasizes the poet's royal connections. As noted in the previous chapter, the nuptials related by *Isle* are in fact a double ceremony uniting (in Speght's reading) both the Gaunt and Blanche figures, and the narrator and Blanche's maidservant – these, biographically speaking, being Chaucer himself and 'a certain Gentlewoman' (argument to *Isle*), i.e. Philippa (Pan) de Roet, who Speght says was, together with her sister Katherine, attendant upon Blanche.[38] *Isle* thus not only rounded out the plot of *BD*; it fortified its canonical value – and, by extension, Chaucer's poetic respectability – by further solidifying Chaucer's connections to the royal court as a brother-in-law of John of Gaunt.

In these ways, the rather peculiar dream-vision now known as the *Isle of Ladies* helped shape the conditions by which Chaucer's inaugural narrative effort was apprehended and rendered intelligible for an early modern readership. Reading *Isle* as part of a matrix of reception of *BD*, rather than a poem merely linked to it by an accident of transmission, adds value to our understanding of *BD*'s making. First, because of the intricacy of *Isle*'s plot in connection to *BD*, an overview is necessary.

In May, a lovesick narrator, weary from hunting, falls asleep beside a well in a forest. After a discussion of dreams that includes the possibility that what follows is a half-waking vision, he relates a dream that begins with his arrival – transported there he knows not how – on an enchanting island walled with glass. A great multitude of ladies inhabits the island, where men are prohibited. The dreamer sees his lady, the object of his waking meditations, accompanying the queen of the island. With them is a knight. The queen recounts how she undertook a journey to gather apples of good fortune when she was abducted by this knight, who insisted he had always loved her. Frightened nearly to death, she was healed by the dreamer's lady with the help of a magical apple. The queen then arranges to determine the knight's full intentions towards her. Confronted thus, he swoons in panic and remorse for his rash actions. Finally revived by the queen, the only word he can utter is 'Mercy' (588); then, he wishes at length for death.[39] The queen speaks mercifully towards him but remains non-committal regarding their future.

At this point the God of Love invades the island with 10,000 ships, and the queen is defeated by Love's arrow; Love also causes the heart of the dreamer's lady to warm towards him. Love assumes dominion over the island, and the queen pledges servitude to him. Courtly pastimes and general celebration ensue. The dreamer's lady then sets out on a journey on which he desperately follows; he nearly drowns, but she revives him with another magic apple. He has just accompanied her to her own country, where mutual happiness awaits, when he wakes from his dream, exhausted and tear-soaked. He is no longer in the forest by the well, but on a bed in a smoke-filled room. He wanders through the house and settles in a painted chamber '[f]ull of storyes old and diverse' (1325), where he falls asleep again and resumes the same dream.

In the continued dream, plans for the wedding of the knight and queen are under way. The knight returns to his own country to gather 60,000 noble attendants for the wedding feast, but he fails to return to the isle by the agreed-upon date. When he arrives on the island, he encounters widespread mourning: the queen has died of sorrow on account of the knight's 'untrothe', and two thirds of her attendant ladies have died along with her, despairing that their feminine sanctuary would now seem 'an open weye ... to every wight' (1674–5). Torn by guilt at his misdeed, the knight promptly dies. A strange songbird alights on the queen's corpse but is frightened away, becomes injured and dies. Other birds bring to their dead fellow a herb that quickly flowers and produces a seed that resurrects the bird. The same seed, applied to the queen, revives her as well. She then resuscitates the knight with the same remedy; his first words upon waking are 'Gramercy, leche' (1946). A double marriage is planned for knight and queen, dreamer and lady. Music from the lavish wedding ceremony startles the dreamer from his sleep. He finds himself in bed, without his lady, surrounded by wall paintings of a hunt – all an illusion, just like his dream ('And, as my dreme, semed that was not' (2176)). He despairs at the loss of his fantasy but hopes his dream bodes well for the future. Failing that, he wishes for a swift return to dreamland, so that he can return to the 'Ile of pleasaunce' with his lady (2201). An envoy addressed to his lady and his own heart, which he bids 'Be diligent, awacke, obye, and dread', completes the poem (2222).

Assessing *Isle* as a Chaucerian production in conjunction with *BD*, as readers of Speght's edition were encouraged to do, opens a new perspective onto Chaucer's poem. There is, to be sure, no evidence that the anonymous author of *Isle* actually intended the poem as an allegory of Gaunt's marriage to Blanche; other topical interpretations have included the union of Gaunt and Katherine Swynford as well as the wedding of Henry V and Catherine of France, but none of these has gained firm acceptance.[40] Stylistically, the poem, like many fifteenth-century Chaucerian imitations, is more thoroughly Lydgatean than Chaucerian.[41] The only interpretation to date of *Isle*'s intertextual relationship with *BD*, by Annika Farber, accounts for the sixteenth-century editorial concatenation of *Isle* and *BD* with reference to *Isle*'s own conscious imitation of *BD*, and it is here that the serendipity of Speght's interpretation lies. In Farber's view, the *Isle*-poet's creative response to *BD* coheres around the compositional strategy of *amplificatio*. In particular, the poet targets and expands upon an underdeveloped part of the plot in *BD*: how the Man in Black met White. We know from *BD* that the Man in Black first encountered White amidst 'the fayrest companye / Of ladyes that evere man with ye / Had seen togedres in oo place' (807–9) and that he attributes his arrival at the scene to Fortune (811). White at first resists Black's advances, but eventually she shows mercy and they live in happy union. *Isle* supplies at length the detail missing in the Man in Black's sparse account of these events. The later poem freely embellishes along romance lines: thus, the 'companye / Of ladyes' becomes a sort of Amazonian island society, 'The Man in Black's botched wooing becomes … a failed abduction', White's granting of pity becomes mythologized as an intervention by the God of Love, and so on.[42] Such belated intervention in the prehistory of a Chaucerian story is by no means unprecedented in fifteenth-century letters: it is quite reminiscent of Lydgate's procedure in the *Siege of Thebes*, for example, which 'continues' Chaucer by supplying the back-story of the *Knight's Tale*.[43]

Farber furthermore identifies several motifs in *Isle* that appear to be sourced in *BD*, particularly given their conjunction: the hunting-as-threshold motif, the narrator's remarks on the inscrutability of the dream, the painted chamber, the dreamer's status as witness, and the noise that startles the dreamer awake.[44] To these elements can be added the narrator's claim that 'Fortunes purveaunce' brought him to the island (194), which echoes the Man in Black's similar statement above; the wooing knight's initial speechlessness and cry for 'Mercy' (cf. *BD* 1219 but also *Tr* 3.98); and the knight's address to Death and desire to encounter him (605–13).

Isle is more than a neat prequel or mosaic of allusions, however. It too is a story about death – a story, in fact, in which the avatar of White dies, and her mourner follows suit (as the Man in Black seems ready to do). As such, it embeds the supreme issue of *BD* – its *raison d'être* and the problem it leaves unsolved – at its midpoint, and neutralizes the threat of sudden death by folding it into a happy ending.[45] Like Charles of Orleans, the *Isle*-poet frames the trials of courtship within the discourse of death, but here love proves revivifying rather than debilitating. The surprise announcement in *Isle* that the queen has died, delivered by one of her grieving ladies, summons lexical associations with the climactic passage of *BD*:

'Allas,' quod she, *'that you ware bore*!
For, for your love, this land is *lore*;
The *quene is ded*, and that is *rothe*,
For sorrow of your great un*trothe*. (*Isle* 1645–8; emphases added)

Chaucer's Man in Black, by comparison, laments 'that I was bore!' (*BD* 1301) and speaks of the loss 'that I hadde lorn' (1303). 'The quene is ded' may echo 'She ys ded!' (1309), and the rhyme of *rothe*/un*trothe* riffs on the signature Chaucerian couplet *trouthe*/*routhe* in the same passage (1309–10), which as we have seen, also informs Lydgate's reworking of this passage in *CLL*. There even seems a Chaucerian cast to the remark, four lines later, that two-thirds of the island's ladies '[n]owe ar ded and clene awaye' (*Isle* 1652); compare the Man in Black's disclosure, in his earlier lyric, that his lady '[i]s fro me ded and ys agoon' (*BD* 479).

It is possible to read this mode of creative response not solely in terms of supplementation, insofar as *Isle* tells an earlier part of *BD*'s story, but reparation: here, in the narrative motion that leads to the revival of the lovers from death and a joyous resolution, is the consolation so conspicuously absent from *BD*. Mourning, and death itself, is finite in a cosmos governed by the God of Love. In connection to this, *Isle* departs from *BD*'s rationale as a narrative of education, avoiding the moral and existential dilemmas it entertains. The knight of *Isle* makes serious mistakes – abducting the lady and failing to keep his date – but unlike in *BD*, where the Man in Black's early fumblings with courtship are rejected for their superficiality, and unlike in Chrétien de Troyes's *Yvain*, which shares the motif of a lover's tardiness, this does not become an opportunity for the hero's ethical reflection and development. Instead, the knight's fallibility is redeemed by miracle, remedied by the queen and, secondarily, by the God of Love. Death, rather than descending at random upon the innocent, is precipitated by the knight's error – he is responsible – and as a result loses the uncanny relation to discourse that marked it in *BD*. In *Isle*, death can be undone by art. The *Isle*-poet seems to suggest that with this series of events in his amatory past – really his textual future – the Man in Black of Chaucer's poem need not feel that all is lost. In this sense, the later poem changes the meaning of the earlier one.

Like Lydgate's *CLL*, *Isle* appropriates *BD*'s narrative structure by presenting a lover-knight whose experience is viewed by a sympathetic narrator. Whereas Lydgate's narrator, unlike Chaucer's, never interacts with the knight and swiftly disavows any emotional congruity with him, the *Isle*-narrator not only documents the action but is himself implicated in it, his love affair paralleling that of the knight and culminating in a double wedding at the end. Herein we find Chaucer's construction of the Man in Black as a kind of alter ego of the dreaming narrator, both figures emotionally preoccupied and struggling with sorrow, registered more directly than in any poetic response surveyed thus far. Although the *Isle*-narrator is not shown to converse with the knight, he does interact with other characters within the dream, has a near-death experience and a private audience with his lady (the content of which he refuses to disclose, lines 1251–66), and periodically comments on aspects of the narrative. His stance on the events of the poem is in a sense more truly dreamlike than that of Chaucer's narrator insofar as his perspective shifts unaccountably from that of participant to observer. In contrast, the dreamer of *BD* becomes an actor within the dream equally with the Man in Black, Octovyen and the rest. Viewed differently, however, the *Isle*-narrator's shifting degrees of omniscience with regard to the action – at some points, he is as surprised by the plot's twists as any other character, but elsewhere he expresses full authorial knowledge of such details as the allegorical significance of the knight's ship – provide insight into the inconsistencies of *BD*'s narrator that, in chapter 2, we saw frequently observed. In portraying his narrator as a dreamer with imperfect authority, both master and subject of his own dream, the *Isle* glosses the problem of how, for example, Chaucer's dreaming narrator can at one moment perfectly understand the source of the Man in Black's grief, and at another, appear innocent of that knowledge and caught up in the story as it unfolds. Indeed, the *Isle*-narrator's complex stance on authorship points to the poem's most striking engagement with *BD*: its appropriation of the fiction of dreaming to intervene in – and become a living component of – an existing story.

Just before the midpoint of *Isle*, during the celebrations marking the God of Love's victory, the dreamer describes a period of nocturnal diversion in which some of Love's subjects compose lays and virelays, others read old romances and still others entertain themselves with 'diverse pleyes' (976). The dreamer's own activities are presented thus: 'And I to me a romaunse toke, / And as I readinge was the booke', he notices the sun rising and a crowd assembling (977–8). This metatextual moment, in which the narrator, dreaming about events that form the prehistory of an earlier poem, reads a book inside his dream, is doubly Chaucerian. In aligning the reading of a book with the experience of a dream, first of all, he follows other fifteenth-century poets (Robert Henryson and the author of the *Kingis Quair* are notable examples) in recapturing the signature bookishness of Chaucer's dream-visions. Secondly, the phrasing here very likely echoes the pivotal moment in *BD* in which the insomniac narrator undertakes his own late-night book-reading:

> And bad oon reche me a book,
> A romaunce, and he it me tok
> To rede and drive the night away;
> For me thoughte it better play
> Then playe either at ches or tables. (*BD* 47–51)

In *Isle*, as in *BD*, the reading of a 'romaunse' is contrasted with other 'diverse pleyes' (*Isle* 976, 977), and the same rhyme on 'toke/booke' further underscores the relation between the two passages. In both cases, the reading occurs at night instead of sleep. *BD*, of course, parlays the content of the 'romaunce' into an opportunity for slumber and, subsequently, into the design of the dream experienced by the narrator. Chaucer also, as we have seen, playfully enfolds the old book read in bed into the new book produced by virtue of the dream – the very book invoked by the narrator, reading the Ovidian story and pitying Alcione's sorrow, when he calls attention to himself as 'I, that made this book' (*BD* 96). The *Isle*-narrator accomplishes a similarly sensational feat when, in the waking interlude that begins at line 1301, he seeks repose in a chamber whose walls are painted with 'storyes old and diverse', later said to feature images of the hunt (1325, 2172–5) and thus recalling the narrator's activity before his dream began at the poem's beginning.

In the midst of this scene's thickly laid narrativization of experience, the dreamer – still between segments of his dream – reflects on the first part of his dream, wishing to keep it all 'in remembraunce', and expresses its status as *story*: 'The dreame, hole as yt me befell, / Wiche was as ye here me tell' (1339–40). More than a pause in the action, what occurs here is a rupture in temporality, and it makes us conscious of the narrator as author and the dream as text in a manner reminiscent of Chaucer's self-presentation *in medias res* as 'I, that made this book'. In *BD*, the narrator's intimation underscores the bookish framework of the dream – especially given the momentary ambiguity we noticed in chapter 3 surrounding *which* book is referred to (the one that prompts the dream, or the one that issues from it?). Similarly in *Isle*, the materials of textuality – the book inside the dream, the wall paintings absorbing the pre-dream hunt into fiction – undergird the experience of the dream and thus highlight its status as a literary creation.

At the end of *Isle*, the narrator, having awoken from the dream's happy ending, again meditates on its capacity as fiction: like the wall paintings of the hunt, the dream 'semed that was not' (i.e. seemed real but was without substance (2176)). Like Chaucer, the *Isle*-narrator here stakes his emotional authority on his status as the author of the very book we are holding: addressing his lady, he swears 'by my trothe … and by this booke' (2213). This wide-reaching consciousness of the value of dreams as fiction and the reciprocity of oneiric imagination and literary creation encourages a distinctly Chaucerian interpretation of the 'romaunse' read by the dreamer inside his dream: not implausibly, what he peruses in this scene is his own book, the very object soon to be mentally concretized in the painted bedroom when the dreamer pauses between stages of his dream – or sections of his poem.

This coyly self-promoting metatextuality is not only a Chaucerian trick: it is also a subtle act of affiliation with Chaucer. Framing *Isle* unusually not as a simple dream-vision but as a series of dreams – according to its most recent editor, no Middle English poem except Langland's *Piers Plowman* is structured thus[46] – the poet develops a clever mechanism for linking past and future iterations of a composite story. The ending of the poem cues this notion explicitly when the narrator expresses hope, since waking reality does not align with fantasy, that he will return to the dream the next time he falls asleep, resuming where he left off in his lady's service on the Isle of Plesaunce (lines 2197–2206). For Chaucer at the end of the *Parliament of Foules*, the reading of new books offers similar future possibilities, and in *Piers Plowman* new dreams also facilitate new levels of understanding in an ongoing intellectual project. What distinguishes *Isle* from these precedents is its conflation of dreaming and book-making – its implication that different stages of the story unfold through dreaming. Somewhat like Jean de Meun, who in his continuation of the *Roman de la rose*, under the pretence of oneiric continuity, 'enters' into a poem – a dream – initiated by Guillaume de Lorris, the *Isle*-poet continues (or, chronologically speaking, prefaces) a dream begun in Chaucer's poem. In short, his determination, in the waking interlude, to return to his own dream-in-progress while conceptualizing it as a written narrative becomes a vehicle for his appropriation of Chaucer's text, which circulates as another kind of unfinished dream. By forecasting future developments of the story through the creative action of dreaming, the *Isle*-poet establishes the pedigree of his narrative in a past text – one whose own attention to textuality and reception it harnessed to make the point.

The Authority of Vigilance: *The Floure and the Leafe* and *The Kingis Quair*

We now shift to two fifteenth-century allegorical visions whose perspective on *BD* is quite different from that of the works we have been examining. Although neither poem advances a wholesale reframing of *BD* such as we have seen in the works considered thus far, both share at least a passing acquaintance with *BD* that is productive of creative conversation. More importantly, these poems offer testimony of *BD*'s broader influence on fifteenth-century courtly poetry, the narrative devices it activated for continued use and the ways in which Chaucer's somewhat idiosyncratic love-vision was homogenized to suit developing literary tastes. Although the literary responses represented by these poems lack the calculated directness of many of those reviewed in the preceding pages, they provide insight into the extent to which *BD* contributed to the fifteenth-century canonization of particular formal registers and motifs. The dream frame, the motif of book-reading and the articulation of vernacular authorship emerge as key sites of reinvention for these poems as they derive from *BD* the building blocks of new literary tableaux.

As Derek Pearsall observes, the *Floure and the Leafe* (*FL*) conveys 'a sense that the boundaries of traditional allegorical love-vision are being deliberately tested', and *BD* figures as a key site of that resistance.[47]

The female narrator, like the narrator of Lydgate's *CLL*, does not actually fall asleep, although in other respects the central experience of the poem resembles a typical dream-vision. She complains of insomnia, in language evocative of the beginning of *BD*:

> but why that I ne might
> Rest, I ne wist ...
> Wherefore I mervaile greatly of my selfe,
> That I so long withouten sleepe lay[.] (18–19, 22–3)

Noteworthy similarities with *BD* – most of which are lacking in the ultimate source of Chaucer's passage, the beginning of Froissart's *Le Paradys d'Amours*, include ignorance of cause ('But men myght axe me why soo / I may not slepe' (*BD* 30–1)), marvel at the unnatural aspect of the condition ('I have gret wonder ... / How that I lyve' (1–2)), and use of dramatic enjambment to accentuate the need for rest ('And I ne may, ne nyght ne morwe, / Slepe' (22–3)). In *FL*, however, the narrator explicitly states that she suffers neither from 'sicknesse nor disease' and that her heart is at ease, thus rejecting the conventional attribution of insomnia to lovesickness to which *BD*, with its ailing narrator, arguably subscribes.[48] Instead, the *Floure*-poet reconceives the opening section of *BD* through the lens of Chaucer's Prologue to the *Legend of Good Women*, hinting at the source of her sleeplessness in her urge to celebrate the coming of spring (24ff.). When she happens upon a little-used, grassy path leading to an arbour from which she espies the companies of the Flower and the Leaf (lines 43–9) and eventually learns a lesson about love, she again follows a Chaucerian precedent – the 'floury grene ... / Ful thikke of gras ... / And litel used; hyt semed thus' (*BD* 398–9, 401) – only to diverge from it into different territory. Rather than struggling with isolation, her position on the outside looking in leads her to enrol in a new community: that of the Leaf. She, rather than the object of her vision, eventually journeys 'homeward' (*FL* 588; cf. *BD* 1315), and what she proudly puts 'in writing' at the end, released for consumption by unknown readers (589; further, 590–5), links the clarity of a waking vision with feminine self-assurance, in contrast with the more oblique authority gained for the male author as sufferer and dreamer within the courtly system advanced in *BD*.

Like *FL*, the *Kingis Quair* (*KQ*), generally believed to have been composed by James I of Scotland during his English imprisonment, bears only a thin and general relation to *BD*, and this in the frame only. Like *BD* (and in certain respects *FL*), *KQ* begins in the voice of a sleepless narrator, 'in bed allone waking' and preoccupied by excessive thought (8; cf. 10–11).[49] Unable to fall asleep 'for craft in erth', he reads a book for diversion – in this case, Boethius' *Consolation of Philosophy* (12). Unlike Chaucer's narrator, who naïvely values his reading in the Ovidian book only as an aid to sleep, the persona of *KQ* revises his practical aim to 'borowe a slepe' through his reading upon discovery of the book's relevance to his own experience as a prisoner (30). He thus models a kind of reflective literacy that escaped *BD*'s narrator, who might well have found more of personal import in Ovid's story than the existence of a god of sleep. For *KQ*'s narrator, responsible reading engenders healthful vigilance rather than the depressive indulgence of dreaming.

Now wide awake and contemplating the Boethian text in detail, he hears the bell for matins, rises from bed (lines 71–84) and resolves to tell his story by writing '[s]um new thing' of his own (89). In the course of the ensuing narration, which concerns his experience in love, there occurs an inset dream-vision of instruction by Venus, Minerva and Fortune. As the editors of *KQ* note, the motif of reading a book related to the narrator's own experience, ultimately derived from *BD*, 'becomes commonplace' in the fifteenth century.[50] In A. C. Spearing's view, *KQ* intentionally defies the precedent of *BD* regarding dreaming by encouraging the assumption that a dream will issue directly from the reading of the book, when instead the narrator fails to fall asleep at all. This directs our attention, Spearing suggests, to James's very different and indeed un-Chaucerian deployment of dreams later in the poem, not in connection to the book, to illuminate and refocus waking life.[51] James's resolution, upon the ringing of the bell, to write a new poem functions similarly, by displacing a Chaucerian moment – the castle bell that startles Chaucer's narrator out of the dream, after which he decides to put it 'in ryme' (*BD* 1332) – to a new position detached from dreaming.[52]

The disentanglement of book-reading, dreaming and writing that occurs in *KQ* has an appealing sense of logic. Many of the problems attendant upon *BD*'s interpretation, as we have seen, derive from its disjointed structure: the meandering opening, the book read and promptly dismissed, the dream that nebulously re-creates the book, the book once more, and the oddly extratemporal ending in which the narrator begins to write the poem that is now finished. Reordering these free-floating elements, *KQ* adapts the decision to write a new poem more logically at the beginning of the narrative proper, in connection to reading the ancient book. As in Robert Henryson's *Testament of Cresseid*, another Scottish response to Chaucer dating from later in the fifteenth century in which a restless narrator reads a book,[53] poetic invention rather than dream experience issues from the act of reading. This may be viewed as a short-circuiting of Chaucerian precedent, in which composition ultimately takes place, but only as a function of dreaming; indeed, the clipped ending of *BD* creates the impression of the poem's writing almost as an incidental fact, an afterthought. James I and Henryson, in effect, transform the book-reading motif canonized by *BD* into a prompt for poetic succession: these readers become writers more transparently and confidently than does Chaucer.

Rather than rejecting the Chaucerian model of dream fiction entirely, these Scottish poets credit it subtly by embedding dreams within the new poetic compositions their poems relate: for James, the dream of the allegorical goddesses, and for Henryson, Cresseid's vision of Cupid and the planetary council. In the process, the device of the dream as a source of creative authority becomes more tangential and less structurally defining than in *BD*. As was also the case in Charles of Orleans's *FS*, dreams become a way of clarifying problems within narrative rather than navigating experience – or shaping a position of authority – more generally. Significantly, the dreams in these fifteenth-century poems all fall within the Macrobian category of *oraculum* – a vision in which the gods or other authorities appear and instruct – rather than the ambiguous middle vision, or *somnium*, exemplified by *BD*, which invites an understanding of experience through mundane means, and is thus more psychologically exploratory.[54] Like the poet of the *Isle of Ladies*, then, James I and, to a lesser extent, Henryson discern in *BD* a conceptual vocabulary for a bookish vernacular authority. Whereas the *Isle*-poet accesses this authority through the communal possibilities of dreaming as a forum of intertextuality, the Scottish poets circumscribe dreaming within a larger (waking) material reality defined by books. Compressing Chaucer's associative and erratic transformation of an old book into a new text while eliding the imaginative fibre of dreaming, these poets source their projects in a more linear notion of poetic succession that capitalizes on the evocative potential of *BD*'s scenario of bedtime reading.

Return to the Source: Edmund Spenser's *Daphnaida*

Of all of *BD*'s literary offspring in the two centuries after its composition, Edmund Spenser's *Daphnaida* (1590 or 1591), a pastoral elegy composed for Sir Arthur Gorges upon the untimely death of his wife, Lady Douglas Howard, is most akin to Chaucer's poem. Whereas most early works modelled on *BD* appropriate it selectively as a narrative about love service, the mechanism of dreaming, or the makings of authorship, *Daphnaida* squarely captures its *raison d'être* as an elegy for a noblewoman, one that transfigures historical reality within a poetic allegory. Spenser's familiarity at this stage of his career with *BD* is confirmed by his clearly discernible incorporation of Chaucer's adaptation of Ovid's Cave of Sleep in the first book of the *Faerie Queene* (1.1.39–43), issued in 1590.[55] The very proximity of *Daphnaida* to *BD* in rationale and form casts into relief not only the temperamental differences of their authors and eras but the relativity of critical commonplaces regarding *BD*, the interpretation of which tends to be represented as more settled than it actually is by students of Spenser's problematic tribute. The question of whether *BD* or *Daphnaida* more fully observes the proprieties of elegy has particularly occupied critics, with opinion generally favouring *BD* as the more variegated, poetically complex expression of an emotional landscape. Indeed, Spenserians tend to speak more favourably of *BD* than do Chaucerians, who, as we have seen, have contended with the early poem's recalcitrant irregularity on formal as well as historical grounds, rarely regarding it as a normative elegy. By contrast, *Daphnaida* has been taken as Spenser's most disappointing foray into Chaucerian reinvention, a pale ghost of his celebrated engagement with Chaucer's precedent in the *Faerie Queene* and *Shepheardes Calender*. It has even been suggested that *Daphnaida* is the more 'medieval' of the two poems – not a compliment, in context – insofar as it is steeped in morbidity and monochromatic in its characterization of the mourning husband as an embodiment of grief.[56] Such arguments, I believe, oversimplify both poems, not to mention their historical periods, and the assumption that Spenser somehow missed the spirit of his predecessor's effort does not go far towards an understanding of the intertextual dialogue at play. A more productive line of inquiry lies in Spenser's distillation – rather than avoidance – of problematic aspects of *BD* that were left unresolved by Chaucer and thus open to creative intervention. The awkward execution of Spenser's elegy, in fact, can help us understand the experimental making of Chaucer's.

Daphnaida contains no dream, little dialogue and no attempt at consolation (apart from the dying lady's own words, as we shall see). It begins on a gloomy autumn evening with the narrator strolling through fields taken by early frost, meditating on 'lifes wretchednesse' (34) and believing himself the '[m]ost miserable man' alive (38).[57] At this point, he encounters a man '[c]lad all in black, that mourning did bewray' (40), his eyes downcast to the earth (46; cf. *BD* 457, 461). Unlike Chaucer's narrator, Spenser's recognizes the man in black, and greets him by his name: Alcyon. The sorrowful narrator offers the shepherd Alcyon company and a sympathetic ear, since '[g]riefe findes some ease by him that like does beare' (67; cf. *BD* 547–57). Alcyon, like Chaucer's knight, rejects the possibility of comfort, albeit in less polite terms: Alcyon's grief is too great for words, and his desire is 'to weepe, and dye alone' (77). Like Chaucer's Man in Black seeking a death that evades him, Alcyon presents his hurt as beyond healing (94–5). (Later in the poem, Alcyon echoes the Man in Black's 'Always deynge and be not ded' when identifying himself as one '[t]hat dying liues, and liuing still does dye' (434)). Taking a harder line than Chaucer's narrator under similar circumstances, Spenser's induces his interlocutor to share his story by suggesting that Alcyon might be thought a criminal if he were to commit suicide for undisclosed reasons. Thus, before he dies, the narrator sensibly urges, 'it were conuenient / To tell the cause' (80–1). Alcyon then recounts his courtship of the lady we later learn is named Daphne, up to the point of her death, by means of an allegorical fiction centring upon a beloved Lioness and a murderous Satyr. The narrator is befuddled by the 'riddle' – Alcyon is in love with an *animal?* – much as his Chaucerian precedent was puzzled over the Man in Black's consternation over a chess piece (177; cf. *BD* 740–1).

At this point, Spenser's elegy departs structurally from Chaucer's, re-mixing its elements into a new form. Alcyon, impatient with the narrator's obtuseness, identifies the Lioness as Daphne and bluntly cries, 'She now is dead' (184). After uttering these words, the equivalent of which occurs only at the end of *BD*, Alcyon falls silent and swoons in a manner reminiscent of the Man in Black's physical reaction after his first, overheard song (185–9; cf. *BD* 487–99). Spenser's narrator, like Chaucer's, attempts to comfort him, but he does not succeed in bringing him into dialogue. From this point on, what little interaction occurs between the narrator and Alcyon is reported in indirect discourse only, and the bulk of what remains is given over to a series of seven complaints against death in Alcyon's voice. Like the Man in Black's complaint, these lyrical ejaculations are addressed to no one; they serve simply to express the enormity of Alcyon's grief and his refusal, or inability, to relinquish it. The final complaint having ended, Alcyon again swoons, in a repetition of the earlier scene, and he again refuses solace. We are told that Alcyon rejects the narrator's offer of lodging at his own house until his spirits improve. Instead, he staggers away, unconsoled, destination obscure – in the poem's final words, 'But what of him became I cannot weene' (567). The lack of human connection here, as earlier, is confirmed by the absence of dialogue: nothing connects the two speakers as at the end of *BD*, and no sense of community or dynastic landscape awaits him in this scene of departure.

Daphnaida is best viewed as an alternative Chaucerian reality: it reveals what *BD* might look like were it to unfold differently. In Spenser's elegy, the solipsism and histrionic rhetoric of the Man in Black's early complaint comes to envelop his entire relation to discourse; consequently, the monologia of lyric displaces the dialogic possibilities of narrative. The sympathetic connection between the narrator and Alcyon, developed from Chaucer's hints in his characterization of the narrator before the dream, proves futile – like cannot cure like in this case, and the semi-comic tension that Chaucer develops between the undiscerning dreamer and the hypersensitive nobleman is left unengaged. The admission that 'She now is dead' becomes a turning point in a different way than in *BD*: rather than bringing the poem to its crisis, it marks the end of dialogue and narrative, and the beginning of lyric. The words 'She now is dead' elicit in Alcyon a torrent of further self-punishing expression as he devotes 350 lines to what is in essence a dilation on the Man in Black's eleven-line complaint in *BD*. In the course of his seven complaints, Alcyon curses nature and the heavens, recalls Daphne's noble virtues, wishes again for death, and declares his hatred of the entire order of creation (on this last point, see especially 400–34). Interestingly, it emerges in the second complaint that Daphne's salvation is assured, when Alcyon recounts how on her deathbed Daphne welcomes her repose among 'Saints and Angels in celestiall thrones' (285) and happily anticipates deliverance from the 'miserie' of life (272). She tells Alcyon that mourning over her death is misplaced, since joy awaits her, and she implores him to cherish the child, Ambrosia, she leaves behind. Such sentiments, of course, are wholly lacking in *BD*, which is conspicuous in its elision of Christian consolation and consideration of heavenly reward (unless one is to seek implicit hints in, for example, the Marian imagery summoned around White). It is all the more striking, then, that Alcyon takes no comfort from any of this, and indeed that his tirade against the world's injustice comes to eclipse his love for Daphne – what the elegy leaves us with is hatred and alienation, not tenderness and communion.

BD, for its part, refuses simple answers to the difficult questions it raises regarding grief, consolation and the value of memory. Modern scholarship has struggled mightily, as the first two chapters of this book illustrate, with the poem's structural cohesion, occasional relevance and tactics of consolation. Spenser's attention to these largely unresolved issues in Chaucer's poem is signalled first of all in his redeployment of Chaucer's Alcione, the Ovidian widow, as Alcyon, the grieving husband. This tribute to the artful narrative layering of *BD* captures the gender reversal from widow to widower already present in Chaucer's poem while amplifying the resonances of the Ovidian-cum-Chaucerian story, in which Alcione's grief is all-encompassing and consolation is futile.[58] With regard to consolation, as we have seen, *BD* subtly argues for the value of human contact and treasured memories, but it does not shrink from acknowledging the imperfection of these salves while refusing the outlet of conventional platitudes. Pathological despair lingers just below the surface of civility, and in one line of interpretation the self-centred melancholy that characterizes the Man in Black's first complaint re-emerges at the end, when reliving his happiness redoubles his loss. Spenser's poem tests this dark reading of what occurs between Chaucer's dreamer and the Man in Black, showing their somewhat one-sided conversation to devolve into pure monologue and the never clearly realized effort at healing to be abandoned entirely. Similarly, in this Spenserian reading of *BD*, the earlier poem's omission of the fate of the soul underscores the importance of Christian ritual and, hence, the mourner's short-sightedness in devaluing heavenly reward.

Finally, *Daphnaida* and *BD* are similarly unconventional as elegies. Neither poem is easily imagined as a public tribute: the obstinate and self-destructive mourners they feature are hardly flattering to their aristocratic models, seeming if anything to suggest how *not* to react in the face of calamity.[59] Both seem to test the limits of poetic expression, *BD* with its final rejection of the various literary filters it employs in the last blunt words exchanged between dreamer and knight, and *Daphnaida* in its status as a 'highly structured song of grief which everywhere denies the efficacy of either song or form'.[60] If *BD*, as was suggested in chapter 1, deconstructs elegy in its very refusal to open up 'She ys ded!' as a field of articulation, *Daphnaida* takes the opposite approach, enfranchising the discourse of death to the extent that the very communication that makes poetry possible falls victim to the mourner's solipsistic grief.

Appropriately enough, although sporadic allusions to *BD* can be discerned in subsequent works (Robert Browning's *My Last Duchess* (1842) being a particularly interesting case[61]), thoroughgoing engagement with it ends here. The apocryphal *Floure and the Leafe* – a kind of anti-*BD*, as we have seen – was in the following centuries, aided by John Dryden's admiring rendition in *Fables, Ancient and Modern* (1700), to eclipse *BD* in reputation as a model Chaucerian love-vision. *BD* quietly survived, *Lenvoy de Chaucer a Bukton* attached, in editions up to the mid-nineteenth century, falling then into a state of critical desuetude that awaited the rigours of early twentieth-century philological scholarship before the kinds of questions asked of it by its early readers would be reopened (deliberately or not) by modern interpretative criticism. In reviving *BD*, cruxes and all, for formal reinvention – in engaging it more faithfully than did any of the venturesome and irreverent makers of the fifteenth century – Spenser divested it of continued life. Finally, we may say, there was an ending.

'NOW HIT YS DOON'

Conclusion

Whatever closure is attempted by the final line of *BD*, the present-tense immediacy of the poem's first sixty-odd lines is a better indication of what continues to entice readers. Militating against any easy conclusion inherent in the declaration that 'hit ys doon', the 'now' that prefaces these words points back temporally to the opening lines, which evoke a perpetual state of wakefulness:

> I have gret wonder, be this lyght,
> How that I lyve …
> For sorwful ymagynacioun
> Ys alway hooly in my mynde. (1–2, 14–15)

In this sense, the poem seems always to begin again, to resist completion, in the very act of its narration. Even as the book is closed, the narrator's experience remains open in a way that troubles conclusions we may wish to draw about a lesson learned or a creative release attained. If, on the one hand, the frame of *BD* confirms Roland Barthes's contention that '[t]he Author … is always conceived as the past of his own book', on the other it insists, strikingly, upon a 'writerly' presence for the narrator-author that epitomizes Barthes's formulation of 'the total being of writing': the extratemporal locus of 'multiple writings, proceeding from several cultures and entering into dialogue, into parody, into contestation'.[1]

The sense that the Chaucerian persona is addressing us across the vast expanse of time is conveyed both by the temporality of these first lines of *BD*, which appropriately relate to the marvel of his continued existence, and their special intimacy, which is more pronounced than in Chaucer's opening discussions of books and dreams in his other love-visions. The complexity of this effect is well captured by the irony, noted by Ardis Butterfield, that this unprecedented (for a narrative poem) foregrounding of 'I' in English is in fact a close translation from the French of Froissart's *Le Paradys d'Amour*.[2] Chaucer's 'I', to echo a famous remark by Arthur Rimbaud in 1871, is *un autre*. The inauthenticity of this 'I' in the framework of translation – it is Froissart's 'je', after all, and he in turn is siphoning the subjectivity of Machaut[3] – prepares for the oblique revelation of the self that occurs in the dreamer's colloquy with his alter ego, the Man in Black. As the Man in Black struggles to articulate the roots of a melancholy that is mirrored in the narrator's waking state, one which the narrator had been unwilling or unable to put in his own words (lines 30–43), the poem becomes a study in translation in its own right. Not only does *BD* itself derive from a network of French writings and feature an Englishing of a Latin fable; it asks us to confront the difficulties of 'translating' personal experience into intelligible words, and 'sweven' into 'ryme' (1332). In doing so, *BD* registers the modern semiological perception, influentially expressed by Umberto Eco, that because languages are 'reciprocally incommensurable', translation is inextricable from interpretation and is never an innocent act.[4] One way of accounting for the richness and intractability of *BD* as confronted by its various readers and critics over time lies in this creative sense of translation: by modelling its own relation to literary precedents, and by staging problems of communication and representation within the dream itself, it inscribes our own intervention as readers in the process of making meaning.

The intimacy of the Chaucerian voice that confides in us, and seems to live on still, in the opening lines of *BD* hints at another, more submerged aspect of the poem's staying power. Although few critics today would assume, as did previous generations, autobiographical veracity in the narrator's account of his waking frustrations, many have unconsciously absorbed this self-portrayal into a construct of Chaucer as author. The chatty, good-hearted, hapless, 'congenial' persona who devours books just as we are encouraged to consume his, and who speaks to us not as a princely adviser, performing minstrel or professional clerk but as a friendly acquaintance with whom we can empathize,[5] has been the essence of 'Chaucer' for much of the poet's reception history. While later poems will, of course, round out this persona with further signature detail, there arguably exists nowhere else in Chaucer's works such a full, compelling and (of course) illusory conjuring of authorial presence.[6] Even the Prologue of the *Legend of Good Women*, which takes a further page from Machaut in its palinodic drama, does not approach the naked intimacy of the Chaucerian persona's self-disclosure here to a concerned reader. In interpellating us as his friend and confidant, only to relate a dream in which he performs a similar function for the Man in Black, Chaucer in *BD* inaugurates what Stephanie Trigg has described as the 'affectionate bonds of affinity and reciprocal love of poet and scholar' that have in various ways defined the history of Chaucer scholarship. This 'identification and sympathy with the author', for Trigg, is a vestige of the sixteenth-century humanist appropriation of Chaucer as the focal point of a scholarly community; the sense of continuity that here offsets the alterity of the medieval text continues to influence scholarship to this day.[7] John Bowers, approaching this issue from the perspective of Chaucer's biography and contemporary English literary production, attributes this construction of Chaucer to the author's own tactical manoeuvring, in a statement we had occasion to note in passing in an earlier section of this study: 'While not making enemies, the affable writer attracted friends during his lifetime and admirers thereafter. His ability at rendering himself lovable succeeded at securing a posterity of affectionate readers.'[8] What Trigg characterizes as the 'sentimental and cozy identifications with Chaucer' that underlie rigorous (especially, in her view, positivist) scholarship are specifically homosocial and 'gentlemanly', replicating the intimacy that Chaucer encourages through his authorial demeanour in exclusive forms of scholarly community centred upon the study of his works.[9]

The point at stake here is that *BD* has a more than incidental relevance to these views of Chaucer's reception history and scholarly rhetoric more generally. It offers a model, as we have seen, of gentle-manly bonds and homosocial communion that extends (in the relation between Chaucer and Ovid) to the development of literary tradition, almost displacing the heterosexual romance that is at the heart of the narrative. It defines an authorial persona who speaks to the reader as an intimate who is receptive to his subjective musings, his medical symptoms, and even his authorial plans and techniques. And in returning us on each reading to a present-tense beginning, it suggests a perpetuity of authorial presence that, in a sense, confirms Chaucer's achievement of canonical status by virtue of producing the book and declaring it 'doon'. The illusion of immediacy and familiarity in the opening passage correlates with Trigg's observation of scholars' attempts, through discourses of affinity, to '"revive" the medieval poet, bringing him into the present and into the presence of new readers'.[10] In these senses, *BD* offers (to borrow a concept from Seth Lerer's study of reception) a 'template' not only for later English developments of the love-vision genre,[11] in which writers such as Lydgate and the poet of *Isle of Ladies* could inhabit a Chaucerian space, but also for a long tradition of critical response to Chaucer for which the dynamic established here between author and reader is formative.

It is not inconsequential that *BD* was for so long – from Thynne's 1532 edition through the nineteenth century – transmitted as the *Dreame of Chaucer*, with alternative titles sometimes supplementing but not replacing this one. No other narrative poem by Chaucer is presented thus in the printed editions, with the exception of the apocryphal *Chaucers dreame*, or the *Isle of Ladies*, which, as we have seen, is conceived as a pendant to *BD*. Although Chaucer's other dream-visions similarly feature a first-person persona that seems a close replica of the author himself – he is called 'Geffrey' in *House of Fame* and is held responsible for Chaucer's known body of writings in *Legend of Good Women* – these poems never receive the biographical imprimatur that distinguishes *BD* throughout its print history as *Chaucer's* dream. It could be said that this bibliographic label both reflects and conditions the perception of a transparently authorial figure in *BD* who confides his personal experience and trade secrets to a collegial reader. It may be that the inscription of a documented historical circumstance in *BD*, albeit not registered from the earliest point, also fostered a sense of the poem as biographically 'real'. Certainly, this dimension of *BD* became important to the royalist and canonical development of Chaucer's 'Life' from Speght's edition onwards. Taken together, these phenomena suggest that *BD*, partly because of its staging of its own writing, has underwritten the history of Chaucer's construction as an author in ways that have not fully been recognized.

A perhaps unexpected example of this can be drawn, not from the 'exclusive' domain of philological scholarship critiqued by Trigg, but from a recent, inclusive 'neomedievalist' attempt to 'offer a Chaucer without canonical fame, to blend specialist medieval scholarship with pop culture, and to throw the medieval and the contemporary together in a way that would inextricably mesh them'.[12] Although 'Geoffrey Chaucer Hath a Blog', to which this quotation refers, is loosely built upon events in the 1380s and, apart from occasional quips about John of Gaunt, does not directly engage *BD*, one could argue that its very premise rests upon the formative construction of Chaucer as an author which we have discerned in *BD*. The blogger username 'LeVostreGC', now also a Twitter handle, was, as Brantley L. Bryant notes, in part 'intended to imply that this Chaucer was "your" Chaucer, a Chaucer with whom readers could speak'.[13] The friendly, forthcoming Chaucer-persona who in various blog entries reflects on his daily life, vents about his domestic and professional troubles, enthuses over books he has read, and shares his plans for future literary works (in this case, the *Canterbury Tales*) has, in a sense, stepped directly out of *BD*, which supplies a precedent for the scattered confessional mode of the Chaucer Blog. The absurdist premise, played for laughs in the Blog, that Chaucer is somehow sharing his innermost thoughts and authorial ambitions with a twenty-first-century audience – that his writing issues from a kind of eternal present that zigzags across received temporal boundaries – is implicitly prepared for by the disruption of temporal coherence we have discerned in *BD*, in which the completion of the book at line 1334 clashes with the indefinite present-tense opening and the intrusion of the author with book 'made' at line 96. Like the Blog, with its 'pleasurable disorientation of the canonical Chaucer',[14] *BD* presents a Chaucer-in-the-making, one whom readers and critics have been tempted to saturate with canonical status and literary convictions that emerge only at a later stage. Furthermore, as we have seen, *BD* experiments with the possibilities of 'making' in the space between languages and linguistic registers – English and French, with all their ingrained cultural and stylistic associations – much as the Blog frames authorial textuality in a murky channel between Middle and Modern English, using these for diverse rhetorical effects in different communicative scenarios.[15]

As a final coordinate on a map of reception that has encompassed a good deal of surprising territory, the Chaucer Blog highlights the importance of textuality and communication to the reading of *BD* advanced in the preceding chapters of this study. By evolving an integrated view of the textual processes of reading, writing and rereading as they cohere around the 'making' of Chaucer's *Book*, we have discerned common patterns in critical reception and creative response, such as the overdetermination of the poem by canonical narratives and its interpretative amalgamation with later Chaucerian works. *Making Chaucer's* Book of the Duchess has dwelled on the 'bookishness' of this first major narrative effort by Chaucer, and its projection of an open, transactional textuality that invites further *inventio*. It has attempted to identify the risks of reading *BD* through the lens of Chaucer's mature poetry, at the same time that it has suggested the fruitfulness of placing it in dialogue with his later considerations of the lives and afterlives of books. Most importantly, this study has aimed to underscore the literary value of *BD* as a Chaucerian work in its own right, one with a rich interpretative history as well as a variegated early modern literary reception that is of consequence for the construction of Chaucer as a canonical author and progenitor of English letters. If an effect of this book is to encourage serious consideration of *BD* in sophisticated critical discussions of Chaucer's poetics more generally, to promote further incorporation of the poem in the teaching of Chaucer and to stimulate a renewed effort to address the gaps in our knowledge of the poem's literary relationships in the sphere of French and English writing, it will have accomplished its central goal. The *Book*, after all, is in our hands.

NOTES

Introduction

1. *BD* is well served by several excellent modern editions, particularly Helen Phillips's free-standing 1982 critical edition. Especially appropriate for student use are Phillips's 1997 edition in the Longman Annotated Texts series and Kathryn L. Lynch's 2007 edition in the Norton Critical Editions series (both of which group *BD* with Chaucer's other dream poems). *BD* is also available in a hypertext edition that facilitates multiple perspectives on the text: Murray McGillivray (ed.), *Geoffrey Chaucer's Book of the Duchess: A Hypertext Edition 2.0*, CD-ROM (Calgary, 1999). Although the current study has benefited from all of these editions, for the sake of consistency and convenience all quotations from *BD* (unless otherwise indicated) are taken from the standard edition of Chaucer's works, *The Riverside Chaucer*, general editor Larry D. Benson, 3rd edn (Boston, 1987). The quotation here is from line 1334; subsequent line numbers are indicated in the main text.

2. My phrasing here is informed by Trevor Ross's observation that 'Chaucer made it possible to think of a literary tradition in English' (*The Making of the English Literary Canon: From the Middle Ages to the Late Eighteenth Century* (Montreal, 1998), p. 44).

1. Reading the *Book* (I): Critical History – An Overview

1. J. M. Manly, *Chaucer and the Rhetoricians* (London, 1940), pp. 5–6.

2. William Godwin, *Life of Geoffrey Chaucer, the Early English Poet: Including Memoirs of His Near Friend and Kinsman, John of Gaunt, Duke of Lancaster*, 2 vols (London, 1803), vol. 2, p. 83; F. J. Furnivall, *Trial-Forewards to My 'Parallel-Text Edition of Chaucer's Minor Poems'* (London, 1871), p. 37 n. 2.

3. Furnivall, *Trial-Forewards*, p. 42.

4. C. S. Lewis, *The Allegory of Love: A Study in Medieval Tradition* (London, 1936), p. 164.

5. Robert Kilburn Root, *The Poetry of Chaucer: A Guide to Its Study and Appreciation*, rev. edn (Boston, 1922), pp. 59–61.

6. Charles Muscatine, *Chaucer and the French Tradition* (Berkeley and Los Angeles, 1966), p. 107.

7. G[eorge] L[yman] Kittredge, 'Chauceriana', *Modern Philology*, 7/4 (1910), 471, and 'Guillaume de Machaut and *The Book of the Duchess*', *PMLA*, 30/1 (1915), 24.

8. Muscatine, *Chaucer and the French Tradition*, p. 98.

9. Quotation from Normand Berlin, 'Chaucer's *The Book of the Duchess* and Spenser's *Daphnaida*: A Contrast', *Studia Neophilologica*, 38/2 (1966), 289.

10. Elizabeth Scala, *Absent Narratives, Manuscript Textuality, and Literary Structure in Late Medieval England* (New York, 2002), pp. 15–16.

11. Steven Davis, 'Guillaume de Machaut, Chaucer's *Book of the Duchess*, and the Chaucer Tradition', *ChR*, 36/4 (2002), 400; John M. Bowers, *Chaucer and Langland: The Antagonistic Tradition* (Notre Dame, IN, 2007), discussing Chaucer's works more broadly, similarly discerns calculation in Chaucer's shaping of his authorial personality and imagined audience: 'His ability at rendering himself lovable succeeded at securing a posterity of affectionate readers' (p. 30).

12. This, of course, excludes French-derived lyrics by Chaucer for which early dates have been posited (though dating here is very uncertain), e.g. *An ABC* and *Complaint unto Pity*. There is no way to know whether the lost 'book of the Leoun' mentioned in Chaucer's *Retraction* (X 1087) preceded *BD* in composition. The 'Leoun' was probably based on Machaut's *Dit dou lyon* (of which *BD* makes passing use), though whether it was a close translation (as the similar title suggests) or a free adaptation is a matter of speculation. It is plausible that Chaucer Englished Machaut's work as preparation for, or a satellite project of, his creative assimilation of multiple *dits amoreux* in *BD*, much as Chaucer's translation of Boethius' *De consolatione Philosophiae* appears to have prepared him for *Troilus and Criseyde* and the *Knight's Tale*. In that event, the inaugural work of English courtly literature may well be one that disappeared without a trace! On Machaut's *Dit dou lyon* as likely source of the 'book of the Leoun', see James I. Wimsatt, *Chaucer and His French Contemporaries: Natural Music in the Fourteenth Century* (Toronto, 1991), pp. 268–9.

13. Steve Guthrie, 'Dialogics and prosody in Chaucer', in Thomas J. Farrell (ed.), *Bakhtin and Medieval Voices* (Gainesville, FL, 1995), p. 102.

14. John Livingstone Lowes, *Geoffrey Chaucer* (Bloomington, IN, 1958), p. 92.

15. Nevill Coghill, *The Poet Chaucer*, rev. edn (London, 1964), pp. 26–7.

16. J. S. P. Tatlock, *The Mind and Art of Chaucer* (New York, 1966), pp. 29–30.

17. W. H. French, 'The Man in Black's Lyric', *JEGP*, 56/2 (1957), 235 n. 12, 236 n. 15.

18. Louise O. [Aranye] Fradenburg, '"Voice memorial": Loss and Reparation in Chaucer's Poetry', spec. issue on 'Reconceiving Chaucer: Literary Theory and Historical Interpretation', ed. Thomas Hahn, *Exemplaria*, 2/1 (1990), 179.

19. Charles W. Owen, 'Chaucer: beginnings', in John M. Hill and Deborah M. Sinnreich-Levi (eds), *The Rhetorical Poetics of the Middle Ages: Reconstructive Polyphony* (Madison and Teaneck, NJ; and London, 2000), pp. 46, 48.

20. Jacques Lacan, 'The function and field of speech and language in psychoanalysis', in *Écrits: A Selection*, trans. Alan Sheridan (New York, 1977), p. 86.

21. Especially recommended resources of this type are the introductions of Phillips's 1982 and 1997 editions; A[lastair] J. Minnis with [V.] [J.]ohn Scattergood and J. J. Smith, *The Shorter Poems*, Oxford Guides to Chaucer (Oxford, 1995), pp. 73–160; William A. Quinn, 'Medieval dream visions: Chaucer's *Book of the Duchess*', in David F. Johnson and Elaine Treharne (eds), *Readings in Medieval Texts: Interpreting Old and Middle English Literature* (Oxford and New York, 2005), pp. 323–36.

22. Advanced in a series of articles, representatively in Margaret Galway, 'Chaucer's Hopeless Love', *MLN*, 60/7 (1945), 431–9.

23. Demonstrated, respectively, in John Livingston Lowes, 'The Dry Sea and the Carrenare', *Modern Philology*, 3/1 (1905), 1–46, and Oliver Farrar Emerson, 'Chaucer and Medieval Hunting', *Romanic Review*, 13 (1922), 115–50.

24. Ian Robinson, *Chaucer and the English Tradition* (Cambridge, 1972), p. 15. An instructive point of contrast is B. A. Windeatt's assertion, in *Chaucer's Dream Poetry: Sources and Analogues* (Woodbridge, Suffolk and Totowa, NJ, 1982), that the proximity of *BD* to its French sources 'show[s] how Chaucer controls his closest verbal borrowings by his control of the context in which those "borrowings" are deployed' (p. xii).

25. Donald C. Baker, 'Imagery and Structure in Chaucer's *Book of the Duchess*', *Studia Neophilologica*, 30/1 (1958), 18, 20, 26. Although Baker does not name them, it is easy to imagine that he is contrasting *BD* with sprawling dream-visions such as the *Roman de la rose* and *Piers Plowman*.

26. Robert O. Payne, *The Key of Remembrance: A Study of Chaucer's Poetics* (New Haven and London, 1963), pp. 115, 121.

27. For this argument, see R. M. Lumiansky, 'The Bereaved Narrator in Chaucer's *The Book of the Duchess*', *Tulane Studies in English*, 9 (1959), 5–17.

28. Muscatine, *Chaucer and the French Tradition*, p. 98.

29. John Gardner, 'Style as Meaning in the *Book of the Duchess*', *Language and Style: An International Journal*, 2 (1969), 145.

30. Bernard Huppé and D. W. Robertson, Jr, *Fruyt and Chaf: Studies in Chaucer's Allegories* (Port Washington, NY and London, 1972), pp. 32–100; reinforced in D. W. Robertson, Jr, 'The historical setting of Chaucer's *Book of the Duchess*', in John Mahoney and John Esten Keller (eds), *Mediaeval Studies in Honor of Urban Tigner Holmes, Jr.* (Chapel Hill, NC, 1965), pp. 169–95 (rpt. in D. W. Robertson, Jr, *Essays in Medieval Culture* (Princeton, 1980), pp. 235–56); cf. D. W. Robertson, Jr, *A Preface to Chaucer: Studies in Medieval Perspectives* (Princeton, 1962), pp. 463–6. An overview is supplied in D. W. Robertson, Jr, 'The *Book of the Duchess*', in Beryl Rowland (ed.), *Companion to Chaucer Studies*, rev. edn (New York and Oxford, 1979), pp. 403–13.

31. The conventional view of *BD* as non-allegorical is represented by W. H. Clemen, *Chaucer's Early Poetry*, trans. C. A. M. Sym (London, 1963),

pp. 48–9, 52–3, which translates and revises Clemen's *Der junge Chaucer* (1938).

32. Steven Justice, 'Who Stole Robertson?', *PMLA*, 124/2 (2009), 609. Another thoughtful, generous reflection on Robertson's impact is Alan T. Gaylord, 'Reflections on D. W. Robertson, Jr., and "Exegetical Criticism"', *ChR*, 40/3 (2006), 311–33. Especially impudent is Robertson's lampoon of New Critical approaches to *BD*, placed creatively in the mouth of Chaucer himself, summarizing his poem: 'Oh, I say. Life, love, and all that. Frightfully ambiguous, what?' ('Historical setting', p. 251).

33. Justice, 'Who Stole Robertson?', 610.

34. On this point, see Lee Patterson, *Negotiating the Past: The Historical Understanding of Medieval Literature* (Madison, WI, 1987), pp. 3–39, and Carolyn Dinshaw, *Chaucer's Sexual Poetics* (Madison, WI, 1989), pp. 28–39.

35. Huppé and Robertson, *Fruyt and Chaf*, p. 95.

36. Robert M. Jordan, 'The Compositional Structure of the *Book of the Duchess*', *ChR*, 9/2 (1974), 108, 111.

37. Judith Ferster, 'Intention and Interpretation in the "Book of the Duchess"', *Criticism*, 22/1 (1980), 1–24. A further development of this topic is Robert S. Sturges, *Medieval Interpretation: Models of Reading in Literary Narrative, 1100–1500* (Carbondale and Edwardsville, IL, 1991), pp. 127–39.

38. Larry Sklute, *Virtue of Necessity: Inconclusiveness and Narrative Form in Chaucer's Poetry* (Columbus, OH, 1984), pp. 23–34; Colleen Donnelly, 'Challenging the Conventions of Dream Vision in *The Book of the Duchess*', *Philological Quarterly*, 66/4 (1987), 421–35, and 'Chaucer's Sense of an Ending', *Journal of the Rocky Mountain Medieval and Renaissance Association*, 11 (1990), 19–32; Rosemarie P. McGerr, *Chaucer's Open Books: Resistance to Closure in Medieval Discourse* (Gainesville, FL, 1998), pp. 44–60.

39. Judith M. Davidoff, *Beginning Well: Framing Fictions in Late Middle English Poetry* (Rutherford, NJ; London and Toronto, 1998), p. 107.

40. Phillip C. Boardman, 'Courtly Language and the Strategy of Consolation in the *Book of the Duchess*', *ELH*, 44/4 (1977), 567–79; Robert Edwards, 'The *Book of the Duchess* and the Beginnings of Chaucer's Narrative', *New Literary History*, 13/2 (1982), 189–204 (rev. in Edwards, *The Dream of Chaucer: Representation and Reflection in the Early Narratives* (Durham, NC and London, 1989), pp. 65–91); Diane M. Ross, 'The Play of Genres in the *Book of the Duchess*', *ChR*, 19/1 (1984), 1–13; Michael B. Herzog, 'The *Book of the Duchess*: The Vision of the Artist as a Young Dreamer', *ChR*, 22/4 (1988), 269–81.

41. Andrew Lynch, '"Taking keep" of the "Book of the Duchess"', in Gregory Kratzmann and James Simpson (eds), *Medieval English Religious and Ethical Literature: Essays in Honour of G. H. Russell* (Cambridge and Dover, NH, 1986), pp. 167–78 (178). Exemplary of this development is John M. Fyler's destabilization of the classic Bronsonian view of psychological continuity between dreamer and knight (see above, p. 14) in his assertion that 'much

of the poem is taken up by the dreamer's failure to realize that the Man in Black is not his alter ego – another somewhat embittered unrequited lover' ('Froissart and Chaucer', in Donald Maddox and Sara Sturm-Maddox (eds), *Froissart across the Genres* (Gainesville, FL, 1998), p. 199)

42. Helen Phillips, 'Fortune and the Lady: Machaut, Chaucer and the Intertextual "Dit"', *Nottingham French Studies*, 38/2 (1999), 128.

43. Kathryn L. Lynch, *Chaucer's Philosophical Visions* (Cambridge, 2000), pp. 31–59; Peter W. Travis, 'White', *SAC*, 22 (2000), 1–66; Peter Brown, *Chaucer and the Making of Optical Space* (Oxford and Bern, 2007), pp. 177–203.

44. Representative instantiations of this trend are Nicholas Watson, 'Censorship and Cultural Change in Late-Medieval England: Vernacular Theology, the Oxford Translation Debate, and Arundel's Constitutions of 1409', *Speculum*, 70 (1995), 822–64; Minnis, *Translations of Authority in Medieval English Literature: Valuing the Vernacular* (Cambridge and New York, 2009); Lynn Arner, *Chaucer, Gower, and the Vernacular Rising: Poetry and the Problem of the Populace after 1381* (University Park, PA, 2013).

45. John Lydgate, *Fall of Princes*, ed. Henry Bergen, EETS e.s., 121–4 (London and Toronto, 1967), 1.305; hereafter cited parenthetically.

46. Kathryn L. Lynch, 'Dating Chaucer', *ChR*, 42/1(2007), 5, with a helpful overview of various arguments for *BD*'s dating on pp. 4–5. Endorsing the pre-1372 dating are Helen Phillips (ed.), *The Book of the Duchess* (Durham, 1982), p. 3; Benson (gen. ed.), *Riverside Chaucer*, p. xxix; Minnis, *The Shorter Poems*, pp. 79–80; Mark Allen and John H. Fisher (eds), *The Complete Poetry and Prose of Geoffrey Chaucer*, 3rd edn (Boston, 2012), p. 537.

47. Problems have also surrounded Blanche's date of birth: see Linda Ann Loschiavo, 'The Birth of "Blanche the Duchesse": 1340 *versus* 1347', *ChR*, 13/2 (1978), 128–32.

48. J. J. N. Palmer, 'The Historical Context of the *Book of the Duchess*: A Revision', *ChR*, 8/4 (1974), 253–61. Further support for the 1368 dating is provided in Sumner Ferris, 'John Stow and the Tomb of Blanche the Duchess', *ChR*, 18/1 (1983), 92–3.

49. Martin M. Crow and Clair C. Olson (eds), *Chaucer Life-Records* (Oxford, 1966), pp. 31–2; discussed in Derek Pearsall, *The Life of Geoffrey Chaucer: A Critical Biography* (Oxford and Cambridge, MA, 1992), p. 54.

50. Marjorie Anderson, 'Blanche, Duchess of Lancaster', *Modern Philology*, 45/3 (1948), 157.

51. J. J. N. Palmer, 'Historical Context', 260.

52. John Norton-Smith (ed.), *Bodleian Library MS Fairfax 16* (London, 1979), fol. 130r.

53. Derek Pearsall, *The Life of Geoffrey Chaucer*, p. 83. For a similar opinion, see Benjamin F. Taggie, 'John of Gaunt, Geoffrey Chaucer and "O noble, o worthy Petro, glorie of Spayne"', *Fifteenth Century Studies*, 10 (1984), 195–228. In a careful analysis of this issue, Nicole Lassahn posits that

in *BD* 'Chaucer is not writing for a patron' and that the poem is an historical, but a deliberately apolitical work ('Literary Representations of History in Fourteenth Century England: Shared Technique and Divergent Practice in Chaucer and Langland', *Essays in Medieval Studies*, 17 (2000), 49–64).

54. Lynn Staley, 'Gower, Richard II, Henry of Derby, and the Business of Making Culture', *Speculum*, 75 (2000), 92, building on points advanced in Lee Patterson, 'The Disenchanted Classroom', *Exemplaria*, 8/2 (1996), 535–41.

55. Robertson, 'Historical Setting', pp. 237–8, and 'The *Book of the Duchess*', p. 403. On *BD*'s oral character more generally, see Ebbe Klitgård, 'Chaucer as Performer: Narrative Strategies in the Dream Visions', *Revista Canaria de Estudios Ingleses*, 47 (2003), 101–6.

56. As Paul Strohm argues, *BD* does not only concern the death of Blanche: it is 'an exploration of Chaucer's own existing and potential relations with Gaunt, in a form at once tactful and quietly self-promotional' (*Social Chaucer* (Cambridge, MA and London, 1989), p. 52). Minnis similarly regards *BD* as a 'princepleasing' poem that celebrates Gaunt's 'superlative quality of life experience and noble sentiment' and encodes Chaucer's readiness to serve him as a courtier (*The Shorter Poems*, p. 134). Alfred David reads the poem as 'the poet's personal plea for acceptance in the world of the court' ('Chaucer's Edwardian poetry', in James M. Dean and Christian K. Zacher (eds), *The Idea of Medieval Literature: New Essays on Chaucer and Medieval Culture in Honor of Donald R. Howard* (Newark, DE; London and Toronto, 1992), p. 41). Less subtly, Beryl Rowland, 'Chaucer as a Pawn in the Book of the Duchess', *AN&Q*, 6 (1967), 3–6, contends that the narrator's eight-year sickness represents the duration of Chaucer's struggle for promotion in the Lancaster household.

57. For the latter possibility, see Gwen M. Vickery, 'The *Book of the Duchess*: The Date of Composition Related to the Theme of Impracticality', *Essays in Literature*, 22/2 (1995), 161–9, and Jane Gilbert, *Living Death in Medieval French and English Literature* (Cambridge and New York, 2011), pp. 198–9.

58. Howard Schless, 'A Dating for the *Book of the Duchess*: Line 1314', *ChR*, 19/4 (1985), 273–6. This de-romanticized view, found increasingly in recent decades' criticism, is a corrective to earlier categorical assumptions that '[i]n order to be at once tactful and relevant in an age when important people remarried with what now seems like indecent haste, Chaucer's poem must have been written shortly after the Duchess' death – certainly by the middle of 1370' (E. T. Donaldson, *Chaucer's Poetry: An Anthology for the Modern Reader* (New York, 1958), p. 951).

59. Bradford B. Broughton, 'Chaucer's "Book of the Duchess": did John [of Gaunt] love Blanche [of Lancaster]?', in Broughton (ed.), *Twenty-Seven to One: A Potpourri of Humanistic Material Presented to Dr. Donald Gale Stillman on the Occasion of His Retirement from Clarkson College of Technology* (Potsdam, NY, 1970), pp. 71–84.

60. Michael Foster, 'On Dating the Duchess: The Personal and Social Context of *Book of the Duchess*', *Review of English Studies*, 59/239 (2007), 185–96.

61. Cf. James Winny, *Chaucer's Dream-Poems* (New York, 1973), p. 45. For a recent consideration of how this might relate to *BD*'s process of revision, see Ben Parsons, 'The *Fall of Princes* and Lydgate's Knowledge of the *Book of the Duchess*', *European English Messenger*, 21/2 (2012), 26–30.

62. Gardner, 'Style as Meaning', 170.

63. Quotation from Robinson, *Chaucer and the English Tradition*, p. 17.

64. J. A. Burrow, 'Politeness and privacy: Chaucer's *Book of the Duchess*', in Anne Marie D'Arcy and Alan J. Fletcher (eds), *Studies in Late Medieval and Early Renaissance Texts in Honour of John Scattergood: 'The key of all good remembrance'* (Dublin, 2005), characterizes *BD* as 'a very extended indirect speech act' that crafts a poetics of inadequacy to honour the 'privacy of grief' (p. 74). Framing the point less positively, Michael Kensak, '"My first matere I wil yow telle": losing (and finding) your place in Chaucer's *The Book of the Duchess*', in T. L. Burton and John F. Plummer (eds), *'Seyd in forme and reverence': Essays on Chaucer and Chaucerians in Memory of Emerson Brown, Jr.* (Adelaide, Australia and Provo, UT, 2005), regards the awkwardness of *BD* as reflective of 'the impossibility of the author's rhetorical situation' (p. 96).

65. A classic reflection on constructs of audience in Chaucer's works is Paul Strohm, 'Chaucer's Audience(s): Fictional, Implied, Intended, Actual', *ChR*, 18/2 (1983), 137–45. On *BD* as flouting available conventions of public elegy, see Ardis Butterfield, 'Lyric and Elegy in *The Book of the Duchess*', *Medium Ævum*, 60 (1991), 40–1.

66. Cf. Michael D. Cherniss, 'The Boethian Dialogue in Chaucer's *Book of the Duchess*', *JEGP*, 68 (1969), 655–65 (663–4).

67. Most fully argued in Schless, 'A Dating'.

68. Phillips (ed.), *Book of the Duchess*, p. 166, line 1314n.

69. For the view that 'this kyng' refers to Octovyen, understood variously as Edward III or Gaunt himself (in the latter reading, Gaunt is not to be identified with the Man in Black), see Cherniss, 'Boethian Dialogue', 664; Edward I. Condren, 'The Historical Context of the *Book of the Duchess*: A New Hypothesis', *ChR*, 5/3 (1971), 195–212, and the same author's 'Of Deaths and Duchesses and Scholars Coughing in Ink', *ChR*, 10/1 (1975), 87–95, and *Chaucer from Prentice to Poet: The Metaphor of Love in Dream Visions and Troilus and Criseyde* (Gainesville, FL, 2008), pp. 24–6, 61; Palmer, 'Historical Context', 258; David Lawton, *Chaucer's Narrators* (Woodbridge, Suffolk and Dover, NH, 1986), p. 55, and 'Voice and public interiorities: Chaucer, Orpheus, Machaut', in Frank Grady and Andrew Galloway (eds), *Answerable Style: The Idea of the Literary in Medieval England* (Columbus, OH, 2013), p. 295.

70. Gardner, 'Style as Meaning', 160.

71. Beginning with Kittredge (*Chaucer and His Poetry*, pp. 68–71), critics have noticed the familiarly dreamlike quality of the poem, whose associative movements do not pause over such curiosities as the dreamer (apparently) mounting a horse inside his bedroom.

72. See, for example, R. A. Shoaf, 'Stalking the Sorrowful H(e)art: Penitential Lore and the Hunt Scene in Chaucer's *The Book of the Duchess*', *JEGP*, 78 (1979), 321–2.

73. Johnye E. Mathews, 'The Black Knight as King of the Castle in "The Book of the Duchess"', *The South Central Bulletin*, 31/4 (1971), 200–1; McGerr, *Chaucer's Open Books*, p. 54; Guillemette Bolens and Paul Beckman Taylor, 'Chess, Clocks, and Counsellors in Chaucer's *Book of the Duchess*', *ChR*, 35/3 (2001), 283–4, 288.

74. See Phillips (ed.), *The Book of the Duchess*, p. 44, and Colin Wilcockson's Explanatory Notes in *Riverside Chaucer*, p. 976, lines 1314–29n.

75. John M. Hill, 'The *Book of the Duchess*, Melancholy, and That Eight-Year Sickness', *ChR*, 9/1 (1974), 35–50.

76. Samuel Schoenbaum, 'Chaucer's Black Knight', *MLN*, 68/2 (1953), 121–2.

77. Cf. Donaldson, *Chaucer's Poetry*, p. 953.

78. Huppé and Robertson, *Fruyt and Chaf*, pp. 51–2; Robertson, 'Historical setting', p. 242; Cherniss, 'Boethian Dialogue', 663–4.

79. Russell A. Peck, 'Theme and number in Chaucer's *Book of the Duchess*', in Alastair Fowler (ed.), *Silent Poetry: Essays in Numerological Analysis* (London, 1970), p. 103.

80. Beryl Rowland, 'Chaucer's "Mistake": The *Book of the Duchess*, Line 455', *AN&Q*, 4 (1966), 99–100; Condren, 'Historical Context', 208, and *Chaucer from Prentice to Poet*, p. 35.

81. See Roger Sherman Loomis, 'Chaucer's Eight Years' Sickness', *MLN*, 59/3 (1944), 178–81.

82. For these several views, see F. G. Fleay, *Guide to Chaucer and Spenser* (London and Glasgow, 1877), pp. 36–7; Galway, 'Chaucer's Hopeless Love'; Huppé and Robertson, *Fruyt and Chaf*, pp. 32–5. Helpful overviews, with bibliography, of theories on the eight-year sickness are provided in Hill, 'The *Book of the Duchess*', 45–7; Phillips (ed.), *The Book of the Duchess*, p. 142, line 37n; *Riverside Chaucer*, p. 967, lines 30–43n.

83. Phillipa Hardman, 'The *Book of the Duchess* as a Memorial Monument', *ChR*, 28/3 (1994), 205–15.

84. For this reason, Phillips favours a date of 'before about 1372 when the influence of the Italians Boccaccio, Dante and Petrarch began to be seen in his work' (*Book of the Duchess*, p. 3). This point holds even if we allow for the mutual enrichment of what used to be schematically regarded as Chaucer's French, Italian and English periods; on this phenomenon, see David Wallace, 'Chaucer and Boccaccio's early writings', in Piero Boitani (ed.), *Chaucer and the Italian Trecento* (Cambridge, 1983), pp. 141–62.

85. This argument is developed in three studies by James Wimsatt: *Chaucer and the French Love Poets: The Literary Background of the* Book of the Duchess (Chapel Hill, NC, 1968), pp. 134–50; 'The *Dit dou bleu chevalier*: Froissart's Imitation of Chaucer', *Mediaeval Studies*, 34 (1972), 388–400; and *Chaucer and His French Contemporaries*, pp. 178–9, 220 (and further, pp. 220–34,

extending the argument to Granson's later *Songe Saint Valentin* and *Livre messire Ode*).

86. In an influential article, Susan Crane disputes *BD*'s influence on Froissart's poem, renewing older arguments for the reverse relationship: 'Froissart's *Dit dou bleu chevalier* as a Source for Chaucer's *Book of the Duchess*', *Medium Ævum*, 61/1 (1992), 59–74. See also William Calin, *The French Tradition and the Literature of Medieval England* (Toronto, 1994), p. 523 n. 20.

87. Ardis Butterfield, 'Chaucer's French inheritance', in Piero Boitani and Jill Mann (eds), *The Cambridge Companion to Chaucer*, 2nd edn (Cambridge, 2003), p. 26.

88. Wimsatt, 'Machaut's *Lay de Confort* and Chaucer's *Book of the Duchess*', in Rossell Hope Robbins (ed.), *Chaucer at Albany* (New York, 1975), pp. 15–16. Cf. Elizabeth Salter, 'Chaucer and Internationalism', *SAC*, 2 (1980), 76.

89. Ardis Butterfield, *The Familiar Enemy: Chaucer, Language and Nation in the Hundred Years War* (Oxford, 2009).

90. The only Chaucerian poem 'plugged' a comparable number of times by its author is the Wife of Bath's Prologue, invoked in the *Clerk's Tale*, *Merchant's Tale* and the *Lenvoy de Chaucer a Bukton*, but the references in these texts are to the Wife herself as a notorious authority rather than to her Prologue, strictly speaking.

91. In his catalogue of Chaucer's works in the *Fall of Princes*, Lydgate jointly cites 'The pitous story off Ceix and Alcione, / And the deth eek of Blaunche the Duchesse' (1.304–5). The sixteenth-century antiquary Bale's three major lists of Chaucer's works supply separate entries for *De Caeyce et Halcyona* and *In obitum Blanchiae ducissae*; see Eleanor Prescott Hammond, *Chaucer: A Bibliographic Manual* (New York, 1933), pp. 8–13, 63–5. In contrast, John Stow in his 1561 edition of Chaucer's works provides 'boke of the Duches' and 'Seis and Alcione' as alternative titles for the same work (quoted in Hammond, *Chaucer*, p. 363). See further Parsons, 'The *Fall of Princes*'.

92. For a review of the possibilities, see Phillips (ed.), *Book of the Duchess*, pp. 32–3.

93. N. F. Blake, 'The Textual Tradition of *The Book of the Duchess*', *English Studies*, 62/3 (1981), 237–48, and '*The Book of the Duchess* Again', *English Studies*, 67/2, (1986), 122–5.

94. Phillips (ed.), *Book of the Duchess*, pp. 64–6, and '*The Book of the Duchess*, Lines 31–96: Are They A Forgery?', *English Studies*, 67/2 (1986), 113–21. James Wimsatt, 'The Sources of Chaucer's "Seys and Alcyone"', *Medium Ævum*, 36/3 (1967), 240–1, further indicates in support of the passage's authenticity its artful integration with the rest of the poem, and its basis in sources used elsewhere in *BD*.

95. Phillips (ed.), *Book of the Duchess*, p. 33.

96. Furnivall, *Trial-Forewords*, p. 36.

97. Lowes, *Geoffrey Chaucer*, p. 93.

98. Schless, 'A Dating', 274.

99. Hardman, 'The *Book of the Duchess*', 206–7.

100. Huppé and Robertson, *Fruyt and Chaf*, pp. 50–2; Robertson, 'Historical setting', p. 252.

101. Lawton, 'Voice and public interiorities', pp. 294–7, also views the references to Gaunt as peripheral to the real subject of the poem, albeit for different reasons from Condren.

102. This argument forms the substance of Condren, 'Historical Context' (cf. J. J. N. Palmer, 'Historical Context', for a rebuttal), 'Of Deaths', and *Chaucer from Prentice to Poet*, pp. 8–62.

103. Condren, 'Historical Context', 211–12 n. 21.

104. Stephanie Trigg, *Congenial Souls: Reading Chaucer from Medieval to Postmodern* (Minneapolis, 2001), pp. 40–5.

105. Alfred L. Kellogg, *Chaucer, Langland, Arthur: Essays in Middle English Literature* (New Brunswick, NJ, 1972), pp. 59–67 (67).

106. One significant dissenting opinion from *BD*'s early reception history was Francis Thynne, who in his *Animadversions* (1599) insisted that the Man in Black's age of twenty-four precludes a connection to Blanche's death, which occurred later. He surmises that White may encode instead another one of Gaunt's mistresses, possibly relating to a surname – a view not unrelated to those considered in the present section. See Francis Thynne, *Chaucer: Animaduersions upon the Annotacions and corrections of some imperfections of impressiones of Chaucer's workes [sett downe before tyme and nowe] reprinted in the yere of our lorde 1598*, EETS o.s., 9 (London and Toronto, 1965), pp. 2–3.

107. Foster, 'On Dating the Duchess', who argues that *BD* propagandizes Gaunt's love for Blanche to defuse suspicion that his affair with Katherine, a source of scandal, began as early as his first marriage.

108. Ian Robinson and Doreen M. Thomas, 'Some riddles about *The Death of Blanche* with hints for a few answers', in Loren C. Gruber (ed.), *Essays on Old, Middle, Modern English and Old Icelandic: In Honor of Raymond P. Tripp, Jr.* (Lewiston, NY, 2000), pp. 447–66 (463).

109. Zacharias P. Thundy, 'The Dreame of Chaucer; Boethian Consolation or Political Celebration?', *Carmina Philosophiae: Journal of the International Boethius Society*, 4 (1995), 91–109 (91, 98).

110. F. [N. M.] Diekstra, 'Chaucer's Way with His Sources: Accident into Substance and Substance into Accident', *English Studies*, 62/3 (1981), 217; Ross, 'Play of Genres', 2.

111. Daniel Chandler, 'An Introduction to Genre Theory' (www document), *http://www.aber.ac.uk/media/Documents/intgenre/chandler_genre_theory.pdf* (accessed 23 August 2013), and, with specific reference to pre-modern forms, Ardis Butterfield, 'Medieval Genres and Modern Genre Theory', *Paragraph: A Journal of Modern Critical Theory*, 13/2 (1990), 184–201.

112. Jean Froissart, *An Anthology of Narrative & Lyric Poetry*, ed. and trans. Kristen M. Figg with R. Barton Palmer (New York and London, 2001), pp. 276–7, lines 246, 248–9.

113. Robertson, 'Historical setting', pp. 236–7; Butterfield, *The Familiar Enemy*, p. 282.
114. Jamie C. Fumo, 'The consolations of philosophy: later medieval elegy', in Karen Weisman (ed.), *The Oxford Handbook of the Elegy* (Oxford, 2010), p. 120.
115. Butterfield, 'Lyric and Elegy', 54 and *passim*.
116. For this reason, it has been argued, the very genre of *BD* is orchestrated as a surprise: what seems at first a love-vision becomes an elegy (French, 'The Man in Black's Lyric', 240).
117. Steve Ellis, 'The Death of the *Book of the Duchess*', *ChR*, 29/3 (1995), 254, 256.
118. Ellen E. Martin, 'Spenser, Chaucer, and the Rhetoric of Elegy', *Journal of Medieval and Renaissance Studies*, 17/1 (1987), 83, 88.
119. Fradenburg, '"Voice memorial"', 184, 192.
120. Wimsatt, *Chaucer and the French Love Poets*, p. 151.
121. R. Barton Palmer, '*The Book of the Duchess* and *Fonteinne Amoureuse*: Chaucer and Machaut Reconsidered', *Canadian Review of Comparative Literature*, 7/4 (1980), 381.
122. Ibid., 381. One of the first important analyses to propose that Chaucer creatively rethinks Machaut's precedent in the narrative structure of *BD* is John Lawlor, 'The Pattern of Consolation in *The Book of the Duchess*', *Speculum*, 31/4 (1956), 626-48 (636-8).
123. R. Barton Palmer, '*The Book of the Duchess* and *Fonteinne Amoureuse*', 383.
124. Ibid., 385.
125. This perspective on *BD* in relation to the *dits amoreux* is most fully developed in Katherine Heinrichs, *The Myths of Love: Classical Lovers in Medieval Literature* (University Park, PA and London, 1990), pp. 211–33.
126. Winny, *Chaucer's Dream-Poems*, p. 74 and further, pp. 64–9.
127. A. C. Spearing, *Medieval Autographies: The 'I' of the Text* (Notre Dame, IN, 2012), pp. 36, 257.
128. Wimsatt, *Chaucer and the French Love Poets*, p. 87.
129. Kittredge, *Chaucer and His Poetry*, p. 58; cf. Clemen, *Chaucer's Early Poetry*, p. 41.
130. French, 'The Man in Black's Lyric', 233–4.
131. Muscatine, *Chaucer and the French Tradition*, p. 102.
132. Steven F. Kruger, *Dreaming in the Middle Ages* (Cambridge, 1992), p. 65; see further A. C. Spearing, *Medieval Dream-Poetry* (Cambridge, 1976), p. 61.
133. Spearing, *Medieval Dream-Poetry*, p. 141. R. Barton Palmer argues that *BD* is in fact indebted to Machaut's *Fonteinne amoureuse* for the idea that 'waking experience ... is fulfilled by unconscious vision' ('*The Book of the Duchess* and *Fonteinne Amoureuse*', 386–7).
134. Beryl Rowland, 'The Whelp in Chaucer's *Book of the Duchess*', *Neuphilologische Mitteilungen*, 66 (1965), 158–60, and 'Chaucer as a Pawn', 3; Spearing, *Medieval Dream-Poetry*, pp. 64–5; Sandra Pierson Prior, '*Routhe*

and *Hert-Huntyng* in the *Book of the Duchess*', *JEGP*, 85 (1986), 3–19; Míceál
F. Vaughan, 'Hunting for the Hurt in Chaucer's *Book of the Duchess*', *Lingua
Humanitatis*, 2/2 (2002), 85–107.

135. Edward E. Foster, 'Allegorical Consolation in *The Book of the Duchess*', *Ball
State University Forum*, 11/4 (1971), 15; Michael D. Cherniss, 'The Narrator
Asleep and Awake in Chaucer's *Book of the Duchess*', *Papers on Language
and Literature*, 8/2 (1972), 124; Steven Kruger, 'Medical and moral authority
in the late medieval dream', in Peter Brown (ed.), *Reading Dreams: The
Interpretation of Dreams from Chaucer to Shakespeare* (Oxford and New
York, 1999), pp. 69–74.

136. See Marshall W. Stearns, 'Chaucer Mentions a Book', *MLN*, 57/1 (1942), 28–31.

137. Piero Boitani, 'Old Books Brought to Life in Dreams: The *Book of the
Duchess*, the *House of Fame*, the *Parliament of Fowls*', in Piero Boitani and
Jill Mann (eds), *The Cambridge Companion to Chaucer*, 2nd edn (Cambridge,
2003), p. 60.

138. William Calin, 'Machaut's legacy: the Chaucerian inheritance reconsidered',
in R. Barton Palmer (ed.), *Chaucer's French Contemporaries: The Poetry/
Poetics of Self and Tradition* (New York, 1999), p. 37; cf. Calin, *The French
Tradition*, pp. 287–8.

139. Quoted in Stephanie A. Viereck Gibbs Kamath, *Authorship and First-Person
Allegory in Late Medieval France and England* (Woodbridge, Suffolk and
Rochester, NY, 2012), p. 67.

140. Spearing, *Medieval Dream-Poetry*, p. 51.

141. Donnelly, 'Challenging the Conventions', 425.

142. McGerr, *Chaucer's Open Books*, p. 60.

143. Lynch, *Chaucer's Philosophical Visions*, pp. 40, 42.

144. More than one critic has sensed a kind of fool/king dynamic here, e.g. Kemp
Malone, *Chapters on Chaucer* (Baltimore, 1951), p. 39; Rose A. Zimbardo,
'The *Book of the Duchess* and the Dream of Folly', *ChR*, 18/4 (1984), 329–46.

145. Robert A. Watson, 'Dialogue and Invention in the *Book of the Duchess*',
Modern Philology, 98/4 (2001), 548; cf. John Finlayson, 'The *Roman de la
rose* and Chaucer's Narrators', *ChR*, 24/3 (1990), 199.

146. G. R. Wilson, Jr, 'The Anatomy of Compassion: Chaucer's *Book of the
Duchess*', *Texas Studies in Literature and Language*, 14/3 (1972), 387.

147. Raymond P. Tripp, Jr, 'The Dialectics of Debate and the Continuity of English
Poetry', *Massachusetts Studies in English*, 7 (1978), 42–3.

148. F. [N. M.] Diekstra, 'Chaucer and the Romance of the Rose', *English Studies*,
69/1 (1988), 18.

149. Malone, *Chapters on Chaucer*, p. 37; Lawlor, 'Pattern of Consolation', 636–8;
Wimsatt, *Chaucer and the French Poets*, pp. 92–3 (quotation from p. 93).

150. For an instructive reading of *Behaingne* in relation to *BD* that emphasizes
this point, see Minnis, *The Shorter Poems*, pp. 100–11.

151. Ardis Butterfield, 'Pastoral and the Politics of Plague in Machaut and
Chaucer', *SAC*, 16 (1994), 24.

152. Nicolette Zeeman, 'Imaginative theory', in Paul Strohm (ed.), *Middle English* (Oxford and New York, 2007), pp. 222, 234.

153. For example, French, 'The Man in Black's Lyric', and Sturges, *Medieval Interpretation*, p. 131.

154. Butterfield, 'Lyric and Elegy', 49.

155. Ross, 'The Play of Genres', 8.

156. Minnis, *The Shorter Poems*, p. 82.

157. Julia Boffey, 'The Lyrics in Chaucer's Longer Poems', *Poetica*, 37 (1993), 18.

158. W. A. Davenport, *Chaucer: Complaint and Narrative* (Cambridge, 1988), p. 67.

159. Wimsatt, *Chaucer and His French Contemporaries*, pp. 126, 128, 131.

160. Martin Irvine, '"Bothe text and gloss": manuscript form, the textuality of commentary, and Chaucer's dream poems', in Charlotte Cook Morse, Penelope Reed Doob and Marjorie Curry Woods (eds), *The Uses of Manuscripts in Literary Studies: Essays in Memory of Judson Boyce Allen* (Kalamazoo, MI, 1992), p. 104.

161. Ibid., p. 87.

162. Umberto Eco, 'The poetics of the open work', in *The Role of the Reader: Explorations in the Semiotics of Texts* (Bloomington, IN, 1979), p. 63.

2. Reading the *Book* (II): Themes, Problems, Interpretations

1. On this topic, see especially Lynch, '"Taking Keep"'; on deterioration of communication in the poem, see Martin Stevens, 'Narrative Focus in *The Book of the Duchess*: A Critical Revaluation', *Annuale Mediaevale*, 7 (1966), 21–4.

2. Clemen, *Chaucer's Early Poetry*, p. 66.

3. A. C. Spearing, 'Literal and Figurative in *The Book of the Duchess*', spec. issue on 'Reconstructing Chaucer', ed. Paul Strohm and Thomas J. Heffernan, *SAC Proceedings*, 1 (1984), 170.

4. Scala, *Absent Narratives*, p. 26.

5. On *BD*'s evocation of 'communicative situations' as they relate to historical audiences, positioned both vertically (John of Gaunt) and horizontally (Chaucer's fellow civil servants), see Strohm, *Social Chaucer*, pp. 51–5.

6. On the emotional unity established here, and the resonances of the *trouthe/routhe* rhyme, see Arthur W. Bahr, 'The Rhetorical Construction of Narrator and Narrative in Chaucer's The *Book of the Duchess*', *ChR*, 35/1 (2000), 54–5.

7. David R. Aers, 'Chaucer's *Book of the Duchess*: An Art to Consume Art', *Durham University Journal* n.s., 8/2 (69/2) (1977), 205; cf. J. Burke Severs, 'Chaucer's Self-Portrait in the *Book of the Duchess*', *Philological Quarterly*, 43/1 (1964), 38. A related view holds that true communication is impeded for much of the dream by the Man in Black's rigid textualization of his own experience through the variety of literary forms he draws on to render his story (lyric, allegorical narrative, courtly romance) (Sturges, *Medieval Interpretation*, pp. 132–3).

8. Minnis, *The Shorter Poems*, p. 84.

9. Robertson, 'Historical setting', p. 254.

10. Donald C. Baker, 'The Dreamer Again in *The Book of the Duchess*', *PMLA*, 70/1 (1955), 282; Georgia Ronan Crampton, 'Transitions and Meaning in *The Book of the Duchess*', *JEGP*, 62 (1963), 498.

11. Michaela Paasche Grudin, *Chaucer and the Politics of Discourse* (Columbia, SC, 1996), p. 27; Ferster, 'Intention and Interpretation', 11.

12. Judith C. Perryman, 'Speech and Meaning in "The Book of the Duchess"', *Neuphilologische Mitteilungen*, 85/2 (1984), 227–38, esp. 233–4, 238.

13. Peter W. Travis, 'White', 5, 34.

14. Stephen Manning, 'That Dreamer Once More', *PMLA*, 71/3 (1956), 540; Kensak, '"My first matere I wil yow telle"', p. 89.

15. Baker, 'The Dreamer Again'; Lawlor, 'Pattern of Consolation', 637–8.

16. Minnis, *The Shorter Poems*, pp. 128–9.

17. French, 'The Man in Black's Lyric', 236–40; Wilson, 'The Anatomy of Compassion', 385; Ruth Morse, 'Understanding the Man in Black', *ChR*, 15/3 (1981), 204–8.

18. Manning, 'That Dreamer Once More', 540.

19. Davis, 'Guillaume de Machaut', 398–9.

20. French, 'The Man in Black's Lyric', 238.

21. James R. Kreuzer, 'The Dreamer in the *Book of the Duchess*', *PMLA*, 66/4 (1951), 546.

22. Stevens, 'Narrative Focus', 27; Burrow, 'Politeness and Privacy', 74.

23. Guillaume de Machaut, *The Fountain of Love (La Fonteinne Amoureuse) and Two Other Love Vision Poems*, ed. and trans. R. Barton Palmer (New York and London, 1993), lines 1439–1542 (hereafter cited parenthetically, by line number). The fact that Chaucer's narrator never corroborates the Man in Black's final revelation with personal documentation of this sort – instead succumbing to near-speechlessness – underscores *BD*'s disruption of literary expectations.

24. Jordan, 'Compositional Structure'.

25. Two pithy overviews of debate on this subject are: Joerg O. Fichte, *Chaucer's 'Art Poetical': A Study in Chaucerian Poetics* (Tübingen, 1980), pp. 44–5, and Helen Phillips, 'Structure and Consolation in the *Book of the Duchess*', *ChR*, 16/2 (1981), 107.

26. Ellis, 'The Death of the *Book of the Duchess*', 254.

27. Denis Walker, 'Narrative Inconclusiveness and Consolatory Dialectic in the *Book of the Duchess*', *ChR*, 18/1 (1983), 1–17.

28. Useful reflections on this point are Lawrence Besserman, *Chaucer's Biblical Poetics* (Norman, OK, 1998), pp. 165–8, and Stephen Knight, 'Classicizing Christianity in Chaucer's dream poems: the *Book of the Duchess*, *Book of Fame* and *Parliament of Fowls*', in Helen Phillips (ed.), *Chaucer and Religion* (Cambridge, 2010), pp. 143–6.

29. Huppé and Robertson, *Fruyt and Chaf*, p. 46; James I. Wimsatt, 'The Apotheosis of Blanche in *The Book of the Duchess*', *JEGP*, 66/1 (1967), 35–7;

Rodney Delasanta, 'Christian Affirmation in *The Book of the Duchess*', *PMLA*, 84 (1969), 251. See further James I. Wimsatt, '*The Book of the Duchess*: secular elegy or religious vision?', in John P. Hermann and John J. Burke, Jr (eds), *Signs and Symbols in Chaucer's Poetry* (University, AL, 1981), pp. 113–29.

30. Huppé and Robertson, *Fruyt and Chaf*, pp. 91–2.

31. Richard Rambuss, '"Processe of tyme": History, Consolation, and Apocalypse in the *Book of the Duchess*', *Exemplaria*, 2/2 (1990), 663.

32. Huppé and Robertson, *Fruyt and Chaf*, p. 100.

33. Delasanta, 'Christian Affirmation', 251.

34. Wimsatt, '*The Book of the Duchess*', p. 123.

35. Cherniss, 'Boethian Dialogue', 655–65, and the same author's *Boethian Apocalypse: Studies in Middle English Vision Poetry* (Norman, OK, 1987), pp. 169–91; Peck, 'Theme and Number', 74–5; Charles P. R. Tisdale, 'Boethian "hert-huntyng": The Elegiac Pattern of *The Book of the Duchess*', *American Benedictine Review*, 24/3 (1973), 365–80.

36. Cherniss, 'Boethian Dialogue', 657–8; Tisdale, 'Boethian "hert-huntyng"', 367 n. 6.

37. Michael St John, *Chaucer's Dream Visions: Courtliness and Individual Identity* (Aldershot and Burlington, VT, 2000), pp. 42–51.

38. Diekstra, 'Chaucer's Way with His Sources', 223; Phillips, 'Fortune and the Lady'.

39. Minnis, *The Shorter Poems*, p. 91.

40. James Dean, 'Chaucer's *Book of the Duchess*: A Non-Boethian Interpretation', *MLQ*, 46/3 (1985), 235–49.

41. Robert A. Watson, 'Dialogue and Invention'; some of these points are anticipated in Dean, 'Chaucer's *Book of the Duchess*'.

42. Joerg O. Fichte, '*The Book of the Duchess* – A Consolation?', *Studia Neophilologica*, 45/1 (1973), 60; Teresa Hooper, 'Chaucer's Whelp: Consolation and the Limits of Reason in the *Book of the Duchess*', *Medieval Perspectives*, 21 (2005), 59.

43. Walker, 'Narrative Inconclusiveness', 15; Robert B. Burlin, *Chaucerian Fiction* (Princeton, 1977), pp. 70–4.

44. The following may be supplemented with the excellent overview of gender analyses of *BD* in Deborah Horowitz, 'An Aesthetic of Permeability: Three Transcapes of the *Book of the Duchess*', *ChR*, 39/3 (2005), 270–5.

45. James R. Lowell, *Conversations on Some of the Old Poets* (Cambridge, MA, 1845), p. 98; quoted in Anderson, 'Blanche, Duchess of Lancaster', 152.

46. *Riverside Chaucer*, p. 973, lines 817–1040n.

47. Quoted from Robertson, 'Historical setting', p. 249; Wimsatt, 'Apotheosis of Blanche', 28.

48. J. J. Anderson, 'The Man in Black, Machaut's Knight, and Their Ladies', *English Studies*, 73/5 (1992), 417–30.

49. Maud Ellmann, 'Blanche', in Jeremy Hawthorn (ed.), *Criticism and Critical Theory* (London and Baltimore, MD, 1984), p. 106. With this point may be compared Alcuin Blamires's consideration of metaphors of illumination in the

portrayals of Blanche and the Wife of Bath, the self-effacement of the former being to an extent 'travest[ied]' by the wilfulness of the latter (*Chaucer, Ethics, and Gender* (Oxford, 2006), p. 139).

50. Elaine Tuttle Hansen, *Chaucer and the Fictions of Gender* (Berkeley, 1992), p. 82.

51. Louise O. [Aranye] Fradenburg, '"My worldes blisse": Chaucer's Tragedy of Fortune', *South Atlantic Quarterly*, 98/3 (1999), 576, and *Sacrifice Your Love: Psychoanalysis, Historicism, Chaucer* (Minneapolis, 2002), pp. 95–6, 100; Gayle Margherita, 'Originary fantasies and Chaucer's *Book of the Duchess*', in Linda Lomperis and Sarah Stanbury (eds), *Feminist Approaches to the Body in Medieval Literature* (Philadelphia, 1993), pp. 122–3.

52. Cyndy Hendershot, 'Male Subjectivity, *fin amor*, and Melancholia in *The Book of the Duchess*', *Mediaevalia*, 21 (1996), 13.

53. Holly A. Crocker, *Chaucer's Visions of Manhood* (New York and Basingstoke, 2007), p. 97. On the mystifying processes of figuration, see Hansen, *Chaucer and the Fictions of Gender*, p. 80.

54. This perspective on femininity helps account for Jane Gilbert's provocative remark that *BD* 'depends on [White's] laudable willingness to leave the land of the living for that of the dead' (*Living Death*, p. 191).

55. Margaret Hallissey, *Clean Maids, True Wives, Steadfast Widows: Chaucer's Women and Medieval Codes of Conduct* (Westport, CT and London, 1993), pp. 141–2; cf. Miriamne Ara Krummel, 'The Tale of Ceïx and Alceone: Alceone's Agency and Gower's "audible mime"', *Exemplaria*, 13/2 (2001), 497–528.

56. Ellmann, 'Blanche', p. 100. Compare R. A. Shoaf's view of White as an 'idol of language' upon which the Man in Black rhetorically fixates, 'someone who can only exist in writing or words' ('"Mutatio amoris": "Penitentia" and the Form of *The Book of the Duchess*', *Genre*, 14 (1981), 167).

57. James Miller, 'How to see through women: medieval blazons and the male gaze', in Robert A. Taylor et al. (eds), *The Centre and Its Compass: Studies in Medieval Literature in Honor of Professor John Leyerle* (Kalamazoo, MI, 1993), p. 373; Fradenburg, *Sacrifice Your Love*, p. 108.

58. Miller, 'How to see through women', pp. 387–8; Gilbert, *Living Death*, p. 191.

59. Margherita, 'Originary fantasies', p. 135.

60. Susan Schibanoff, *Chaucer's Queer Poetics: Rereading the Dream Trio* (Toronto, 2006), pp. 65–97.

61. Steven F. Kruger, 'Medical and moral authority', pp. 77–8.

62. Deanne Williams, 'The dream visions', in Seth Lerer (ed.), *The Yale Companion to Chaucer* (New Haven and London, 2006), pp. 150–1.

63. D. Vance Smith, 'Plague, Panic Space, and the Tragic Medieval Household', *South Atlantic Quarterly*, 98/3 (1999), 390.

64. David K. Coley, '*Pearl* and the Narrative of Pestilence', *SAC*, 35 (2013), 250–2. An earlier, more general consideration of plague as a context for *BD* is Norman D. Hinton, 'The Black Death and the Book of the Duchess', in

Donald E. Hayden (ed.), *His Firm Estate: Essays in Honor of Franklin James Eikenberry* (Tulsa, 1967), pp. 72–8.

65. The view of English obliquity is classically formulated in Siegfried Wenzel, 'Pestilence and Middle English literature: Friar John Grimestone's poems on death', in Daniel Williman (ed.), *The Black Death: The Impact of the Fourteenth-Century Plague* (Binghamton, NY, 1982), pp. 131–59. Compare Coley's revisionist approach to this issue, which highlights the quiet profundity of English vernacular response to the plague ('*Pearl* and the Narrative of Pestilence'), 209–62.

66. Glending Olson, *Literature as Recreation in the Later Middle Ages* (Ithaca and London, 1982), esp. pp. 85–9, 164–83 (quotation at p. 89).

67. Louise M. Bishop, *Words, Stones, & Herbs: The Healing Word in Medieval and Early Modern England* (Syracuse, NY, 2007), p. 8.

68. For a medical diagnosis of the latter, see Joseph E. Grennen, '*Hert-huntyng* in the *Book of the Duchess*', *MLQ*, 25/2 (1964), 131–9.

69. On *BD* as a 'curative distraction or source of healing delight' for those touched by the plague, see Patricia Prandini Buckler, 'Love and death in Chaucer's *The Book of the Duchess*', in JoAnna Stephens Mink and Janet Doubler Ward (eds), *Joinings and Disjoinings: The Significance of Marital Status in Literature* (Bowling Green, OH, 1991), p. 7.

70. Butterfield, 'Pastoral and the Politics of Plague'.

71. Ibid., 23.

72. Kruger, 'Medical and moral authority', p. 73. This argument reframes, from a medical perspective, the psychoanalytic reading of the Man in Black as a therapeutic projection of the Dreamer's own anxieties seminally advanced in Bertrand H. Bronson, '*The Book of the Duchess* Re-opened', *PMLA*, 67/5 (1952), 863–81. For the argument that the narrator does not himself reach a state of restored health, despite the therapy he provides the Man in Black, see Míceál {F.} Vaughan, 'Hunting for the Hurt'.

73. Robert B. Burlin, *Chaucerian Fiction*, pp. 68–9.

74. First formulated by W. Owen Sypherd, 'Chaucer's Eight Years' Sickness', *MLN*, 20/8 (1905), 240–3, this position is reinforced in Minnis, *The Shorter Poems*, pp. 104–5. Notable dissenting opinions include R. M. Lumiansky, 'The Bereaved Narrator', and J. Burke Severs, 'Chaucer's Self-Portrait'. The classic account of medical aspects of lovesickness is Mary F. Wack, *Lovesickness in the Middle Ages: The* Viaticum *and Its Commentaries* (Philadelphia, 1990).

75. John M. Hill, 'The *Book of the Duchess*'; Judith S. Neaman, 'Brain Physiology and Poetics in *The Book of the Duchess*', *Res Publica Litterarum: Studies in the Classical Tradition*, 3 (1980), 101–13 (109). On writer's block, see also Lisa J. Kiser, 'Sleep, Dreams, and Poetry in Chaucer's *Book of the Duchess*', *Papers on Language and Literature*, 19/1 (1983), 3–12.

76. Jessica Rosenfeld, *Ethics and Enjoyment in Late Medieval Poetry: Love after Aristotle* (Cambridge and New York, 2011), p. 98.

77. Helen Phillips, 'Fortune and the Lady', 128.

78. Carol Falvo Heffernan, *The Melancholy Muse: Chaucer, Shakespeare and Early Medicine* (Pittsburgh, 1995), p. 41.

79. On confessional discourse in *BD*, see Shoaf, 'Stalking the Sorrowful H(e)art', and Robert A. Watson, 'Dialogue and Invention'.

80. On this distinction, see Mirko D. Grmek, 'The concept of disease', in Mirko D. Grmek (ed.), *Western Medical Thought from Antiquity to the Middle Ages*, trans. Antony Shugaar (Cambridge, MA and London, 1998), pp. 241–58.

81. The medical resonances of this phrase form the subject of a valuable recent essay collection: Jennifer C. Vaught (ed.), *Rhetorics of Bodily Disease and Health in Medieval and Early Modern England* (Farnham, Surrey and Burlington, VT, 2010).

82. For an account of this paradox, see Rossell Hope Robbins, 'Geoffroi Chaucier, poète français, Father of English Poetry', *ChR*, 13/2 (1978), 93–115 (100).

83. Thomas Tyrwhitt, *The Canterbury Tales of Chaucer. To Which Are Added an Essay on His Language and Versification, and an Introductory Discourse: Together with Notes and a Glossary*, 2nd edn, 2 vols (Oxford, 1798), vol. 2, p. 515.

84. Kittredge, 'Guillaume de Machaut'; Wimsatt, *Chaucer and the French Love Poets*, pp. 155–62 ('Appendix'); Windeatt, *Chaucer's Dream Poetry*, pp. 167–8.

85. Wimsatt, *Chaucer and the French Love Poets*, p. 151.

86. Muscatine contrasts *BD*'s 'wholesale borrowing of themes and passages from Guillaume de Machaut and his followers' with the more successful absorption and rechannelling of French influence in Chaucer's later poems (*Chaucer and the French Tradition*, p. 99).

87. E.-G. Sandras, *Étude sur G. Chaucer, considéré comme imitateur des trouvères* (Paris, 1859), pp. 89–95 (95); my translation.

88. Furnivall, *Trial-Forewords*, pp. 43, 49.

89. Ibid., p. 49.

90. Kemp Malone, *Chapters on Chaucer*, p. 22.

91. Kittredge, 'Guillaume de Machaut', 24.

92. W. Owen Sypherd, '*Le songe vert* and Chaucer's Dream-Poems', *MLN*, 24/2 (1909), 46–7; further, J. Burke Severs, 'The Sources of "The Book of the Duchess"' *Mediaeval Studies*, 25 (1963), 355–62.

93. Constance L. Rosenthal, 'A Possible Source of Chaucer's *Booke of the Duchesse – Li Regret de Guillaume* by Jehan de la Mote', *MLN*, 48/8 (1933), 511–14; Wimsatt, *Chaucer and the French Love Poets*, pp. 147–9.

94. The two texts are *La complainte de l'an nouvel* and *Complainte de saint Valentin*. See Haldeen Braddy, 'Chaucer's *Book of the Duchess* and Two of Granson's *Complaintes*', *MLN*, 52/7 (1937), 487–91, and the same author's *Chaucer and the French Poet, Graunson* (Baton Rouge, 1947), pp. 57–61.

95. Normand R. Cartier, 'Le *Bleu chevalier* de Froissart et le *Livre de la Duchesse* de Chaucer', *Romania*, 88 (1967), 232–52; Crane, 'Froissart's *Dit dou Bleu chevalier*'.

96. A sense of the difficulties involved in the latter is well conveyed in Kristen M. Figg, 'The Narrative of Selection in Jean Froissart's Collected Poems: Omissions and Additions in BN MSS fr. 830 and 831', *Journal of the Early Book Society*, 5 (2002), 37–55.

97. Wimsatt's position is summarized in *Chaucer and the French Love Poets*, p. 146.

98. Cartier, 'Le *Bleu chevalier*', 250–1; Wimsatt, '*Dit dou bleu chevalier*', 388, and the same author's *Chaucer and His French Contemporaries*, pp. 178–80. See also Stephanie Downes's illuminating consideration of Chaucer's currency in fourteenth-century France: 'After Deschamps: Chaucer's French fame', in Isabel Davis and Catherine Nall (eds), *Chaucer and Fame: Reputation and Reception* (Cambridge, 2015), pp. 127–42.

99. Calin, 'Machaut's legacy'. Calin notes furthermore that this bias among Chaucerians is partly inherited from French literary criticism in the first half of the twentieth century, which held the artifice and allegory of the *dits* in relatively low esteem (a view no longer current).

100. Elizabeth Salter, 'Chaucer and Internationalism', 76.

101. Ibid., 77.

102. Steve Guthrie, 'Dialogics and prosody', p. 103.

103. Ibid.

104. See Larry D. Benson, 'The beginnings of Chaucer's English style', in Theodore M. Andersson and Stephen A. Barney (eds), *Contradictions: from* Beowulf *to* Chaucer (Aldershot and Brookfield, VT, 1995), pp. 243–65, esp. 263–5.

105. Butterfield, 'Lyric and Elegy'.

106. Benson, 'The beginnings of Chaucer's English style', pp. 249–50.

107. Guthrie, 'Dialogics and prosody', p. 107.

108. Barbara Nolan, 'The art of expropriation: Chaucer's narrator in *The Book of the Duchess*', in Donald M. Rose (ed.), *New Perspectives in Chaucer Criticism* (Norman, OK, 1981), pp. 203–21 (205, 213). On parody of French style, cf. Edward I. Condren, 'Historical Context', 206–8.

109. John M. Bowers, *Chaucer and Langland*, p. 53.

110. Alessandro Barchiesi, *Speaking Volumes: Narrative and Intertext in Ovid and Other Latin Poets*, ed. and trans. Matt Fox and Simone Marchesi (London, 2001), p. 142.

111. R. Barton Palmer, 'Rereading Guillaume de Machaut's vision of love: Chaucer's *Book of the Duchess* as bricolage', in David Galef (ed.), *Second Thoughts: A Focus on Rereading* (Detroit, 1998), pp. 170–1. This conceptual vocabulary is also applied to *BD* in Phillips, 'Fortune and the Lady'.

112. R. Barton Palmer, 'Rereading Guillaume de Machaut's vision of love', p. 186. See also Fyler, 'Froissart and Chaucer', pp. 196–9.

113. Butterfield, *The Familiar Enemy*, p. 283.

114. Deanne Williams, *The French Fetish from Chaucer to Shakespeare* (Cambridge, 2004), p. 21.

115. Butterfield, 'Chaucer's French inheritance', p. 275 (emphasis in original).

3. All This Black: Reading and Making

1. Kevin Brownlee, *Poetic Identity in Guillaume de Machaut* (Madison, WI, 1984), pp. 188–9.
2. For this possibility, see Wimsatt, *Chaucer and the French Love Poets*, p. 12.
3. The fact that this line appears at the very end of the sixty-five-line passage extant only in Thynne's edition, the authenticity of which has occasionally been doubted, renders the oblique assertion of authorship – the Chaucerian 'I' – almost postmodern. It is as if Eolus blew Chaucer's claim to his work out of Fame's house in the wrong direction.
4. In Tanner MS 348, the title 'Chaucer's Dream' is added in a seventeenth-century hand after Thynne's 1532 edition.
5. The *explicit* of the *Retraction* refers to 'the book of the tales of Caunterbury'. It is unclear whether this rubric is scribal; a case for its authorial design has persuasively been made by Stephen Partridge, '"The Makere of this Boke": Chaucer's *Retraction* and the author as scribe and compiler', in Stephen Partridge and Erik Kwakkel (eds), *Author, Reader, Book: Medieval Authorship in Theory and Practice* (Toronto, 2012), pp. 106–53.
6. Although *LGW* almost wholly eschews the vocabulary of 'books', it does similarly compartmentalize translations ('Boece' and 'Of the Wreched Engendrynge of Mankynde' (G 413–14)) as distinct from original works, a point that factors into Chaucer's defence in the charges brought by the God of Love (see G 340–5, 349–52).
7. Partridge, '"The Makere of this Boke"', p. 129; Linne R. Mooney, 'Chaucer's Scribe', *Speculum*, 81 (2006), 97–138.
8. Daniel Poirion, 'DIT, genre littéraire', *Encyclopædia Universalis* (online), consulted 17 August 2014. *http://www.universalis.fr/encyclopedie/dit-genre-litteraire/*; my translation.
9. Joseph A. Dane, *Who Is Buried in Chaucer's Tomb? Studies in the Reception of Chaucer's Book* (East Lansing, MI, 1998), p. 138. Dane provides a full survey of the critical development of the 'booklet theory' in chapter 7.
10. Jesse M. Gellrich, *The Idea of the Book in the Middle Ages: Language Theory, Mythology, and Fiction* (Ithaca and London, 1985), p. 20.
11. These tropes are surveyed in Ernst Robert Curtius, *European Literature and the Latin Middle Ages*, trans. Willard R. Trask (New York, 1953), ch. 16; Gellrich, *Idea of the Book*, p. 248.
12. Eric Jager, *The Book of the Heart* (Chicago and London, 2000), pp. 38, 47 and *passim*.
13. Herbert Grabes, *The Mutable Glass: Mirror-Imagery in Titles and Texts of the Middle Ages and the English Renaissance* (Cambridge, 1982).
14. Laurel Amtower, *Engaging Words: The Culture of Reading in the Later Middle Ages* (New York, 2000), p. 7.
15. Mary [J.] Carruthers, *The Book of Memory: A Study of Memory in Medieval Culture* (Cambridge, 1990).

16. Martha Dana Rust, *Imaginary Worlds in Medieval Books: Exploring the Manuscript Matrix* (New York, 2007), p. 5.

17. Ibid., p. 8.

18. Mary [J.] Carruthers, '"The Mystery of the Bed Chamber": mnemotechnique and vision in Chaucer's *The Book of the Duchess*', in John M. Hill and Deborah M. Sinnreich-Levi (eds), *The Rhetorical Poetics of the Middle Ages: Reconstructive Polyphony – Essays in Honor of Robert O. Payne* (Madison and Teaneck, NJ; London, 2000), pp. 67–87.

19. Rust, *Imaginary Worlds*, p. 25.

20. Appropriately, the vocabulary of 'finding' suffuses the final lines of *BD*, where wordplay occurs on forms of the verb 'finden' (*MED* s.v. 'finden' v. 3(a), to discover) and 'fonden' (*MED* s.v. 'fonden' v. 7(a), to attempt or endeavour), thus suggesting the latent relevance of *MED* s.v. 'finden' v. 23(a), 'to compose or produce by way of artistic endeavor'. See *BD* 1325, 1329 and 1332, and compare the first appearance of 'finden' in *BD* to relate the narrator's selection of the tale of Seys (line 60).

21. Martine Gamaury, 'Le livre du rêve, le rêve du livre: réflexions sur l'écriture du rêve dans *Le Livre de la Duchesse* de Chaucer (1368)', in *L'articulation langue-littérature dans les textes médiévaux anglais: Actes du colloque des 25 et 26 juin 1999 à l'Université de Nancy II*, ed. Colette Stévanovitch, Publications de l'AMAES, Collection GRENDEL 3 (Nancy, 1999), pp. 175–92, esp. 186–92.

22. Jamie C. Fumo, 'Ovid: artistic identity and intertextuality', in Suzanne Conklin Akbari (ed.), *Oxford Handbook to Chaucer* (Oxford, forthcoming), and 'Ancient Chaucer: temporalities of fame', in Isabel Davis and Catherine Nall (eds), *Chaucer and Fame: Reputation and Reception* (Cambridge, 2015), pp. 201–20.

23. Barchiesi, *Speaking Volumes*, p. 26 (emphasis in original).

24. Martine Irvine, '"Bothe text and gloss"'.

25. For example, by Phillipa Hardman, '"Ars celare artem": Interpreting the Black Knight's "Lay" in Chaucer's *Book of the Duchess*', *Poetica*, 37 (1992), 55–7, and Rust, *Imaginary Worlds*, pp. 27–8. Fichte, '*The Book of the Duchess*', highlights the Man in Black's poetic efforts as among the evidence for what he regards as *BD*'s unusual status (for a medieval text) as a consolation that affirms eternity through art.

26. See, for example, Dean, 'Chaucer's *Book of the Duchess*', 244; Lynch, *Chaucer's Philological Visions*, pp. 52–6; St John, *Chaucer's Dream Visions*, pp. 50–2; David Burnley, 'Some Terminology of Perception in the *Book of the Duchess*', *ELN*, 23/3 (1986), 17–19.

27. Paula Neuss, 'Images of Writing and the Book in Chaucer's Poetry', *Review of English Studies* n.s., 32/128 (1981), 387, 396; Suzanne Conklin Akbari, *Seeing through the Veil: Optical Theory and Medieval Allegory* (Toronto, 2004), p. 191.

28. Ellmann, 'Blanche', p. 106.

29. Margherita, 'Originary fantasies'.
30. Ellmann, 'Blanche', pp. 106–7.
31. See Laura F. Hodges, 'Sartorial Signs in *Troilus and Criseyde*', *ChR*, 35/3 (2001), 223–59, esp. 226, and Rust, *Imaginary Worlds*, pp. 89–90. Neither Hodges nor Rust considers this imagery in relation to *BD*.
32. Rust, *Imaginary Worlds*, p. 90.
33. Martine Yvernault, '"I have lost more than thow wenest": Past, Present, and (Re)presentation in *The Book of the Duchess*', *Bulletin des Anglicistes Médiévistes*, 72 (2007), 32.
34. Butterfield, 'Chaucer's French inheritance', p. 31. For an example of how this observation has been enlisted towards a (rather strained) reading of *BD* as thematically unified, see Lynn Veach Sadler, 'Chaucer's *The Book of the Duchess* and the "Law of Kinde"', *Annuale Mediaevale*, 11 (1970), 58. On the subject of temporality in relation to framing and authorship in love-visions, see further Helen Phillips's excellent analysis in 'Frames and narrators in Chaucerian poetry', in Helen Cooper and Sally Mapstone (eds), *The Long Fifteenth Century: Essays for Douglas Gray* (Oxford, 1997), pp. 82–3.
35. David Lawton, *Chaucer's Narrators*, pp. 54, 56.
36. Deborah Horowitz, 'An Aesthetic of Permeability', 267–8.
37. Guthrie, 'Dialogics and prosody', p. 107.
38. Marcella Ryan, 'The Concept of Textual Unity in Chaucer's Dream-Visions', spec. issue on 'Narrative Issues', ed. John Hay and Marie Maclean, *AUMLA: Journal of the Australasian Universities Language and Literature Association*, 74 (1990), 25–33 (29).
39. Yvernault, '"I have lost more than thow wenest"', 42.
40. The edition referenced is Jean Froissart, *Le Paradys d'Amours*, in *Œuvres de Froissart: Poésies*, ed. August Scheler, vol. 1 (Brussels, 1870); translations are from Windeatt, *Chaucer's Dream Poetry*.
41. Only in this qualified sense is Wimsatt's claim accurate that 'each poet [i.e. Froissart's and Chaucer's narrators] ... closes on a professional note with a statement about the poetic material which the dream has provided' (*Chaucer and the French Love Poets*, p. 124).
42. Ambrosius Aurelius Theodosius Macrobius, *Commentary on the Dream of Scipio*, trans. William Harris Stahl (New York and London, 1952), p. 88.
43. Here I disagree with Cherniss's assertion that progress occurs for the narrator only while in the dream state, and that 'at the end of his dream he is no nearer his "cure" than he had been before he picked up his book of "fables"' ('The Narrator Asleep and Awake', 121).
44. Quoted from Guillaume de Lorris and Jean de Meun, *Le Roman de la rose*, ed. Félix Lecoy, 3 vols (Paris, 1973–5), vol. 1, lines 29–30; translation from Guillaume de Lorris and Jean de Meun, *The Romance of the Rose*, trans. Frances Horgan (Oxford, 1994), p. 3.
45. Lori Walters, 'Reading the "Rose": Literacy and the Presentation of the "Roman de la Rose" in Medieval Manuscripts', *Romanic Review*, 85/1 (1994), 2.

46. Deborah McGrady, *Controlling Readers: Guillaume de Machaut and His Late Medieval Audience* (Toronto, 2006), p. 46. Cf. Butterfield, 'Chaucer's French inheritance', p. 31.

47. Wimsatt, *Chaucer and the French Love Poets*, pp. 84–5.

48. Jocelyn Wogan-Browne et al. (eds), *The Idea of the Vernacular: An Anthology of Middle English Literary Theory, 1280–1520* (Exeter, 1999), and esp., included in this volume, Ruth Evans et al., 'The notion of vernacular theory', pp. 314–30.

49. Mícéál [F.] Vaughan, '"Til I gan awake": The Conversion of Dreamer into Narrator in *Piers Plowman* B', *Yearbook of Langland Studies*, 5 (1991), 175–92.

50. Citations of *Piers Plowman* are from William Langland, *The Vision of Piers Plowman*, ed. A. V. C. Schmidt (London and Rutland, VT, 1995).

51. Nicholas Watkins and Jacqueline Jenkins (eds), *A Revelation of Love*, in *The Writings of Julian of Norwich: A Vision Showed to a Devout Woman and A Revelation of Love* (University Park, PA, 2006), ch. 32, line 6. All citations are from this edition, by chapter and line number.

52. See Watkins and Jenkins (eds), *The Writings of Julian of Norwich*, pp. 32–3, and chs 51, 86 of *A Revelation*.

53. On the development of this hermeneutic construct in the 'Aristotelian prologue', see the classic account by Minnis, *Medieval Theory of Authorship: Scholastic Literary Attitudes in the Later Middle Ages* (London, 1984), pp. 75–84.

54. Watson and Jenkins (eds), *The Writings of Julian of Norwich*, p. 378.

55. The text of this injunction is given by Watson and Jenkins on p. 415.

56. Citations are from John Gower, *Confessio amantis*, vol. 1, ed. Russell A. Peck with Andrew Galloway, 2nd edn (Kalamazoo, MI, 2006), here Prologue, line *51 (from the Ricardian recension).

4. Rereading the *Book* (I): The Materials of Transmission

1. A description of the MSS and of Thynne's text is given in Phillips (ed.), *Book of the Duchess*, pp. 62–6. On Thynne's procedures, see Blake, 'Textual Tradition' and '*The Book of the Duchess* Again'. Revisitations of the textual difficulties and their editorial implications appear in M. C. Seymour, 'Chaucer's *Book of the Duchess*: A Proposal', *Medium Ævum*, 74/1 (2005), 60–70, and Murray McGillivray, 'Editing Chaucer's Early Poems: A Rationale for Virtual Copy-Text', *Florilegium*, 27 (2010), 159–76.

2. Aage Brusendorff advanced this theory in *The Chaucer Tradition* (1925; Oxford, 1967), pp. 178–207. Quotation from Pamela Robinson (ed.), *Manuscript Tanner 346: A Facsimile* (Norman, OK and Woodbridge, Suffolk, 1980), p. xxv. On the cultural attraction of Chaucerian anthologies for a gentry audience, see Seth Lerer, *Chaucer and His Readers: Imagining the Author in Late-Medieval England* (Princeton, 1993), pp. 57–84, and Kathleen

Forni, *The Chaucerian Apocrypha: A Counterfeit Canon* (Gainesville, FL, 2001), pp. 23–6.

3. Theories advanced, respectively, in N. F. Blake, 'Textual Tradition', 247, and M. C. Seymour, 'Chaucer's *Book of the Duchess*', 63.

4. See John H. Fisher's advancement of this view in his now classic article, 'A Language Policy for Lancastrian England', *PMLA*, 107/5 (1992), 1168–80; see further Bowers, *Chaucer and Langland*, pp. 183–90.

5. See Derek Pearsall, 'Thomas Speght (ca. 1550–?)', in Paul G. Ruggiers (ed.), *Editing Chaucer: The Great Tradition* (Norman, OK, 1984), p. 81, and Seymour, 'Chaucer's *Book of the Duchess*', 69.

6. Forni, *The Chaucerian Apocrypha*, p. 25.

7. Speght, *The workes of our antient and learned English poet, Geffrey Chaucer, newly printed* (London, 1598), 'Arguments', c5v.

8. Ibid., c6v.

9. Ibid., b3v.

10. Thomas Speght, *The workes of ovr Ancient and learned English Poet, Geoffrey Chavcer, newly printed* (London, 1602), fol. 347r.

11. Pearsall, 'Thomas Speght', p. 88, and *The Life of Geoffrey Chaucer*, pp. 83–4. On Speght's integration of Chaucer's works with 'the facts of royal biography', see further Forni, *The Chaucerian Apocrypha*, pp. 76–80.

12. Laila Z. Gross indicates in the Explanatory Notes to *An ABC* in the *Riverside Chaucer*, p. 1076, that 'Speght may have used a MS once owned by Humphrey, Duke of Gloucester, Blanche's grandson, and could therefore have recorded a family tradition'. Pearsall allows that Cambridge University Library MS Gg. 4.27, which is missing four leaves at the relevant point, may once have included the heading reproduced by Speght. On points of intersection between *An ABC* and *BD*, see Wimsatt, 'Apotheosis of Blanche', 44 n. 44; Robbins, 'Geoffroi Chaucier', p. 100; Williams, *French Fetish*, pp. 29–30.

13. John Urry, *The Works of Geoffrey Chaucer* (London, 1721). The prefatory matter in Urry's edition is unpaged; these quotations, from 'The life of Geoffrey Chaucer', correspond to pp. iv, xix–xx.

14. Godwin, *Life of Geoffrey Chaucer*, vol. 2, pp. 85–95.

15. Compare Helen Phillips's account of the conventional *dit amoreux* narrator as embodying 'the point of reception, combining writer and reader', at once 'an alter ego of the author' and 'the alter ego of the reader or audience, experiencing the process of gradually entering the realm of fiction' ('Frames and narrators', p. 80).

16. See Walter W. Skeat (ed.), *Chaucerian and Other Pieces*, vol. 7 of *Supplement to the Works of Geoffrey Chaucer* (London, 1897), pp. lxii, 359–60; Eleanor Prescott Hammond, *Chaucer*, pp. 406–7; and Norton-Smith (ed.), *Bodleian Library MS Fairfax 16*, p. xxv. On this poem's context in Tanner 346, see Lerer, *Chaucer and His Readers*, pp. 82–3.

17. Tyrwhitt, *The Canterbury Tales of Chaucer*, p. 529. For an overview of this aberration as well as the publication history of *Bukton*, see Hammond,

Chaucer, pp. 366–7. See also George B. Pace and Alfred David (eds), *The Minor Poems: Part One*, vol. 5 of *A Variorum Edition of the Works of Geoffrey Chaucer* (Norman, OK, 1982), p. 142 n. 1; p. 144, line 1n. My review of the printed editions does not support Pace and David's observation that '&c.' is changed to 'AC' or 'A.C.' beginning with Thynne's 1542 edition. Instead of 'AC', I read '&c.' with the Tironian nota for *et* instead of ampersand.

18. Pace and David (eds), *The Minor Poems*, p. 142 n. 2.

19. James E. Blodgett, 'William Thynne (d. 1546)', in Paul G. Ruggiers (ed.), *Editing Chaucer: The Great Tradition* (Norman, OK, 1984), p. 39.

20. R. F. Yeager, 'Literary Theory at the Close of the Middle Ages: William Caxton and William Thynne', *SAC*, 6 (1984), 159–62; Forni, *The Chaucerian Apocrypha*, p. 65.

21. Pace and David (eds), *The Minor Poems*, p. 144.

22. Thynne's text of several of the minor poems suggests that he used a MS related to the Oxford group that was closer to the exemplar than the extant MSS (Blodgett, 'William Thynne', p. 40). As Blake points out in his discussion of *BD*, the relationship among the extant MSS and Thynne's text necessitates – if one assumes that Thynne did not forge the lines missing elsewhere – that Thynne used more than one MS in preparing *BD*, a practice that has precedent in his edition. Blake, '*The Book of the Duchess*', 123.

23. Julia Boffey, 'The Reputation and Circulation of Chaucer's Lyrics in the Fifteenth Century', *ChR*, 28/1 (1993), 35.

24. Forni, *The Chaucerian Apocrypha*, p. 58.

25. Ibid., p. 58; cf. Blodgett, 'William Thynne', p. 41.

26. Forni, *The Chaucerian Apocrypha*, p. 56.

27. Skeat, *Chaucerian and Other Pieces*, p. lxx. An edition of the poem itself appears on pp. 405–7, to which citations in the text refer; a description is given in Hammond, *Chaucer*, p. 440.

28. See chapter 1's treatment of this point, and cf. Parsons, 'The *Fall of Princes*'.

29. Urry, *The Works of Geoffrey Chaucer*, p. 413; the list of contents presents it similarly.

30. Tyrwhitt, *The Canterbury Tales of Chaucer*, p. 529.

31. Details based on Hammond, *Chaucer*, pp. 139, 366–7.

32. Paul Strohm, *Social Chaucer*, p. 72.

33. This point is differently registered in the analyses of the poem's ironic structure in Jane Chance, 'Chaucerian Irony in the Verse Epistles "Wordes Unto Adam," "Lenvoy a Scogan," and "Lenvoy a Bukton"', *Papers on Language & Literature*, 21/2 (1985), 115–28, and Jay Ruud, '*Many a song and many a lecherous lay*': *Tradition and Individuality in Chaucer's Lyric Poetry* (New York and London, 1992), pp. 107–20.

34. G[eorge]. L[yman]. Kittredge, 'Chaucer's *Envoy to Bukton*', *MLN*, 24 (1909), 14–15 (15).

35. Richard P. Horvath, 'Chaucer's Epistolary Poetic: The Envoys to Bukton and Scogan', *ChR*, 37/2 (2002), 173–89 (185).

36. Trigg, *Congenial Souls*, p. 31. In an interesting variation on this point, a recent consideration of *Bukton* by Geoffrey W. Gust critiques narrowly autobiographical readings of Chaucer's envoy by speculating, 'What if we did *not* have the traditional title [of *Lenvoy de Chaucer a Bukton*] ... and line one simply read "my maister" rather than "my maister Bukton"?' (*Constructing Chaucer: Author and Autofiction in the Critical Tradition* (New York, 2009), p. 93). Remarkably, Gust appears unaware that *Bukton* was presented almost exactly in these terms for the first five centuries of its transmission history, revealing how deeply submerged the early textual representation of *Bukton* (and the *BD/Bukton* link) has become for modern critics.

37. Gross, Explanatory Notes to *Bukton* in *Riverside Chaucer*, p. 1087.

38. Warren S. Ginsberg, Explanatory Notes to the *Clerk's Tale* in *Riverside Chaucer*, p. 883, line 1177n.

39. Not to be confused with *Lenvoy de Chaucer a Bukton*. The present discussion refers to the latter poem exclusively as *Bukton*; as already noted, the longer title now used in editions of the poem is absent in early printed editions.

40. See Thomas J. Farrell, 'The "Envoy de Chaucer" and the *Clerk's Tale*', *ChR*, 24/4 (1990), 329–36.

41. Forni, *The Chaucerian Apocrypha*, p. 65.

42. William Thynne, *The workes of Geffray Chaucer newly printed, wyth dyuers workes whych were neuer in print before* (London, 1542), fol. 357v.

43. See, for example, Gwen M. Vickery, 'The *Book of the Duchess*', and Edward E. Foster, 'On Dating the Duchess'. On these trends in scholarship, see chapter 1.

44. This characterization of *Remedy of Loue* is by Alexandra Gillespie, *Print Culture and the Medieval Author: Chaucer, Lydgate, and Their Books 1473–1557* (Oxford, 2007), p. 143, who does not consider the connection to *Bukton*.

45. Forni, *The Chaucerian Apocrypha*, p. 69.

46. Ibid., p. 73.

47. John Stow, *The workes of Geffrey Chaucer, newlie printed, with diuers addicions, whiche were neuer in print before: with the siege and destruccion of the worthy citee of Thebes, compiled by Ihon Lidgate, Monke of Berie* (London, 1561), fol. 340r.

48. Stow, fol. 340r–v; Skeat, *Chaucerian and Other Pieces*, pp. xlix–l, 291–4 (to which quotations, by line number, refer). Alain Renoir and C. David Benson, 'John Lydgate', in Albert E. Hartung (gen. ed.), *A Manual of the Writings in Middle English 1050–1500*, vol. 6 (New Haven, 1980), no. 37, p. 1828.

49. On this point, compare Scattergood's discussion of the proverbial nature of *Bukton* in Minnis, *The Shorter Poems*, pp. 497–500, and '*Chaucer a Bukton* and Proverbs', *Nottingham Medieval Studies*, 31 (1987), 98–107.

50. The edition used, cited by line number, is that in Kathleen Forni (ed.), *The Chaucerian Apocrypha: A Selection* (Kalamazoo, MI, 2005), p. 116.

51. Forni, *The Chaucerian Apocrypha*, p. 75.

52. F. G. Fleay, *Guide to Chaucer and Spenser*, pp. 36–7, quoted in Sypherd, 'Chaucer's Eight Years' Sickness', 241.

53. Spearing, *Medieval Autographies*, p. 83.

54. Minnis, *Fallible Authors: Chaucer's Pardoner and Wife of Bath* (Philadelphia, 2008), pp. 250–64.

55. Lee Patterson, *Chaucer and the Subject of History* (Madison, WI, 1991), p. 316.

56. Spearing, *Medieval Autographies*, ch. 3.

5. Rereading the *Book* (II): Literary Reception up to the Sixteenth Century

1. On Gower's French influences, see especially Ardis Butterfield, '*Confessio Amantis* and the French tradition', in Siân Echard (ed.), *A Companion to Gower* (Cambridge and Rochester, NY, 2004), pp. 165–80, and Peter Nicholson, *Love and Ethics in Gower's* Confessio Amantis (Ann Arbor, 2005), pp. 3–40.

2. See, for example, Miramne Ara Krummel, 'The Tale of Ceïx and Alceone', and Ellen Shaw Bakalian, *Aspects of Love in John Gower's* Confessio Amantis (New York and London, 2004).

3. Phillips, '*The Book of the Duchess*, Lines 31–96', 116–17 n. 19, outlines the parallels.

4. John Gower, *The English Works of John Gower*, ed. G. C. Macaulay, EETS e.s., 81–2, 2 vols. (London, 1969), 1.2973n; Phillips (ed.), *The Book of the Duchess*, line 134n; Phillips, '*The Book of the Duchess*, Lines 31–96', 116–17 n. 19.

5. Quotations are from John Gower, *Confessio Amantis*, vol. 2, ed. Russell A. Peck with Andrew Galloway (Kalamazoo, MI, 2003), by book and line number.

6. Ovid, *Metamorphoses*, ed. and trans. Frank Justus Miller, 3rd edn (Cambridge, MA and London, 1977), 2 vols; cited by book and line number.

7. From Peck and Galloway's edition of the *Confessio*, vol. 2, p. 408, 4.3020–1n.

8. Andrew Galloway, 'Reassessing Gower's dream-visions', in Elisabeth Dutton with John Hines and R. F. Yeager (eds), *John Gower, Trilingual Poet: Language, Translation, and Tradition* (Cambridge, 2010), 293–4.

9. A similar position is maintained by Froissart at the end of *Le Paradys d'Amours*, an erotic wish-fulfilment dream *par excellence*; see Froissart, *Le Paradys d'Amours*, lines 1719–21.

10. Compare Froissart: 'Pensées et merancolies / Qui me sont ens au coer liies / Et pas ne les puis deslyer, / Car ne voeil la belle oublyer / Pour quele amour en ce traveil / Je sui entrés et tant je veil' (Sad thoughts and melancholy … bind my heart tightly, and I cannot loosen them, for I do not want to forget the fair one, for love of whom I entered into this torment and suffer such sleeplessness) (*Le Paradys d'Amours*, lines 7–12; Windeatt, *Chaucer's Dream Poetry*, p. 41).

11. Dated thus by John Norton-Smith, from whose edition quotations are cited parenthetically by line number (John Lydgate, *Poems*, ed. John Norton-Smith (Oxford, 1966), p. 168). The dating is conjectural, and Derek Pearsall favours a later period, the 1420s (*John Lydgate (1371–1449): A Bio-bibliography*, ELS Monograph Series, 71 (Victoria, B.C., 1997), p. 14).

12. Hammond, *Chaucer*, pp. 413–15. See further Forni, *The Chaucerian Apocrypha*, pp. 21–6, and Dana M. Symons (ed.), *Chaucerian Dream Visions and Complaints* (Kalamazoo, MI, 2004), p. 79.

13. Derek Pearsall's claim that 'it is rarely necessary to go beyond Chaucer for Lydgate's specific borrowings' in *CLL* (*John Lydgate* (London, 1970), p. 84) has been challenged by Susan Bianco and Dana M. Symons, who demonstrate Lydgate's French influences and his conscious experimentation with inherited forms. See Bianco, 'A Black Monk in the Rose Garden: Lydgate and the *Dit Amoureux* Tradition', *ChR*, 34/1 (1999), 60–8, and 'New perspectives on Lydgate's courtly verse', in Helen Cooney (ed.), *Nation, Court and Culture: New Essays on Fifteenth-Century English Poetry* (Dublin and Portland, OR, 2001), pp. 95–115; Symons (ed.), *Chaucerian Dream Visions and Complaints*, pp. 3–5.

14. Symons (ed.), *Chaucerian Dream Visions and Complaints*, pp. 3, 5.

15. Ibid., pp. 5–6; A. C. Spearing, *The Medieval Poet as Voyeur: Looking and Listening in Medieval Love Narratives* (Cambridge, 1993), pp. 218–30.

16. Spearing, *The Medieval Poet as Voyeur*, p. 226.

17. See Cherniss, 'The Narrator Asleep and Awake'; Winny, *Chaucer's Dream-Poems*, pp. 52–5.

18. Raymond P. Tripp, Jr, 'The Loss of Suddenness in Lydgate's *A Complaynt of a Loveres Lyfe*', *Fifteenth Century Studies*, 6 (1983), 253–69 (259).

19. See Norton-Smith's note to lines 130–1 (John Lydgate, *Poems*, p. 168).

20. On this interpretation, see chapter 4, p. 110.

21. Julia Boffey, 'Charles of Orleans reading Chaucer's dream visions', in Piero Boitani and Anna Torti (eds), *Mediaevalitas: Reading the Middle Ages* (Cambridge and Rochester, NY, 1996), p. 44.

22. On the duke's library, see Boffey, 'Charles of Orleans', p. 61; on his literary influences more generally, see Charles of Orleans, *Fortunes Stabilnes: Charles of Orleans's English Book of Love*, ed. Mary-Jo Arn (Binghamton, NY, 1994), pp. 39–49. All citations of *FS* refer to Arn's edition, by poem and line number.

23. Arn (ed.), *Fortunes Stabilnes*, p. 2. See also A. E. B. Coldiron's stimulating consideration of Charles's practices of *translatio*, and the fruitful incommensurability of his French and English sequences, in *Canon, Period, and the Poetry of Charles of Orleans: Found in Translation* (Ann Arbor, 2000). Coldiron further observes the inclusion of one of Charles's English ballades in the fifth quire of MS Fairfax 16, the Chaucerian miscellany that also features *BD*, together with nineteen other ballades in a similar vein (p. 81).

24. Arn (ed.), *Fortunes Stabilnes*, p. 540, line 6531n.

25. Boffey finds similarities to *BD* later in *FS* (lines 4799–4861) when, in an inset dream-vision, Venus encourages the still grieving Charles to recollect his dead lady at length ('Charles of Orleans', p. 53). Allusions to *BD* are conspicuously absent in this section of the poem, however, where the immediate model is instead the last two books of *Troilus and Criseyde*. Rather than constructing a memorial tableau of his lost lady, as does the Man in Black, the dreamer follows Troilus in revisiting the intimate sites of their love affair, while Venus plays the role of Pandarus, advocating a shift of affection. The emphasis lies in the latter trajectory.

26. Eleanor Prescott Hammond, *English Verse between Chaucer and Surrey* (New York, 1969), p. 471.

27. On this conception of chess in *BD*, see Jenny Adams, 'Pawn Takes Knight's Queen: Playing with Chess in the *Book of the Duchess*', *ChR*, 34/2 (1999), 125–38, and *Power Play: The Literature and Politics of Chess in the Late Middle Ages* (Philadelphia, 2006), pp. 96–7.

28. For these and related views, see S. W. Stevenson, 'Chaucer's Ferses Twelve', *ELH*, 7/3 (1940), 215–22; Franklin D. Cooley, 'Two Notes on the Chess Terms in *The Book of the Duchess*', *MLN*, 63/1 (1948), 30–5; W. H. French, 'Medieval Chess and the *Book of the Duchess*', *MLN*, 64/4 (1949), 261–4; Beryl Rowland, 'The Chess Problem in Chaucer's *Book of the Duchess*', *Anglia*, 80 (1962), 384–9, and 'Chaucer's *Duchess* and Chess', *Florilegium*, 16 (1999), 41–59; Margaret Connolly, 'Chaucer and Chess', *ChR*, 29/1 (1994), 40–4; Guillemette Bolens and Paul Beekman Taylor, 'The Game of Chess in Chaucer's *Book of the Duchess*', *ChR*, 32/4 (1998), 325–34; Mark N. Taylor, 'Chaucer's Knowledge of Chess', *ChR*, 38/4 (2004), 299–313.

29. French, 'Medieval Chess'.

30. Vickery, 'The *Book of the Duchess*', 167.

31. On the pre-Chaucerian sources of this motif, see Colin Wilcockson's Explanatory Notes in the *Riverside Chaucer*, p. 971, lines 599–616n.

32. On the differences of opinion regarding the direction of influence, see chapter 2, notes 92 and 97. Wimsatt, *Chaucer and the French Love Poets*, p. 146, briefly observes *FS*'s relationship to *Songe vert* in conjunction with *BD*.

33. The argument for its inauthenticity is summarized in Charles Flint McClumpha, 'Chaucer's Dream', *MLN*, 4/3 (1889), 65–7.

34. Speght does qualify this (the full heading reads 'The Booke commonly entituled Chaucer's Dreame'), perhaps referring to popular usage rather than best practice, but he perpetuates the flawed title nonetheless. An overview of *Isle*'s textual history with an indispensable chart of titles and attributions is provided by Kathleen Forni, '"Chaucer's Dreame": A Bibliographer's Nightmare', *Huntington Library Quarterly*, 64/1–2 (2001), 139–50. See also Ellis, 'The Death of the *Book of the Duchess*'. Fairfax 16 and Bodley 638 designate *BD* '*The Booke of the Duchesse*'; Tanner 346 supplies '*Chaucer's Dream*' in a seventeenth-century hand.

35. Quoted from Speght's 1602 edition, fol. 334r.
36. As Annika Farber notes, Speght, influenced by Francis Thynne's objections to this historical analogy, qualifies this argument in his 1602 edition (fol. 227r), indicating that the woman mourned is merely 'supposed to bee Blanch the Duchesse' ('Usurping "Chaucers dreame": *Book of the Duchess* and the Apocryphal *Isle of Ladies*', *Studies in Philology*, 105/2 (2008), 209).
37. Farber, 'Usurping "Chaucers dreame"', 207–25.
38. These points are consistent across Speght's 1598 and 1602 editions. The quotation, from Speght's 1602 edition, appears on fol. 334r; the other details, from 'Chaucers life', on b3v.
39. All citations, by line number, from *The Isle of Ladies* in *The Floure and the Leafe, The Assembly of Ladies, The Isle of Ladies*, ed. Derek Pearsall (Kalamazoo, MI, 1990), pp. 63–140.
40. Rossell Hope Robbins, 'XI. The Chaucerian apocrypha', in Albert E. Hartung (gen. ed.), *A Manual of the Writings in Middle English 1050–1500*, vol. 4 (New Haven, 1973), p. 1097.
41. *The Isle of Ladies*, ed. Pearsall, p. 67.
42. Farber, 'Usurping "Chaucers dreame"', 219–23 (222).
43. In this sense, *Isle*'s technique is consistent with the exploitation of Chaucerian structures for inventive purposes described in Phillips, 'Frames and narrators', esp. pp. 75–7.
44. Farber, 'Usurping "Chaucers dreame"', 219–23.
45. Compare Farber's suggestion that *Isle* shows 'love still persists despite death and therefore … death is not as great a loss as the Man in Black believes it is' (ibid., 223).
46. *The Isle of Ladies*, ed. Pearsall, p. 136, lines 1301–49n.
47. *The Floure and the Leafe*, in *The Floure and the Leafe, The Assembly of Ladies, The Isle of Ladies*, ed. Derek Pearsall (Kalamazoo, MI, 1990, pp. 1–29 (2). All quotations, by line number, are from this edition.
48. This further serves to ally the *Floure*-narrator with the company of the Leaf, which eschews amatory turbulence: see Ad Putter, 'Fifteenth-century Chaucerian visions', in Julia Boffey and A. S. G. Edwards (eds), *A Companion to Fifteenth-Century English Poetry* (Cambridge, 2013), pp. 143–4.
49. All citations from *The Kingis Quair* in Linne R. Mooney and Mary-Jo Arn (eds), *The Kingis Quair and Other Prison Poems* (Kalamazoo, MI, 2005), pp. 17–112, by line number.
50. *The Kingis Quair*, ed. Mooney and Arn, p. 82, lines 8–14n.
51. A. C. Spearing, 'Dreams in *The Kingis Quair* and the Duke's Book', in Mary-Jo Arn (ed.), *Charles d'Orléans in England (1415–1440)* (Cambridge and Rochester, NY, 2000), pp. 127–9.
52. On this point, see Joanna Summers, *Late-Medieval Prison Writing and the Politics of Autobiography* (Oxford, 2004), p. 74.
53. Phillips, '*The Book of the Duchess*, Lines 31–96', p. 115 n. 16 adduces *BD* as a possible source for lines 15 and 231 of Henryson's *Testament of Cresseid*,

but the conventional imagery in these lines does not support a connection. Phillips does not consider the points raised here.

54. See the discussion of *BD*'s stance on dreaming in chapter 1, pp. 38–42.

55. This parallel is noted in Thomas William Nadal, 'Spenser's *Daphnaïda*, and Chaucer's *Book of the Duchess*', *PMLA*, 23/4 (1908), 647 n. 1, and demonstrated more fully in Donald Cheney, 'Grief and creativity in Spenser's *Daphnaïda*', in Jennifer C. Vaught (ed.), *Grief and Gender: 700–1700* (New York and Houndmills, Hants., 2003), pp. 125–7.

56. Normand Berlin, 'Chaucer's *The Book of the Duchess* and Spenser's *Daphnaïda*', 282–9.

57. The edition used is Edmund Spenser, *The Minor Poems*, ed. Charles Grosvenor Osgood and Henry Gibbons Lotspeich, vol. 1 (Baltimore, 1943), pp. 125–42, cited by line number.

58. Cheney, 'Grief and creativity', p. 130.

59. On this point, see William A. Oram, '*Daphnaida* and Spenser's Later Poetry', *Spenser Studies*, 2 (1981), 141–58.

60. Duncan Harris and Nancy L. Steffen, 'The Other Side of the Garden: An Interpretive Comparison of Chaucer's *Book of the Duchess* and Spenser's *Daphnaïda*', *Journal of Medieval and Renaissance Studies*, 8/1 (1978), 27.

61. See Lou Thompson, 'Browning's My Last Duchess', *Explicator*, 42/1 (1983), 23–4.

'Now hit ys doon': Conclusion

1. Roland Barthes, 'The death of the author', in *The Rustle of Language*, trans. Richard Howard (New York, 1986), pp. 52, 54. For Barthes's definition of a 'writerly' (*scriptible*) text as occupying a 'perpetual present', see Barthes, *S/Z*, trans. Richard Miller (New York, 1974), p. 5.

2. Butterfield, 'Chaucer's French inheritance', p. 28.

3. Compare Coldiron's discussion of the 'intersection of imitation and self-fashioning' in early modern lyric, in which 'the translator-poet necessarily takes another's words to construct the lyric persona, "I", self, or subject' (*Canon, Period, and the Poetry of Charles of Orleans*, p. 41).

4. Umberto Eco, *Experiences in Translation*, trans. Alastair McEwen (Toronto, 2001), p. 21.

5. *Pace* Klitgård, 'Chaucer as Performer', 101–6, who argues for a context of oral performance despite the textual orientation of comments such as 'I, that made this book'.

6. For a theorization of Chaucer's 'autofictional persona' that emphasizes its illusory nature, see Gust, *Constructing Chaucer*, pp. 1–50.

7. Trigg, *Congenial Souls*, pp. 140, 196.

8. Bowers, *Chaucer and Langland*, p. 30.

9. Trigg, *Congenial Souls*, p. 196; cf. p. 134.

10. Ibid., p. 140.

11. See Lerer, *Chaucer and His Readers*, p. 21.

12. Brantley L. Bryant, *Geoffrey Chaucer Hath a Blog: Medieval Studies and New Media* (New York and Basingstoke, 2010), p. 20; Kathleen Forni, *Chaucer's Afterlife: Adaptations in Recent Popular Culture* (Jefferson, NC and London, 2013), p. 17.
13. Bryant, *Geoffrey Chaucer Hath a Blog*, p. 19.
14. Ibid., p. 22.
15. Chaucer's intractable son Lowys, for example, speaks Modern English in a hip-hop argot, in contrast to which Chaucer's semi-modern Middle English sounds hopelessly old-fashioned; the two inevitably have difficulty communicating ('April 19, 2006: Straight Out of London', in Bryant, *Geoffrey Chaucer Hath a Blog*, pp. 77–8).

BIBLIOGRAPHY

Primary Sources

Charles of Orleans, *Fortunes Stabilnes: Charles of Orleans's English Book of Love*, ed. Mary-Jo Arn (Binghamton, NY, 1994).

Chaucer, Geoffrey, *The Book of the Duchess*, ed. Helen Phillips (Durham, 1982).

—— 'The Book of the Duchess', ed. Helen Phillips, in *Chaucer's Dream Poetry*, ed. Helen Phillips and Nick Havely (London and New York, 1997), pp. 29–111.

—— *The Complete Poetry and Prose of Geoffrey Chaucer*, ed. Mark Allen and John H. Fisher, 3rd edn (Boston, 2012).

—— *Dream Visions and Other Poems*, ed. Kathryn L. Lynch (New York and London, 2007).

—— *The Minor Poems: Part One*, in *A Variorum Edition of the Works of Geoffrey Chaucer*, ed. George B. Pace and Alfred David, vol. 5 (Norman, OK, 1982).

—— *The Riverside Chaucer*, gen. ed. Larry D. Benson, 3rd edn (Boston, 1987).

Crow, Martin M. and Clair C. Olson (eds), *Chaucer Life-Records* (Oxford, 1966).

Donaldson, E. T., *Chaucer's Poetry: An Anthology for the Modern Reader* (New York, 1958).

Forni, Kathleen (ed.), *The Chaucerian Apocrypha: A Selection* (Kalamazoo, MI, 2005).

Froissart, Jean, *An Anthology of Narrative & Lyric Poetry*, ed. and trans. Kristen M. Figg with R. Barton Palmer (New York and London, 2001).

—— *Le Paradys d'Amours*, in *Œuvres de Froissart: Poésies*, ed. August Scheler, vol. 1 (Brussels, 1870), pp. 1–32.

Gower, John, *Confessio Amantis*, ed. Russell A. Peck with Andrew Galloway, 2nd edn, vol. 1 (Kalamazoo, MI, 2006).

—— *Confessio Amantis*, ed. Russell A. Peck with Andrew Galloway, vol. 2 (Kalamazoo, MI, 2003).

—— *The English Works of John Gower*, ed. G. C. Macaulay, EETS e.s., 81–2, 2 vols (London, 1969).

Guillaume de Lorris and Jean de Meun, *Le Roman de la Rose*, ed. Félix Lecoy, 3 vols (Paris, 1973–5).

—— *The Romance of the Rose*, trans. Frances Horgan (Oxford, 1994).

Langland, William, *The Vision of Piers Plowman*, ed. A. V. C. Schmidt (London and Rutland, VT, 1995).

Lydgate, John, *Fall of Princes*, ed. Henry Bergen, EETS e.s., 121–4 (London and Toronto, 1967).

—— *Poems*, ed. John Norton-Smith (Oxford, 1966).

Machaut, Guillaume de, *The Fountain of Love (La Fonteinne Amoureuse) and Two Other Love Vision Poems*, ed. and trans. R. Barton Palmer (New York and London, 1993).

Macrobius, Ambrosius Aurelius Theodosius, *Commentary on the Dream of Scipio*, trans. William Harris Stahl (New York and London, 1952).

McGillivray, Murray, *Geoffrey Chaucer's Book of the Duchess: A Hypertext Edition 2.0*. CD-ROM (Calgary, 1999).

Mooney, Linne R. and Mary-Jo Arn (eds), *The Kingis Quair and Other Prison Poems* (Kalamazoo, MI, 2005).

Norton-Smith, John (ed.), *Bodleian Library MS Fairfax 16* (London, 1979).

Ovid, *Metamorphoses*, ed. and trans. Frank Justus Miller, 3rd edn, 2 vols (Cambridge, MA and London, 1977).

Pearsall, Derek (ed.), *The Floure and the Leafe, The Assembly of Ladies, The Isle of Ladies* (Kalamazoo, MI, 1990).

Robinson, Pamela (ed.), *Manuscript Bodley 638: A Facsimile* (Norman, OK and Woodbridge, Suffolk, 1982).

—— *Manuscript Tanner 346: A Facsimile* (Norman, OK and Woodbridge, Suffolk, 1980).

Skeat, Walter W. (ed.), *Chaucerian and Other Pieces*, in *Supplement to the Works of Geoffrey Chaucer*, vol. 7 (London, 1897).

Speght, Thomas, *The workes of our antient and learned English poet, Geffrey Chaucer, newly printed* (London, 1598).

—— *The workes of our Ancient and learned English Poet, Geoffrey Chavcer, newly printed* (London, 1602).

Spenser, Edmund, *The Minor Poems*, ed. Charles Grosvenor Osgood and Henry Gibbons Lotspeich, vol. 1 (Baltimore, 1943).

Stow, John, *The workes of Geffrey Chaucer, newlie printed, with diuers addicions, whiche were neuer in print before: with the siege and destruccion of the worthy citee of Thebes, compiled by Ihon Lidgate, Monke of Berie* (London, 1561).

Symons, Dana M. (ed.), *Chaucerian Dream Visions and Complaints* (Kalamazoo, MI, 2004).

Thynne, Francis, *Chaucer: Animaduersions uppon the Annotacions and corrections of some imperfections of impressiones of Chaucer's workes [sett downe before tyme and nowe] reprinted in the yere of our lorde 1598*, EETS o.s., 9 (London and Toronto, 1965).

Thynne, William, *The workes of Geffray Chaucer newlye printed, wyth dyuers workes whych were neuer in print before* (London, 1542).

Tyrwhitt, Thomas, *The Canterbury Tales of Chaucer. To Which Are Added an Essay on His Language and Versification, and an Introductory Discourse: Together with Notes and a Glossary*, 2nd edn, 2 vols (Oxford, 1798).

Urry, John, *The Works of Geoffrey Chaucer* (London, 1721).

Watkins, Nicholas and Jacqueline Jenkins (eds), *The Writings of Julian of Norwich:* A Vision Showed to a Devout Woman *and* A Revelation of Love (University Park, PA, 2006).

Secondary Sources

Adams, Jenny, 'Pawn Takes Knight's Queen: Playing with Chess in the *Book of the Duchess*', *ChR*, 34/2 (1999), 125–38.

—— *Power Play: The Literature and Politics of Chess in the Late Middle Ages* (Philadelphia, 2006).

Aers, David R., 'Chaucer's *Book of the Duchess*: An Art to Consume Art', *Durham University Journal* n.s., 38/2 (69/2) (1977), 201–5.

Akbari, Suzanne Conklin, *Seeing through the Veil: Optical Theory and Medieval Allegory* (Toronto, 2004).

Amtower, Laurel, *Engaging Words: The Culture of Reading in the Later Middle Ages* (New York, 2000).

Anderson, J. J., 'The Man in Black, Machaut's Knight, and Their Ladies', *English Studies*, 73/5 (1992), 417–30.

Anderson, Marjorie, 'Blanche, Duchess of Lancaster', *Modern Philology*, 45/3 (1948), 152–9.

Arner, Lynn, *Chaucer, Gower, and the Vernacular Rising: Poetry and the Problem of the Populace after 1381* (University Park, PA, 2013).

Bahr, Arthur W., 'The Rhetorical Construction of Narrator and Narrative in Chaucer's The *Book of the Duchess*', *ChR*, 35/1 (2000), 43–59.

Bakalian, Ellen Shaw, *Aspects of Love in John Gower's* Confessio Amantis (New York and London, 2004).

Baker, Donald C., 'The Dreamer Again in *The Book of the Duchess*', *PMLA* 70/1 (1955), 279–82.

—— 'Imagery and Structure in Chaucer's *Book of the Duchess*', *Studia Neophilologica*, 30/1 (1958), 17–26.

Barchiesi, Alessandro, *Speaking Volumes: Narrative and Intertext in Ovid and Other Latin Poets*, ed. and trans. Matt Fox and Simone Marchesi (London, 2001).

Barootes, Benjamin S. W., 'The poetics of the elegiac dream vision in Middle English literature' (unpublished PhD thesis, McGill University, 2014).

Barthes, Roland, 'The death of the author', in *The Rustle of Language*, trans. Richard Howard (New York, 1986), pp. 49-64.

—— *S/Z*, trans. Richard Miller (New York, 1974).

Benson, Larry D., 'The beginnings of Chaucer's English style', in Theodore M. Andersson and Stephen A. Barney (eds), *Contradictions: from Beowulf to Chaucer* (Aldershot and Brookfield, VT, 1995), pp. 243–65.

Berlin, Normand, 'Chaucer's *The Book of the Duchess* and Spenser's *Daphnaida*: A Contrast', *Studia Neophilologica*, 38/2 (1966), 282–9.

Besserman, Lawrence, *Chaucer's Biblical Poetics* (Norman, OK, 1998).

Bianco, Susan, 'A Black Monk in the Rose Garden: Lydgate and the *Dit Amoureux* Tradition', *ChR*, 34/1 (1999), 60–8.

—— 'New perspectives on Lydgate's courtly verse', in Helen Cooney (ed.), *Nation, Court and Culture: New Essays on Fifteenth-Century English Poetry* (Dublin and Portland, OR, 2001), pp. 95–115.

Bishop, Louise M., *Words, Stones, and Herbs: The Healing Word in Medieval and Early Modern England* (Syracuse, NY, 2007).

Blake, N. F., '*The Book of the Duchess* Again', *English Studies*, 67/2 (1986), 122–5.

—— 'The Textual Tradition of *The Book of the Duchess*', *English Studies*, 62/3 (1981), 237–48.

Blamires, Alcuin, *Chaucer, Ethics, and Gender* (Oxford, 2006).

Blodgett, James E., 'William Thynne (d. 1546)', in Ruggiers (ed.), *Editing Chaucer*, pp. 35–52.

Boardman, Phillip C.,'Courtly Language and the Strategy of Consolation in the *Book of the Duchess*', *ELH*, 44/4 (1977), 567–79.

Boffey, Julia, 'Charles of Orleans reading Chaucer's dream visions', in Piero Boitani and Anna Torti (eds), *Mediaevalitas: Reading the Middle Ages* (Cambridge and Rochester, NY, 1996), pp. 43–62.

—— 'The Lyrics in Chaucer's Longer Poems', *Poetica*, 37 (1993), 15–37.

—— 'The Reputation and Circulation of Chaucer's Lyrics in the Fifteenth Century', *ChR*, 28/1 (1993), 23–40.

Boitani, Piero, 'Old books brought to life in dreams: The *Book of the Duchess*, the *House of Fame*, the *Parliament of Fowls*', in Boitani and Mann (eds), *The Cambridge Companion to Chaucer*, pp. 58–77.

Boitani, Piero and Jill Mann (eds), *The Cambridge Companion to Chaucer*, 2nd edn (Cambridge, 2003).

Bolens, Guillemette and Paul Beckman Taylor, 'Chess, Clocks, and Counsellors in Chaucer's *Book of the Duchess*', *ChR*, 35/3 (2001), 281–93.

—— 'The Game of Chess in Chaucer's *Book of the Duchess*', *ChR*, 32/4 (1998), 325–34.

Bowers, John M., *Chaucer and Langland: The Antagonistic Tradition* (Notre Dame, IN, 2007).

Braddy, Haldeen, *Chaucer and the French Poet, Graunson* (Baton Rouge, 1947).

—— 'Chaucer's *Book of the Duchess* and Two of Granson's *Complaintes*', *MLN*, 52/7 (1937), 487–91.

Bronson, Bertrand H., '*The Book of the Duchess* Re-Opened', *PMLA*, 67/5 (1952), 863–81.

Broughton, Bradford B., 'Chaucer's "Book of the Duchess": did John [of Gaunt] love Blanche [of Lancaster]?', in Broughton (ed.), *Twenty-Seven to One: A Potpourri of Humanistic Material Presented to Dr. Donald Gale Stillman on the Occasion of His Retirement from Clarkson College of Technology* (Potsdam, NY, 1970), 71–84.

Brown, Peter, *Chaucer and the Making of Optical Space* (Oxford and Bern, 2007).

Brownlee, Kevin, *Poetic Identity in Guillaume de Machaut* (Madison, WI, 1984).

Brusendorff, Aage, *The Chaucer Tradition* (1925; Oxford, 1967).

Bryant, Brantley L., *Geoffrey Chaucer Hath a Blog: Medieval Studies and New Media* (New York and Basingstoke, 2010).

Buckler, Patricia Prandini, 'Love and death in Chaucer's *The Book of the Duchess*', in JoAnna Stephens Mink and Janet Doubler Ward (eds), *Joinings and Disjoinings: The Significance of Marital Status in Literature* (Bowling Green, OH, 1991), pp. 6–18.

Burlin, Robert B., *Chaucerian Fiction* (Princeton, 1977).

Burnley, David, 'Some Terminology of Perception in the *Book of the Duchess*', *ELN*, 23/3 (1986), 15–22.

Burrow, J. A., 'Politeness and privacy: Chaucer's *Book of the Duchess*', in Anne Marie D'Arcy and Alan J. Fletcher (eds), *Studies in Late Medieval and Early Renaissance Texts in Honour of John Scattergood: 'The key of all good remembrance'* (Dublin, 2005), pp. 65–75.

Butterfield, Ardis, 'Chaucer's French inheritance', in Boitani and Mann (eds), *The Cambridge Companion to Chaucer*, pp. 20–35.

—— '*Confessio Amantis* and the French tradition', in Siân Echard (ed.), *A Companion to Gower* (Cambridge and Rochester, NY, 2004), pp. 165–80.

—— *The Familiar Enemy: Chaucer, Language and Nation in the Hundred Years War* (Oxford, 2009).

—— 'Lyric and Elegy in *The Book of the Duchess*', *Medium Ævum*, 60 (1991), 33–60.

—— 'Medieval Genres and Modern Genre Theory', *Paragraph: A Journal of Modern Critical Theory*, 13/2 (1990), 184–201.

—— 'Pastoral and the Politics of Plague in Machaut and Chaucer', *SAC*, 16 (1994), 3–27.

Calin, William, *The French Tradition and the Literature of Medieval England* (Toronto, 1994).

—— 'Machaut's legacy: the Chaucerian inheritance reconsidered', in R. Barton Palmer (ed.), *Chaucer's French Contemporaries: The Poetry/Poetics of Self and Tradition* (New York, 1999), pp. 29–46.

Carruthers, Mary [J.], *The Book of Memory: A Study of Memory in Medieval Culture* (Cambridge, 1990).

—— '"The mystery of the bed chamber": mnemotechnique and vision in Chaucer's *The Book of the Duchess*', in Hill and Sinnreich-Levi (eds), *The Rhetorical Poetics of the Middle Ages*, pp. 67–87.

Cartier, Normand R., 'Le *Bleu chevalier* de Froissart et le *Livre de la Duchesse* de Chaucer', *Romania*, 88 (1967), 232–52.

Cawsey, Kathy, *Twentieth-Century Chaucer Criticism: Reading Audiences* (Farnham and Burlington, VT, 2011).

Chance, Jane, 'Chaucerian Irony in the Verse Epistles "Wordes Unto Adam," "Lenvoy a Scogan," and "Lenvoy a Bukton"', *Papers on Language & Literature*, 21/2 (1985), 115–28.

Chandler, Daniel, 'An Introduction to Genre Theory' (www document), *http://www.aber.ac.uk/media/Documents/intgenre/chandler_genre_theory.pdf* (accessed 23 August 2013).

Cheney, Donald, 'Grief and creativity in Spenser's *Daphnaïda*', in Jennifer C. Vaught (ed.), *Grief and Gender: 700–1700* (New York and Houndmills, Hants., 2003), pp. 123–31.

Cherniss, Michael [D.], *Boethian Apocalypse: Studies in Middle English Vision Poetry* (Norman, OK, 1987).

—— 'The Boethian Dialogue in Chaucer's *Book of the Duchess*', *JEGP*, 68 (1969), 655–65.

—— 'The Narrator Asleep and Awake in Chaucer's *Book of the Duchess*', *Papers on Language and Literature*, 8/2 (1972), 115–26.

Clemen, W. H., *Chaucer's Early Poetry*, trans. C. A. M. Sym (London, 1963).

Coghill, Nevill, *The Poet Chaucer*, rev. edn (London, 1964).

Coldiron, A. E. B., *Canon, Period, and the Poetry of Charles of Orleans: Found in Translation* (Ann Arbor, 2000).

Coley, David K., '*Pearl* and the Narrative of Pestilence', *SAC*, 35 (2013), 209–62.

Condren, Edward I., *Chaucer from Prentice to Poet: The Metaphor of Love in Dream Visions and* Troilus and Criseyde (Gainesville, FL, 2008).

—— 'Of Deaths and Duchesses and Scholars Coughing in Ink', *ChR*, 10/1 (1975), 87–95.

—— 'The Historical Context of the *Book of the Duchess:* A New Hypothesis', *ChR*, 5/3 (1971), 195–212.

Connolly, Margaret, 'Chaucer and Chess', *ChR*, 29/1 (1994), 40–4.

Cooley, Franklin D., 'Two Notes on the Chess Terms in *The Book of the Duchess*', *MLN*, 63/1 (1948), 30–5.

Crampton, Georgia Ronan, 'Transitions and Meaning in *The Book of the Duchess*', *JEGP*, 62 (1963), 486–500.

Crane, Susan, 'Froissart's *Dit dou bleu chevalier* as a Source for Chaucer's *Book of the Duchess*', *Medium Ævum*, 61/1 (1992), 59–74.

Crocker, Holly A., *Chaucer's Visions of Manhood* (New York and Basingstoke, 2007).

Curtius, Ernst Robert, *European Literature and the Latin Middle Ages*, trans. Willard R. Trask (New York, 1953).

Dane, Joseph A., *Who Is Buried in Chaucer's Tomb?: Studies in the Reception of Chaucer's Book* (East Lansing, MI, 1998).

Davenport, W. A., *Chaucer: Complaint and Narrative* (Cambridge, 1988).

David, Alfred, 'Chaucer's Edwardian poetry', in James M. Dean and Christian K. Zacher (eds), *The Idea of Medieval Literature: New Essays on Chaucer and Medieval Culture in Honor of Donald R. Howard* (Newark, DE; London and Toronto, 1992), pp. 35–54.

Davidoff, Judith M., *Beginning Well: Framing Fictions in Late Middle English Poetry* (Rutherford, NJ; London and Toronto, 1998).

Davis, Steven, 'Guillaume de Machaut, Chaucer's *Book of the Duchess*, and the Chaucer Tradition', *ChR*, 36/4 (2002), 391–405.

Dean, James, 'Chaucer's *Book of the Duchess*: A Non-Boethian Interpretation', *MLQ*, 46/3 (1985), 235–49.

Delasanta, Rodney, 'Christian Affirmation in *The Book of the Duchess*', *PMLA*, 84 (1969), 245–51.

Diekstra, F. [N. M.], 'Chaucer and the Romance of the Rose', *English Studies*, 69/1 (1988), 12–26.

—— 'Chaucer's Way with His Sources: Accident into Substance and Substance into Accident', *English Studies*, 62/3 (1981), 215–36.

Dinshaw, Carolyn, *Chaucer's Sexual Poetics* (Madison, WI, 1989).

Donnelly, Colleen, 'Challenging the Conventions of Dream Vision in *The Book of the Duchess*', *Philological Quarterly*, 66/4 (1987), 421–35.

—— 'Chaucer's Sense of an Ending', *Journal of the Rocky Mountain Medieval and Renaissance Association*, 11 (1990), 19–32.

Downes, Stephanie, 'After Deschamps: Chaucer's French fame', in Isabel Davis and Catherine Nall (eds), *Chaucer and Fame: Reputation and Reception* (Cambridge, 2015), pp. 127–42.

Eco, Umberto, *Experiences in Translation*, trans. Alastair McEwen (Toronto, 2001).

—— 'The poetics of the open work', in *The Role of the Reader: Explorations in the Semiotics of Texts* (Bloomington, IN, 1979), pp. 47–66.

Edwards, Robert, 'The *Book of the Duchess* and the Beginnings of Chaucer's Narrative', *New Literary History*, 13/2 (1982), 189–204.

—— *The Dream of Chaucer: Representation and Reflection in the Early Narratives* (Durham, NC and London, 1989).

Ellis, Steve, *Chaucer at Large: The Poet in the Modern Imagination* (Minneapolis, 2000).

—— 'The Death of the *Book of the Duchess*', *ChR*, 29/3 (1995), 249–58.

Ellmann, Maud, 'Blanche', in Jeremy Hawthorn (ed.), *Criticism and Critical Theory* (London and Baltimore, MD, 1984), pp. 99–110.

Emerson, Oliver Farrar, 'Chaucer and Medieval Hunting', *Romanic Review*, 13 (1922), 115–50.

Evans, Ruth et al., 'The notion of vernacular theory', in Wogan-Browne et al. (eds), *The Idea of the Vernacular*, pp. 314–30.

Farber, Annika, 'Usurping "Chaucers dreame": *Book of the Duchess* and the Apocryphal *Isle of Ladies*', *Studies in Philology*, 105/2 (2008), 207–25.

Farrell, Thomas J., 'The "Envoy de Chaucer" and the *Clerk's Tale*', *ChR*, 24/4 (1990), 329–36.

Ferris, Sumner, 'John Stow and the Tomb of Blanche the Duchess', *ChR*, 18/1 (1983), 92–3.

Ferster, Judith, 'Intention and Interpretation in the "Book of the Duchess"', *Criticism*, 22/1 (1980), 1–24.

Fichte, Joerg O., '*The Book of the Duchess* – A Consolation?', *Studia Neophilologica*, 45/1 (1973), 53–67.

—— *Chaucer's 'Art Poetical': A Study in Chaucerian Poetics* (Tübingen, 1980).

Figg, Kristen M., 'The Narrative of Selection in Jean Froissart's Collected Poems: Omissions and Additions in BN MSS fr. 830 and 831', *Journal of the Early Book Society*, 5 (2002), 37–55.

Finlayson, John, 'The *Roman de la rose* and Chaucer's Narrators', *ChR*, 24/3 (1990), 187–210.

Fisher, John H., 'A Language Policy for Lancastrian England', *PMLA*, 107/5 (1992), 1168–80.

Fleay, F. G., *Guide to Chaucer and Spenser* (London and Glasgow, 1877).

Forni, Kathleen, *The Chaucerian Apocrypha: A Counterfeit Canon* (Gainesville, FL, 2001).

—— *Chaucer's Afterlife: Adaptations in Recent Popular Culture* (Jefferson, NC and London, 2013).

—— '"Chaucer's Dreame": A Bibliographer's Nightmare', *Huntington Library Quarterly*, 64/1–2 (2001), 139–50.

Foster, Edward E., 'Allegorical Consolation in *The Book of the Duchess*', *Ball State University Forum*, 11/4 (1971), 14-20.

Foster, Michael, 'On Dating the Duchess: The Personal and Social Context of *Book of the Duchess*', *Review of English Studies*, 59/239 (2007), 185–96.

Fradenburg, Louise O. [Aranye], '"My worldes blisse": Chaucer's Tragedy of Fortune', *South Atlantic Quarterly*, 98/3 (1999), 563–92.

—— *Sacrifice Your Love: Psychoanalysis, Historicism, Chaucer* (Minneapolis, 2002).

—— '"Voice memorial": Loss and Reparation in Chaucer's Poetry', spec. issue on 'Reconceiving Chaucer: Literary Theory and Historical Interpretation', ed. Thomas Hahn, *Exemplaria*, 2/1 (1990), 169–202.

French, W. H., 'The Man in Black's Lyric', *JEGP*, 56/2 (1957), 231–41.

—— 'Medieval Chess and the *Book of the Duchess*', *MLN*, 64/4 (1949), 261–4.

Fumo, Jamie C., 'Ancient Chaucer: temporalities of fame', in *Chaucer and Fame: Reputation and Reception*, ed. Isabel Davis and Catherine Nall (Cambridge, 2015), pp. 201–20.

—— 'The consolations of philosophy: later medieval elegy', in Karen
　　Weisman (ed.), *The Oxford Handbook of the Elegy* (Oxford, 2010),
　　pp. 118–34.

—— 'Ovid: artistic identity and intertextuality', in *Oxford Handbook to
　　Chaucer*, ed. Suzanne Conklin Akbari (Oxford, forthcoming).

Furnivall, Frederick James, *Trial-Forewards to My 'Parallel-Text Edition of
　　Chaucer's Minor Poems'* (London, 1871).

Fyler, John M., 'Froissart and Chaucer', in Donald Maddox and Sara
　　Sturm-Maddox (eds), *Froissart across the Genres* (Gainesville, FL,
　　1998), pp. 195–218.

Galloway, Andrew, 'Reassessing Gower's dream-visions', in Elisabeth Dutton
　　with John Hines and R. F. Yeager (eds), *John Gower, Trilingual Poet:
　　Language, Translation, and Tradition* (Cambridge, 2010), pp. 288–303.

Galway, Margaret, 'Chaucer's Hopeless Love,' *MLN*, 60/7 (1945), 431–9.

Gamaury, Martine, 'Le Livre du rêve, le rêve du livre: réflexions sur
　　l'écriture du rêve dans *Le Livre de la Duchesse* de Chaucer (1368)', in
　　Colette Stévanovitch (ed.), *L'articulation langue-littérature dans les
　　textes médiévaux anglais: Actes du colloque des 25 et 26 juin 1999 à
　　l'Université de Nancy II*, Publications de l'AMAES, Collection GRENDEL
　　no. 3 (Nancy, 1999), pp. 175–92.

Gardner, John, 'Style as Meaning in the *Book of the Duchess*', *Language
　　and Style: An International Journal*, 2 (1969), 143–71.

Gaylord, Alan T., 'Reflections on D. W. Robertson, Jr., and "Exegetical
　　Criticism"', *ChR*, 40/3 (2006), 311–33.

Gellrich, Jesse M., *The Idea of the Book in the Middle Ages: Language
　　Theory, Mythology, and Fiction* (Ithaca and London, 1985).

Gilbert, Jane, *Living Death in Medieval French and English Literature*
　　(Cambridge and New York, 2011).

Gillespie, Alexandra. *Print Culture and the Medieval Author: Chaucer,
　　Lydgate, and Their Books 1473–1557* (Oxford, 2007).

Godwin, William, *Life of Geoffrey Chaucer, the Early English Poet:
　　Including Memoirs of His Near Friend and Kinsman, John of Gaunt,
　　Duke of Lancaster*, 2 vols (London, 1803).

Grabes, Herbert, *The Mutable Glass: Mirror-Imagery in Titles and Texts of
　　the Middle Ages and the English Renaissance* (Cambridge, 1982).

Grennen, Joseph E., '*Hert-huntyng* in the *Book of the Duchess*', *MLQ*,
　　25/2 (1964), 131–9.

Grmek, Mirko D., 'The concept of disease', in Mirko D. Grmek (ed.),
　　Western Medical Thought from Antiquity to the Middle Ages, trans.
　　Antony Shugaar (Cambridge, MA and London, 1998), pp. 241–58.

Grudin, Michaela Paasche, *Chaucer and the Politics of Discourse* (Columbia, SC, 1996).

Gust, Geoffrey W., *Constructing Chaucer: Author and Autofiction in the Critical Tradition* (New York and Basingstoke, 2009).

Guthrie, Steve, 'Dialogics and prosody in Chaucer', in Thomas J. Farrell (ed.), *Bakhtin and Medieval Voices* (Gainesville, FL, 1995), pp. 94–108.

Hallissey, Margaret, *Clean Maids, True Wives, Steadfast Widows: Chaucer's Women and Medieval Codes of Conduct* (Westport, CT and London, 1993).

Hammond, Eleanor Prescott, *Chaucer: A Bibliographic Manual* (New York, 1933).

—— *English Verse between Chaucer and Surrey* (New York, 1969).

Hansen, Elaine Tuttle, *Chaucer and the Fictions of Gender* (Berkeley, 1992).

Hardman, Phillipa, '"Ars celare artem": Interpreting the Black Knight's "Lay" in Chaucer's *Book of the Duchess*', *Poetica*, 37 (1992), 49–57.

—— 'The *Book of the Duchess* as a Memorial Monument', *ChR*, 28/3 (1994), 205–15.

Harris, Duncan and Nancy L. Steffen, 'The Other Side of the Garden: An Interpretive Comparison of Chaucer's *Book of the Duchess* and Spenser's *Daphnaida*', *Journal of Medieval and Renaissance Studies*, 8/1 (1978), 17–36.

Heffernan, Carol Falvo, *The Melancholy Muse: Chaucer, Shakespeare and Early Medicine* (Pittsburgh, 1995).

Heinrichs, Katherine, *The Myths of Love: Classical Lovers in Medieval Literature* (University Park, PA and London, 1990).

Hendershot, Cyndy, 'Male subjectivity, *fin amor*, and melancholia in *The Book of the Duchess*', *Mediaevalia*, 21 (1996), 1–26.

Herzog, Michael B., 'The *Book of the Duchess*: The Vision of the Artist as a Young Dreamer', *ChR*, 22/4 (1988), 269–81.

Hill, John M., 'The *Book of the Duchess*, Melancholy, and That Eight-Year Sickness', *ChR*, 9/1 (1974), 35–50.

Hill, John M. and Deborah M. Sinnreich-Levi (eds), *The Rhetorical Poetics of the Middle Ages: Reconstructive Polyphony – Essays in Honor of Robert O. Payne* (Madison and Teaneck, NJ; London, 2000).

Hinton, Norman D., 'The Black Death and the Book of the Duchess', in Donald E. Hayden (ed.), *His Firm Estate: Essays in Honor of Franklin James Eikenberry* (Tulsa, 1967), pp. 72–8.

Hodges, Laura F., 'Sartorial Signs in *Troilus and Criseyde*', *ChR*, 35/3 (2001), 223–59.

Hooper, Teresa, 'Chaucer's Whelp: Consolation and the Limits of Reason in the *Book of the Duchess*', *Medieval Perspectives*, 21 (2005), 58–75.

Horowitz, Deborah, 'An Aesthetic of Permeability: Three Transcapes of the *Book of the Duchess*', *ChR*, 39/3 (2005), 259–79.

Horvath, Richard P., 'Chaucer's Epistolary Poetic: The Envoys to Bukton and Scogan', *ChR*, 37/2 (2002), 173–89.

Huppé, Bernard and D. W. Robertson, Jr, *Fruyt and Chaf: Studies in Chaucer's Allegories* (Port Washington, NY and London, 1972).

Irvine, Martin, '"Bothe text and gloss": manuscript form, the textuality of commentary, and Chaucer's dream poems', in Charlotte Cook Morse, Penelope Reed Doob and Marjorie Curry Woods (eds), *The Uses of Manuscripts in Literary Studies: Essays in Memory of Judson Boyce Allen* (Kalamazoo, MI, 1992), pp. 81–120.

Jager, Eric, *The Book of the Heart* (Chicago and London, 2000).

Jordan, Robert M., 'The Compositional Structure of the *Book of the Duchess*', *ChR*, 9/2 (1974), 99–117.

Justice, Steven, 'Who Stole Robertson?', *PMLA*, 124/2 (2009), 609–15.

Kamath, Stephanie A. Viereck Gibbs, *Authorship and First-Person Allegory in Late Medieval France and England* (Woodbridge, Suffolk and Rochester, NY, 2012).

Kellogg, Alfred L., *Chaucer, Langland, Arthur: Essays in Middle English Literature* (New Brunswick, NJ, 1972).

Kensak, Michael, '"My first matere I wil yow telle": losing (and finding) your place in Chaucer's *The Book of the Duchess*', in T. L. Burton and John F. Plummer (eds), *'Seyd in forme and reverence': Essays on Chaucer and Chaucerians in Memory of Emerson Brown, Jr.* (Adelaide, Australia and Provo, UT, 2005), pp. 83–96.

Kiser, Lisa J., 'Sleep, Dreams, and Poetry in Chaucer's *Book of the Duchess*', *Papers on Language and Literature*, 19/1 (1983), 3–12.

Kittredge, G[eorge]. L[yman], 'Chauceriana', *Modern Philology*, 7/4 (1910), 465–83.

—— 'Chaucer's *Envoy to Bukton*', *MLN*, 24 (1909), 14–15.

—— 'Guillaume de Machaut and *The Book of the Duchess*', *PMLA*, 30/1 (1915), 1–24.

Klitgård, Ebbe. 'Chaucer as Performer: Narrative Strategies in the Dream Visions', *Revista Canaria de Estudios Ingleses*, 47 (2003), 101–14.

Knedlik, Will Roger, 'Chaucer's *Book of the Duchess*: a bibliographical compendium of the first 600 years' (unpublished PhD thesis, University of Washington, 1978).

Knight, Stephen, 'Classicizing Christianity in Chaucer's dream poems: the *Book of the Duchess*, *Book of Fame* and *Parliament of Fowls*', in Helen Phillips (ed.), *Chaucer and Religion* (Cambridge, 2010), pp. 143–55.

Kreuzer, James R., 'The Dreamer in the *Book of the Duchess*', *PMLA*, 66/4 (1951), 543–7.

Kruger, Steven F., *Dreaming in the Middle Ages* (Cambridge, 1992).

—— 'Medical and moral authority in the late medieval dream', in Peter Brown (ed.), *Reading Dreams: The Interpretation of Dreams from Chaucer to Shakespeare* (Oxford and New York, 1999), pp. 51–83.

Krummel, Miriamne Ara, 'The Tale of Ceïx and Alceone: Alceone's Agency and Gower's "audible mime"', *Exemplaria*, 13/2 (2001), 497–528.

Lacan, Jacques, 'The function and field of speech and language in psychoanalysis', in *Écrits: A Selection*, trans. Alan Sheridan (New York, 1977), pp. 30-113.

Lassahn, Nicole, 'Literary Representations of History in Fourteenth Century England: Shared Technique and Divergent Practice in Chaucer and Langland', *Essays in Medieval Studies*, 17 (2000), 49–64.

Lawlor, John, 'The Pattern of Consolation in *The Book of the Duchess*', *Speculum*, 31/4 (1956), 626–48.

Lawton, David, *Chaucer's Narrators* (Woodbridge, Suffolk and Dover, NH, 1986).

—— 'Voice and public interiorities: Chaucer, Orpheus, Machaut', in Frank Grady and Andrew Galloway (eds), *Answerable Style: The Idea of the Literary in Medieval England* (Columbus, OH, 2013), pp. 284–306.

Lerer, Seth, *Chaucer and His Readers: Imagining the Author in Late-Medieval England* (Princeton, 1993).

Lewis, C. S., *The Allegory of Love: A Study in Medieval Tradition* (London, 1936).

Loomis, Roger Sherman, 'Chaucer's Eight Years' Sickness', *MLN*, 59/3 (1944), 178–81.

Loschiavo, Linda Ann. 'The Birth of "Blanche the Duchesse": 1340 *versus* 1347', *ChR*, 13/2 (1978), 128–32.

Lowell, James R., *Conversations on Some of the Old Poets* (Cambridge, MA, 1845).

Lowes, John Livingston, 'The Dry Sea and the Carrenare', *Modern Philology*, 3/1 (1905), 1–46.

—— *Geoffrey Chaucer* (Bloomington, IN, 1958).

Lumiansky, R. M., 'The Bereaved Narrator in Chaucer's *The Book of the Duchess*', *Tulane Studies in English*, 9 (1959), 5–17.

Lynch, Andrew, "'Taking keep" of the "Book of the Duchess"', in
  Gregory Kratzmann and James Simpson (eds), *Medieval English
  Religious and Ethical Literature: Essays in Honour of G. H. Russell*
  (Cambridge and Dover, NH, 1986), pp. 167–78.
Lynch, Kathryn L., *Chaucer's Philosophical Visions* (Cambridge, 2000).
—— 'Dating Chaucer', *ChR*, 42/1 (2007), 1–22.
Malone, Kemp, *Chapters on Chaucer* (Baltimore, 1951).
Manly, J. M., *Chaucer and the Rhetoricians* (London, 1940).
Manning, Stephen, 'That Dreamer Once More', *PMLA*, 71/3 (1956), 540–1.
Margherita, Gayle, 'Originary fantasies and Chaucer's *Book of the
  Duchess*', in Linda Lomperis and Sarah Stanbury (eds), *Feminist
  Approaches to the Body in Medieval Literature* (Philadelphia, 1993),
  pp. 116–41.
Martin, Ellen E., 'Spenser, Chaucer, and the Rhetoric of Elegy', *Journal of
  Medieval and Renaissance Studies*, 17/1 (1987), 83–109.
Mathews, Johnye E., 'The Black Knight as King of the Castle in "The
  Book of the Duchess"', *The South Central Bulletin*, 31/4 (1971), 200–1.
McClumpha, Charles Flint, 'Chaucer's Dream', *MLN*, 4/3 (1889), 65–7.
McGerr, Rosemarie P., *Chaucer's Open Books: Resistance to Closure in
  Medieval Discourse* (Gainesville, FL, 1998).
McGillivray, Murray. 'Editing Chaucer's Early Poems: A Rationale for
  Virtual Copy-Text', *Florilegium*, 27 (2010), 159–76.
McGrady, Deborah, *Controlling Readers: Guillaume de Machaut and His
  Late Medieval Audience* (Toronto, 2006).
Miller, James, 'How to see through women: medieval blazons and
  the male gaze', in Robert A. Taylor et al. (eds), *The Centre and Its
  Compass: Studies in Medieval Literature in Honor of Professor John
  Leyerle* (Kalamazoo, MI, 1993), pp. 367–88.
Minnis, A[lastair]. J., *Fallible Authors: Chaucer's Pardoner and Wife of
  Bath* (Philadelphia, 2008).
—— *Medieval Theory of Authorship: Scholastic Literary Attitudes in the
  Later Middle Ages* (London, 1984).
—— *Translations of Authority in Medieval English Literature: Valuing the
  Vernacular* (Cambridge and New York, 2009).
Minnis, A. J. with V. J. Scattergood and J. J. Smith, *The Shorter Poems*,
  Oxford Guides to Chaucer (Oxford, 1995).
Mooney, Linne R., 'Chaucer's Scribe', *Speculum*, 81 (2006), 97–138.
Morse, Ruth, 'Understanding the Man in Black', *ChR*, 15/3 (1981), 204–8.
Muscatine, Charles, *Chaucer and the French Tradition* (Berkeley and
  Los Angeles, 1966).

Nadal, Thomas William, 'Spenser's *Daphnaïda*, and Chaucer's *Book of the Duchess*', *PMLA*, 23/4 (1908), 646–61.

Neaman, Judith S., 'Brain Physiology and Poetics in *The Book of the Duchess*', *Res Publica Litterarum: Studies in the Classical Tradition*, 3 (1980), 101–13.

Neuss, Paula, 'Images of Writing and the Book in Chaucer's Poetry', *Review of English Studies* n.s., 32/128 (1981), 385–97.

Nicholson, Peter, *Love and Ethics in Gower's* Confessio Amantis (Ann Arbor, 2005).

Nolan, Barbara, 'The art of expropriation: Chaucer's narrator in *The Book of the Duchess*', in Donald M. Rose (ed.), *New Perspectives in Chaucer Criticism* (Norman, OK, 1981), pp. 203–22.

Olson, Glending, *Literature as Recreation in the Later Middle Ages* (Ithaca and London, 1982).

Oram, William A., '*Daphnaida* and Spenser's Later Poetry', *Spenser Studies*, 2 (1981), 141–58.

Owen, Charles W., 'Chaucer: beginnings', in Hill and Sinnreich-Levi (eds), *The Rhetorical Poetics of the Middle Ages*, pp. 45–66.

Palmer, J. J. N., 'The Historical Context of the *Book of the Duchess*: A Revision', *ChR*, 8/4 (1974), 253–61.

Palmer, R. Barton, '*The Book of the Duchess* and *Fonteinne Amoureuse*: Chaucer and Machaut Reconsidered', *Canadian Review of Comparative Literature*, 7/4 (1980), 380–93.

—— 'Rereading Guillaume de Machaut's vision of love: Chaucer's *Book of the Duchess* as bricolage', in David Galef (ed.), *Second Thoughts: A Focus on Rereading* (Detroit, 1998), pp. 169–95.

Parsons, Ben, 'The *Fall of Princes* and Lydgate's Knowledge of the *Book of the Duchess*', *European English Messenger*, 21/2 (2012), 26–30.

Partridge, Stephen, '"The Makere of this Boke": Chaucer's *Retraction* and the author as scribe and compiler', in Stephen Partridge and Erik Kwakkel (eds), *Author, Reader, Book: Medieval Authorship in Theory and Practice* (Toronto, 2012), pp. 106–53.

Patterson, Lee, *Chaucer and the Subject of History* (Madison, WI, 1991).

—— 'The Disenchanted Classroom', *Exemplaria*, 8/2 (1996), 513–45.

—— *Negotiating the Past: The Historical Understanding of Medieval Literature* (Madison, WI, 1987).

Payne, Robert O., *The Key of Remembrance: A Study of Chaucer's Poetics* (New Haven and London, 1963).

Pearsall, Derek, *John Lydgate* (London, 1970).

—— *John Lydgate [1371–1449]: A Bio-bibliography*, ELS Monograph Series, 71 (Victoria, B.C., 1997).

—— *The Life of Geoffrey Chaucer: A Critical Biography* (Oxford and Cambridge, MA, 1992).

—— 'Thomas Speght (ca. 1550–?)', in Ruggiers (ed.), *Editing Chaucer*, pp. 71–92.

Peck, Russell A., 'Theme and number in Chaucer's *Book of the Duchess*', in Alastair Fowler (ed.), *Silent Poetry: Essays in Numerological Analysis* (London, 1970), pp. 72–115.

Perryman, Judith C., 'Speech and Meaning in "The Book of the Duchess"', *Neuphilologische Mitteilungen*, 85/2 (1984), 227–38.

Phillips, Helen, '*The Book of the Duchess*, Lines 31–96: Are They A Forgery?', *English Studies*, 67/2 (1986), 113–21.

—— 'Fortune and the Lady: Machaut, Chaucer and the Intertextual "Dit"', *Nottingham French Studies*, 38/2 (1999), 120–36.

—— 'Frames and narrators in Chaucerian poetry', in Helen Cooper and Sally Mapstone (eds), *The Long Fifteenth Century: Essays for Douglas Gray* (Oxford, 1997), pp. 71–97.

—— 'Structure and Consolation in the *Book of the Duchess*', *ChR*, 16/2 (1981), 107–18.

Poirion, Daniel, 'DIT, genre littéraire', *Encyclopædia Universalis* (online), consulted 17 August 2014. *http://www.universalis.fr/encyclopedie/ dit-genre-litteraire/*.

Prior, Sandra Pierson, '*Routhe* and *Hert-Huntyng* in the *Book of the Duchess*', *JEGP*, 85 (1986), 3–19.

Putter, Ad, 'Fifteenth-century Chaucerian visions', in Julia Boffey and A. S. G. Edwards (eds), *A Companion to Fifteenth-Century English Poetry* (Cambridge, 2013), pp. 143–56.

Quinn, William A., 'Medieval dream visions: Chaucer's *Book of the Duchess*', in David F. Johnson and Elaine Treharne (eds), *Readings in Medieval Texts: Interpreting Old and Middle English Literature* (Oxford and New York, 2005), pp. 323–36.

Rambuss, Richard, '"Processe of tyme": History, Consolation, and Apocalypse in the *Book of the Duchess*', *Exemplaria*, 2/2 (1990), 659–83.

Renoir, Alain and C. David Benson, 'XVI. John Lydgate', in Albert E. Hartung (gen. ed.), *A Manual of the Writings in Middle English 1050– 1500*, vol. 6 (New Haven, 1980), pp. 1809–1920, 2071–2175.

Robbins, Rossell Hope, 'XI. The Chaucerian apocrypha', in Albert E. Hartung (gen. ed.), *A Manual of the Writings in Middle English 1050– 1500*, vol. 4 (New Haven, 1973), pp. 1061–1101, 1285–1306.

—— 'Geoffroi Chaucier, poète français, Father of English Poetry', *ChR*, 13/2 (1978), 93–115.

Robertson, D. W., Jr, 'The *Book of the Duchess*', in Beryl Rowland (ed.), *Companion to Chaucer Studies*, rev. edn (New York and Oxford, 1979), pp. 403–13.

—— 'The historical setting of Chaucer's *Book of the Duchess*', in John Mahoney and John Esten Keller (eds), *Mediaeval Studies in Honor of Urban Tigner Holmes, Jr* (Chapel Hill, NC, 1965), pp. 169–95; rpt. in D. W. Robertson, Jr., *Essays in Medieval Culture* (Princeton, 1980), pp. 235–56.

—— *A Preface to Chaucer: Studies in Medieval Perspectives* (Princeton, 1962).

Robinson, Ian, *Chaucer and the English Tradition* (Cambridge, 1972).

Robinson, Ian and Doreen M. Thomas, 'Some riddles about *The Death of Blanche* with hints for a few answers', in Loren C. Gruber (ed.), *Essays on Old, Middle, Modern English and Old Icelandic: In Honor of Raymond P. Tripp, Jr.* (Lewiston, NY, 2000), pp. 447–66.

Root, Robert Kilburn, *The Poetry of Chaucer: A Guide to Its Study and Appreciation*, rev. edn (Boston, 1922).

Rosenfeld, Jessica, *Ethics and Enjoyment in Late Medieval Poetry: Love after Aristotle* (Cambridge and New York, 2011).

Rosenthal, Constance L., 'A Possible Source of Chaucer's *Booke of the Duchesse – Li Regret de Guillaume* by Jehan de la Mote', *MLN*, 48/8 (1933), 511–14.

Ross, Diane M., 'The Play of Genres in the *Book of the Duchess*', *ChR*, 19/1 (1984), 1–13.

Ross, Trevor, *The Making of the English Literary Canon: From the Middle Ages to the Late Eighteenth Century* (Montreal, 1998).

Rowland, Beryl, 'Chaucer as a Pawn in The Book of the Duchess', *AN&Q*, 6/1 (1967), 3–6.

—— 'Chaucer's *Duchess* and Chess', *Florilegium*, 16 (1999), 41–59.

—— 'Chaucer's "Mistake": *The Book of the Duchess*, Line 455', *AN&Q*, 4/7 (1966), 99–100.

—— 'The Chess Problem in Chaucer's *Book of the Duchess*', *Anglia*, 80 (1962), 384–9.

—— 'The Whelp in Chaucer's *Book of the Duchess*', *Neuphilologische Mitteilungen*, 66 (1965), 148–60.

Ruggiers, Paul G. (ed.), *Editing Chaucer: The Great Tradition* (Norman, OK, 1984).

Rust, Martha Dana, *Imaginary Worlds in Medieval Books: Exploring the Manuscript Matrix* (New York, 2007).

Ruud, Jay, *'Many a song and many a lecherous lay': Tradition and Individuality in Chaucer's Lyric Poetry* (New York and London, 1992).

Ryan, Marcella, 'The Concept of Textual Unity in Chaucer's Dream-Visions', spec. issue on 'Narrative Issues', ed. John Hay and Marie Maclean, *AUMLA: Journal of the Australasian Universities Language and Literature Association*, 74 (1990), 25–33.

Sadler, Lynn Veach, 'Chaucer's *The Book of the Duchess* and the "Law of Kinde"', *Annuale Mediaevale*, 11 (1970), 51–64.

St John, Michael, *Chaucer's Dream Visions: Courtliness and Individual Identity* (Aldershot and Burlington, VT, 2000).

Salter, Elizabeth, 'Chaucer and Internationalism', *SAC*, 2 (1980), 71–9.

Sandras, E.-G., Étude sur G. Chaucer, considéré comme imitateur des trouvères (Paris, 1859).

Scala, Elizabeth, *Absent Narratives, Manuscript Textuality, and Literary Structure in Late Medieval England* (New York, 2002).

Scattergood, [V.] [J.]ohn, '*Chaucer a Bukton* and Proverbs', *Nottingham Medieval Studies*, 31 (1987), 98–107.

Schibanoff, Susan, *Chaucer's Queer Poetics: Rereading the Dream Trio* (Toronto, 2006).

Schless, Howard, 'A Dating for the *Book of the Duchess*: Line 1314', *ChR*, 19/4 (1985), 273–6.

Schoenbaum, Samuel, 'Chaucer's Black Knight', *MLN*, 68/2 (1953), 121–2.

Severs, J. Burke, 'Chaucer's Self-Portrait in the *Book of the Duchess*', *Philological Quarterly*, 43/1 (1964), 27–39.

—— 'The Sources of "The Book of the Duchess"', *Mediaeval Studies*, 25 (1963), 355–62.

Seymour, M. C., 'Chaucer's *Book of the Duchess:* A Proposal', *Medium Ævum*, 74/1 (2005), 60–70.

Shoaf, R. A., '"Mutatio amoris": "Penitentia" and the Form of *The Book of the Duchess*', *Genre*, 14 (1981), 163–89.

—— 'Stalking the Sorrowful H(e)art: Penitential Lore and the Hunt Scene in Chaucer's *The Book of the Duchess*', *JEGP*, 78 (1979), 313–24.

Sklute, Larry, *Virtue of Necessity: Inconclusiveness and Narrative Form in Chaucer's Poetry* (Columbus, OH, 1984).

Smith, D. Vance, 'Plague, Panic Space, and the Tragic Medieval Household', *South Atlantic Quarterly*, 98/3 (1999), 367–414.

Spearing, A. C., 'Dreams in *The Kingis Quair* and the Duke's Book', in Mary-Jo Arn (ed.), *Charles d'Orléans in England (1415–1440)* (Cambridge and Rochester, NY, 2000), pp. 123–44.

—— 'Literal and Figurative in *The Book of the Duchess*', spec. issue on 'Reconstructing Chaucer', ed. Paul Strohm and Thomas J. Heffernan, *SAC Proceedings*, 1 (1984), 165–71.

—— *Medieval Autographies: The 'I' of the Text* (Notre Dame, IN, 2012).

—— *Medieval Dream-Poetry* (Cambridge, 1976).

—— *The Medieval Poet as Voyeur: Looking and Listening in Medieval Love Narratives* (Cambridge, 1993).

Staley, Lynn, 'Gower, Richard II, Henry of Derby, and the Business of Making Culture', *Speculum*, 75 (2000), 68–96.

Stearns, Marshall W., 'Chaucer Mentions a Book', *MLN*, 57/1 (1942), 28–31.

Stevens, Martin, 'Narrative Focus in *The Book of the Duchess*: A Critical Revaluation', *Annuale Mediaevale*, 7 (1966), 16–32.

Stevenson, S. W., 'Chaucer's Ferses Twelve', *ELH*, 7/3 (1940), 215–22.

Strohm, Paul, 'Chaucer's Audience(s): Fictional, Implied, Intended, Actual', *ChR*, 18/2 (1983), 137–45.

—— *Social Chaucer* (Cambridge, MA and London, 1989).

Sturges, Robert S., *Medieval Interpretation: Models of Reading in Literary Narrative, 1100–1500* (Carbondale and Edwardsville, IL, 1991).

Summers, Joanna, *Late-Medieval Prison Writing and the Politics of Autobiography* (Oxford, 2004).

Sypherd, W. Owen, 'Chaucer's Eight Years' Sickness', *MLN*, 20/8 (1905), 240–3.

—— *'Le songe vert* and Chaucer's Dream-Poems', *MLN*, 24/2 (1909), 46–7.

Taggie, Benjamin F., 'John of Gaunt, Geoffrey Chaucer and "O noble, o worthy Petro, glorie of Spayne"', *Fifteenth Century Studies*, 10 (1984), 195–228.

Tatlock, J. S. P., *The Mind and Art of Chaucer* (New York, 1966).

Taylor, Mark N., 'Chaucer's Knowledge of Chess', *ChR*, 38/4 (2004), 299–313.

Thompson, Lou, 'Browning's My Last Duchess', *Explicator*, 42/1 (1983), 23–4.

Thundy, Zacharias P., 'The Dreame of Chaucer; Boethian Consolation or Political Celebration?', *Carmina Philosophiae: Journal of the International Boethius Society*, 4 (1995), 91–109.

Tisdale, Charles P. R., 'Boethian "hert-huntyng": The Elegiac Pattern of *The Book of the Duchess*', *American Benedictine Review*, 24/3 (1973), 365–80.

Travis, Peter W., 'White', *SAC*, 22 (2000), 1–66.

Trigg, Stephanie, *Congenial Souls: Reading Chaucer from Medieval to Postmodern* (Minneapolis, 2001).

Tripp, Raymond P., Jr, 'The Dialectics of Debate and the Continuity of English Poetry', *Massachusetts Studies in English*, 7 (1978), 41–51.

—— 'The Loss of Suddenness in Lydgate's *A Complaynt of a Loveres Lyfe*', *Fifteenth Century Studies*, 6 (1983), 253–69.

Vaughan, Mícheál [F.], 'Hunting for the Hurt in Chaucer's *Book of the Duchess*', *Lingua Humanitatis*, 2/2 (2002), 85–107.

—— '"Til I gan awake": The Conversion of Dreamer into Narrator in *Piers Plowman* B', *Yearbook of Langland Studies*, 5 (1991), 175–92.

Vaught, Jennifer C. (ed.), *Rhetorics of Bodily Disease and Health in Medieval and Early Modern England* (Farnham, Surrey and Burlington, VT, 2010).

Vickery, Gwen M., 'The *Book of the Duchess*: The Date of Composition Related to the Theme of Impracticality', *Essays in Literature*, 22/2 (1995), 161–9.

Wack, Mary F., *Lovesickness in the Middle Ages: The* Viaticum *and Its Commentaries* (Philadelphia, 1990).

Walker, Denis, 'Narrative Inconclusiveness and Consolatory Dialectic in the *Book of the Duchess*', *ChR*, 18/1 (1983), 1–17.

Wallace, David, 'Chaucer and Boccaccio's early writings', in Piero Boitani (ed.), *Chaucer and the Italian Trecento* (Cambridge, 1983), pp. 141–62.

Walters, Lori, 'Reading the "Rose": Literacy and the Presentation of the "Roman de la Rose" in Medieval Manuscripts', *Romanic Review*, 85/1 (1994), 1-26.

Watson, Nicholas, 'Censorship and Cultural Change in Late-Medieval England: Vernacular Theology, the Oxford Translation Debate, and Arundel's Constitutions of 1409', *Speculum*, 70 (1995), 822–64.

Watson, Robert A., 'Dialogue and Invention in the *Book of the Duchess*', *Modern Philology*, 98/4 (2001), 543–76.

Wenzel, Siegfried, 'Pestilence and Middle English literature: Friar John Grimestone's poems on death', in Daniel Williman (ed.), *The Black Death: The Impact of the Fourteenth-Century Plague* (Binghamton, NY, 1982), pp. 131–59.

Williams, Deanne, 'The dream visions', in Seth Lerer (ed.), *The Yale Companion to Chaucer* (New Haven and London, 2006), pp. 147–78.

—— *The French Fetish from Chaucer to Shakespeare* (Cambridge, 2004).

Wilson, G. R., Jr, 'The Anatomy of Compassion: Chaucer's *Book of the Duchess*', *Texas Studies in Literature and Language*, 14/3 (1972), 381–8.

Wimsatt, James [I.], 'The Apotheosis of Blanche in *The Book of the Duchess*', *JEGP*, 66/1 (1967), 26–44.

—— 'The Book of the Duchess: secular elegy or religious vision?', in John P. Hermann and John J. Burke, Jr (eds), *Signs and Symbols in Chaucer's Poetry* (University, AL, 1981), pp. 113–29.

—— *Chaucer and the French Love Poets: The Literary Background of the* Book of the Duchess (Chapel Hill, NC, 1968).

—— *Chaucer and His French Contemporaries: Natural Music in the Fourteenth Century* (Toronto, 1991).

—— 'The *Dit dou bleu chevalier*: Froissart's Imitation of Chaucer', *Mediaeval Studies*, 34 (1972), 388–400.

—— 'Machaut's *Lay de Confort* and Chaucer's *Book of the Duchess*', in Rossell Hope Robbins (ed.), *Chaucer at Albany* (New York, 1975), pp. 11–26.

—— 'The Sources of Chaucer's "Seys and Alcyone"' *Medium Ævum*, 36/3 (1967), 231–41.

Windeatt, B. A., *Chaucer's Dream Poetry: Sources and Analogues* (Woodbridge, Suffolk and Totowa, NJ, 1982).

Winny, James, *Chaucer's Dream-Poems* (New York, 1973).

Wogan-Browne, Jocelyn et al. (eds), *The Idea of the Vernacular: An Anthology of Middle English Literary Theory, 1280–1520* (Exeter, 1999).

Yeager, R. F., 'Literary Theory at the Close of the Middle Ages: William Caxton and William Thynne', *SAC*, 6 (1984), 135–64.

Yvernault, Martine, '"I have lost more than thow wenest": Past, Present, and (Re)presentation in *The Book of the Duchess*', *Bulletin des Anglicistes Médiévistes*, 72 (2007), 31–45.

Zeeman, Nicolette, 'Imaginative theory', in Paul Strohm (ed.), *Middle English* (Oxford and New York, 2007), pp. 222–40.

Zimbardo, Rose A. 'The *Book of the Duchess* and the Dream of Folly', *ChR*, 18/4 (1984), 329–46.

INDEX

Note: the abbreviation *BD* in
the index denotes the *Book of the
Duchess*

ABC, An (Chaucer) 41, 110, 111
Against Women Unconstant
    (Chaucer) 126
Alan of Lille: *De planctu Naturae*
    145
allegory 15, 36, 57–8, 91–4, 150
ambiguity 11, 16, 17, 38–9, 42, 68
amplificatio 151, 159
Anderson, Robert 121
Anelida and Arcite (Chaucer) 118
Animadversions (Francis Thynne)
    116, 156, 190 n. 106
annexation 6, 113–30
anthologies 86, 106, 107, 117
aporia 53, 132, 143
Arn, Mary-Jo 146
Assembly of Ladies (anon.) 118
audience 9–10, 17, 50, 56, 113,
    121–2, 182 n. 11
authority 5, 9, 40, 81, 85, 98, 168–9
authorship 4, 5, 6, 9–10, 40, 76,
    79–104, 162–4, 167–8
autography 37–8

Baker, Donald C. 14
Bale, John 28
Barchiesi, Alessandro 77
Barthes, Roland 77, 175
Bell, John 121
Belle Dame Sans Mercy, La (Roos)
    118
Benson, C. David 3

Bersuire, Pierre: *Ovidius moralizatus*
    133
Beware of Doublenesse (Lydgate)
    126–7
biographical readings (*BD*) 4, 13,
    25, 108–10, 156–7, 176–9
Black Death *see* plague
Blake, N. F. 28–9
Blanche of Lancaster 1, 18–27,
    29–30, 32, 34, 62, 108, 109–11,
    142, 156, 159
Boccaccio, Giovanni 66, 70, 114
Bodley 638 manuscript 82, 105, 113
Boece (Chaucer) 59, 84
Boethianism 5, 36, 37, 55, 58–61
Boethius: *Consolation of Philosophy*
    37, 58–61, 84, 132, 145, 167
Boitani, Piero 40
Boke of Cupide (Clanvowe) 113,
    116
Book of the Duchess (Chaucer)
    and allegory 15, 36, 57–8, 91–4,
        150
    and ambiguity 16, 17, 38–9, 42,
        68
    annexation 6, 113–30
    audience 17, 50, 56
    and authorship 5, 6, 9–10, 40, 76,
        79–104, 162–4
    biographical readings 4, 13, 25,
        108–10, 156–7, 176–9
    Bodley 638 manuscript 82, 105,
        113
    and Boethianism 5, 36, 37, 55,
        58–61
    and *chanson d'aventure* 34, 45

Book of the Duchess (Chaucer) (CONTD.)
   characterization 11, 13, 16–17,
      53–5, 172
   and Chaucer's mature poetry
      4–5, 10–12, 18, 59, 106–7, 180
   chess analogy 11, 23–4, 39, 140,
      143, 148–50
   and Christianity 15, 35, 55, 56–8,
      59, 62, 150, 172, 173
   and closure 4, 17, 35, 42, 61,
      119, 124, 175
   and collaboration 4, 74, 77–8
   collocation with *Lenvoy de*
      Chaucer a Bukton 6, 114–30,
      154–5, 174
   and commemoration 21, 25–6,
      34–5, 66
   and commentary 34, 46–7, 90
   and communication 5, 17, 50–55,
      61, 69, 76, 141, 144
   and complaint 46, 75, 171, 172
   compositional history 5, 27–33
   and consistency 8, 11, 53–5, 162
   and consolation 5, 14, 15, 35,
      55–61, 161, 172–3
   critical studies of 2–3, 5, 7–18
   dating 5, 18–27
   and debate 34, 42–4
   dissemination 6, 105–30, 138
   and *dit amoreux* 27, 33, 36–8,
      44–6, 94–9, 114, 130, 135–6,
      146, 154
   dreamer *see* narrator (*BD*)
   and dream-vision 1, 3, 33,
      36, 38–42, 65, 72, 75, 94–8,
      100–102, 107–8, 135–6, 178
   early creative responses to *see*
      early creative responses (to *BD*)
   in editions of Chaucer's works *see*
      Works (Chaucer)
   and elegy 8, 21, 33, 34–6, 50, 72,
      169–70, 173–4
   and the English language 10, 18,
      34, 37, 65, 70, 74–6, 78, 146,
      154, 176, 180
   and Englishness 5, 18, 69–78,
      133, 146, 180

Fairfax 16 manuscript 20, 82,
      105, 108, 112–18, 120, 121,
      122, 124, 126, 156
   and first-person narration 79,
      81–2, 176, 178
   and forgetting 65–6
   and French literary traditions 1,
      10, 13, 26–7, 36–8, 45–6, 60,
      65, 68, 70–78, 94–9, 135–6,
      146, 154, 155, 176, 183 n. 24
   and Frenchness 5, 18, 69–78,
      146, 180
   and gender 5, 61–5, 91–2
   and genre 5, 33–47, 191 n. 116
   imagery 11, 13, 39, 57–8, 91–4,
      148–50
   influence on French poetry 26–7,
      73–4
   and interlingualism 5, 43, 69–78,
      146, 154, 180
   interpretive issues 5, 8–9, 12,
      49–78
   and intertextuality 5, 18, 44,
      77–8, 131–74
   and irony 17, 21–2, 59, 176
   and lyric 34, 36, 45–6, 51–5,
      75–6, 90–91, 96, 141, 144, 171,
      172
   Man in Black *see* Man in Black
      (*BD*)
   manuscript glosses 20, 112–13
   manuscript preservation 6, 86,
      105–7
   and melancholy 1, 14, 35–6, 40,
      65, 67, 68, 96, 139, 172–3
   and memory 15, 43, 46, 57, 60,
      61, 66, 172, 173
   modern resonances 5, 179–80
   and motivation 8, 11, 16
   and multivalence 16, 17, 38–9,
      42, 68
   narrative structure 1–2, 13–14,
      161, 173
   narrator *see* narrator (*BD*)
   occasion 5, 18–27, 108, 120
   and parody 76
   and pastoral 34, 44–5

and plain speech 22, 50–51, 75–6
and polyglossia 74–6
revision 5, 25–6, 29, 33, 120, 187
 n. 61
and secularism 16, 58
and self-consciousness 5, 6, 17,
 36, 74, 94–104, 162–4
Seys and Alcione story 28–9, 37,
 40, 46–7, 63, 82, 89, 90, 105,
 133–7, 173
and sickness 5, 13, 25–6, 28, 29,
 31, 65–9, 105, 129
and simplicity 7, 14–15, 51
sources 5, 8, 13, 18, 60, 67,
 70–74, 76, 96, 183 n. 24
and subversion 76–7
supplementation 6, 111–13
Tanner 346 manuscript 86, 105,
 113, 120
and temporality 12, 80, 81–2,
 94–104, 163, 168, 175–6,
 179–80, 202 n. 34
and translation 176
transmission 6, 105–30, 138
and uses of the word 'book' 6,
 82–9, 103, 104
White *see* White (*BD*)
booklets 86, 106, 117
books
and clothing 92–3
and dreams 40–41, 93–4, 162–5,
 167–9
and embodiment 91–4
as having agency 3–4, 90
and memory 87–8
as physical objects 3, 80, 83,
 85–90, 104
and poetic inspiration 167–9
and the self 86–8, 104
uses of the word 'book' 6, 82–9,
 103, 104
see also anthologies; authorship;
 booklets
Bowers, John M. 77, 177
Braddy, Haldeen 13
Bronson, Bertrand H. 14, 54
Brown, Peter 18

Browning, Robert: *My Last Duchess*
 174
Brownlee, Kevin 81
Brusendorff, Aage 106
Bryant, Brantley L. 179
Bukton, Sir Peter 115
Bukton, Sir Robert 115
Butterfield, Ardis 18, 27, 35, 44–5,
 67, 95, 176

Calin, William 41, 73
Canterbury Tales (Chaucer) 8, 10,
 11, 38, 44, 82, 84, 105, 129,
 133
 Clerk's Tale 123–4, 129
 Franklin's Tale 125, 143
 General Prologue 92
 Knight's Tale 59, 70, 159
 Man of Law's Tale, Introduction
 28, 33, 82, 83, 89
 Manciple's Tale 99
 Nun's Priest's Tale 34
 Retraction 1, 28, 82, 83–5, 90
 Wife of Bath's Prologue 65, 122,
 126, 130, 189 n. 90
 see also Wife of Bath (character)
Canticus Troili (Chaucer) 142
Canzoniere (Petrarch) 152
Carruthers, Mary J. 87
Cartier, Normand 73
Catherine of France 159
Cawsey, Kathy 9
Caxton, William 108
Ceys and Alcione story *see* Seys and
 Alcione story
chanson d'aventure 34, 45
characterization 11, 13, 16–17, 53–5,
 172
Charles of Orleans: *Fortunes
 Stabilnes* 6, 145–55, 168
Chaucer, Alice 109
Chaucer, Geoffrey
 An ABC 41, 110, 111, 182 n. 12
 Against Women Unconstant 126
 Anelida and Arcite 118
 authorial persona 2, 4, 9, 10, 130,
 175–80

Chaucer, Geoffrey (CONTD.)
  Boece 59, 84, 182 n. 12
  Book of the Duchess see *Book of the Duchess* (Chaucer)
  Book of the Leoun 84, 85, 182 n. 12
  Canterbury Tales see *Canterbury Tales* (Chaucer)
  Canticus Troili 142
  Clerk's Tale 123–4, 129, 189 n. 90
  Complaint of Chaucer to His Purse 118
  Complaint of Mars 116
  Complaint of Venus 72, 116
  Complaint Unto Pity 118, 138, 182 n. 12
  as courtier 1, 4, 19
  Franklin's Tale 125, 143
  General Prologue 92
  House of Fame 23, 26, 59, 83, 84, 89, 92, 105, 129–30, 131, 178
  and John of Gaunt 1, 19, 20, 21, 26
  Knight's Tale 59, 70, 159, 182 n. 12
  Legend of Good Women 11, 19, 28, 62, 83, 84, 90, 105, 107, 118–20, 156, 166, 177, 178
  Lenvoy de Chaucer 123–4, 126, 127, 129
  Lenvoy de Chaucer a Bukton 6, 114–30, 154–5, 174, 189 n. 90
  Lenvoy de Chaucer a Scogan 118
  literary canon 2, 4, 10–12, 106, 116–17, 125–6, 130, 138, 155, 178, 179, 180
  Man of Law's Tale, Introduction 28, 33, 82, 83, 89
  Manciple's Tale 99
  mature poetry 4–5, 10–12, 18, 59, 106–7, 180
  Merchant's Tale, 189 n. 90
  Nun's Priest's Tale 34
  Parliament of Foules 44, 83, 105, 118, 119, 130, 144, 164
  Retraction 1, 28, 82, 83–5, 90, 182 n. 12

  Troilus and Criseyde 10, 11, 12, 28, 38, 54, 58, 59, 65, 70, 84, 90, 92, 93, 105, 114, 118, 134, 136, 138, 141–2, 152–3, 182 n. 12, 209 n. 25
  Wife of Bath's Prologue 65, 122, 126, 130, 189 n. 90
  Works see *Works* (Chaucer)
Chaucer, Philippa 1, 31–2, 109, 130, 157
chess analogies 11, 23–4, 39, 140, 143, 148–50
Chrétien de Troyes: *Yvain* 161
Christianity 15, 35, 55, 56–8, 59, 62, 150, 172
Clanvowe, Sir John: *Boke of Cupide* 113, 116
Clerk's Tale (Chaucer) 123–4, 129
closure 4, 17, 35, 42, 61, 119, 124, 144–5, 175
clothing 92–3, 155
Coghill, Nevill 11
collaboration 4, 74, 77–8
colour symbolism 63, 72, 91–3, 140–41, 155
Commedia (Dante) 57
commemoration 21, 25–6, 34–5, 66
commentary 34, 46–7, 90, 101, 139
communication 5, 17, 50–55, 61, 69, 76, 141, 144, 171–2
complaint 46, 75, 139, 171, 172
Complaint of Chaucer to His Purse (Chaucer) 118
Complaint of Mars (Chaucer) 116
Complaint of Venus (Chaucer) 72, 116
Complaint of the Black Knight see *Complaynt of a Loveres Lyfe* (Lydgate)
Complaint Unto Pity (Chaucer) 118, 138
Complainte de l'an nouvel (Granson) 26–7
Complainte de Saint Valentin (Granson) 26–7

Complaynt of a Loveres Lyfe (Lydgate)
    107, 110, 111, 138–45, 160,
    161, 166
compositional history (*BD*) 5, 27–33
Condren, Edward I. 25, 29–30
Confessio Amantis (Gower) 80, 99,
    103–4, 132–8
consistency 8, 11, 53–5, 162
consolation 5, 14, 15, 35, 55–61,
    161, 172–3
Consolation of Philosophy (Boethius)
    37, 58–61, 84, 132, 145, 167
Constance of Castile 23, 31, 109, 125
counter-pastoral 45, 67
courtly love 15, 63, 64, 75, 76,
    125, 130, 139, 152–4; *see also*
    courtly verse; *dit amoreux*
courtly verse 2, 10, 36–8, 70,
    129, 146, 155, 165; *see also*
    dit amoreux

Dane, Joseph A. 86
Dante 26, 57, 136
Daphnaida (Spenser) 169–74
Dart, John 110
dating (*BD*) 5, 18–27, 73
Davis, Steven 9–10, 54, 76–7, 78
de la Pole, William 109
De planctu Naturae (Alan of Lille)
    145
de Worde, Wynken 108
debate 34, 42–4, 139
Deguileville, Guillaume de:
    *Le Pèlerinage de la vie
    humaine* 41, 110
Deschamps, Eustache 36, 73
Diekstra, F. N. M. 43–4
Dinshaw, Carolyn 3
dissemination (*BD*) 6, 105–30, 138
dit amoreux 27, 33, 36–8, 44–6, 85,
    91, 94–9, 114, 130, 132, 134–9,
    145–6, 154
Dit de la fonteinne amoreuse
    (Machaut) 37, 54–5, 81–2, 85,
    134, 135, 191 n. 133
Dit dou bleu chevalier (Froissart) 27,
    72, 85, 139

Dit dou lyon (Machaut) 85
Donnelly, Colleen 42
dream-vision 1, 3, 33, 36, 38–42, 65,
    72, 75, 94–8, 100–102, 105,
    107–8, 134–7, 139, 151–2,
    157–69, 178
dreamer *see* narrator (*BD*)
Dryden, John: *Fables, Ancient and
    Modern* 174

early creative responses (to *BD*)
    Complaynt of a Loveres Lyfe
        (Lydgate) 138–45
    Confessio Amantis (Gower)
        132–8
    Daphnaida (Spenser) 169–74
    The Floure and the Leafe 165–7
    Fortunes Stabilnes (Charles of
        Orleans) 145–55
    Isle of Ladies 155–65
    The Kingis Quair (James I) 167–9
    overview 6, 131–2
Eco, Umberto 47, 176
Edward III 1, 23, 30
elegy 8, 21, 33, 34–6, 50, 72, 169–70,
    173–4
Ellis, Steve 9, 35–6
Ellmann, Maud 62, 63–4, 91
English language 10, 18, 34, 37, 65,
    70, 74–6, 78, 107, 145–6, 154,
    176, 180
Englishness 5, 18, 69–78, 133, 146,
    180
Envoy to Alison (anon.) 113–14, 124,
    129
exegetical criticism 15–16, 37

Fables, Ancient and Modern
    (Dryden) 174
Faerie Queene (Spenser) 169, 170
Fairfax 16 manuscript 20, 82, 105,
    108, 112–18, 120, 121, 122,
    124, 126, 156
Fall of Princes (Lydgate) 19
Farber, Annika 159–60
feminist criticism 17, 22, 62–4, 91
Ferster, Judith 17

fin'amors see courtly love
first-person narration 36, 37–8, 79, 81–2, 97, 176, 178
Fleay, Frederick Gard 129–30
Floure and the Leafe, The (anon.) 6, 165–6, 174
Floure of Curtesy (Lydgate) 118
forgetting 65–6
formalist criticism 13–14, 16
Forni, Kathleen 108, 117–18, 125, 126
Fortune 23, 37, 58–9, 99, 143, 148–9, 150–51, 159, 160
Fortunes Stabilnes (Charles of Orleans) 145–55, 168
Fradenburg, Louise O. 11, 36
Franklin's Tale (Chaucer) 125, 143
French language 70, 78, 180
French literary traditions 1, 2, 10, 13, 26–7, 36–8, 45–6, 60, 65, 68, 70–78, 85, 94–9, 134–7, 138–9, 145–6, 154, 155, 176; *see also* courtly verse; *dit amoreux*; dream-vision
Frenchness 5, 18, 69–78, 146, 180
French, W. H. 11, 53–4
Freud, Sigmund 38, 56, 62
Froissart, Jean 34, 36, 80, 94
    Dit dou bleu chevalier 27, 72, 85, 139
    Joli buisson de jonece 34, 35
    Paradys d'Amours 68, 72, 75, 96–7, 98, 135, 137, 166, 176, 207 nn. 9, 10
Furnivall, Frederick James 7, 29, 51, 71

Galway, Margaret 13
Gamaury, Martine 88–9
Gardner, John 14–15, 23
Gawain-poet 23, 75
gender 5, 61–5, 91–2, 125–30
General Prologue (Chaucer) 92
Genette, Gérard 77
genre 5, 33–47, 191 n. 116
'Geoffrey Chaucer Hath a Blog' 179–80

Godwin, William 8, 111
Gorges, Sir Arthur 169
Gower, John 146
    Confessio Amantis 6, 80, 99, 103–4, 132–8
    Mirour de l'omme 136
Granson, Oton de 26–7, 72, 188–9 n. 85
Guthrie, Steve 75, 76

Hansen, Elaine Tuttle 62–3
Hardman, Phillipa 25–6, 29
Henry IV 2, 32–3, 107
Henry V 107, 159
Henryson, Robert: *Testament of Cresseid* 117, 118, 162, 168, 169
hermeneutics 17, 95
Hoccleve, Thomas 114
homosociality 63, 64, 91, 177, 178
Horvath, Richard P. 122
House of Fame (Chaucer) 23, 26, 59, 83, 84, 89, 92, 105, 129–30, 131, 178
Howard, Lady Douglas 169
hunting motifs 23, 39, 45, 157, 160, 163
Huppé, Bernard 15–16, 25, 30, 37, 57–8, 59

insomnia 1, 21, 53, 65, 68, 95, 96, 127–8, 129, 135–8, 166, 167
interlingualism 5, 43, 69–78, 146, 154, 180
intertextuality 5, 18, 44, 74, 77–8; *see also* early creative responses (to *BD*)
inventio 4, 45, 87, 88, 180
irony 17, 21–2, 37, 59, 121–2, 124–5, 126–7, 150, 176
Irvine, Martin 47, 90
Isle of Ladies (anon.) 6, 107, 109, 110–11, 155–65, 169, 178
Italian literary traditions 26, 70

Jager, Eric 87
James I 167–9

Jehan de la Mote: *Regret Guillaume Comte de Hainault* 35, 72, 73
Jenkins, Jacqueline 102
John of Gaunt 1–2, 19–26, 29–32, 72, 107, 109–11, 120, 125, 129, 142, 149, 156, 159, 179
Joli buisson de jonece (Froissart) 34, 35
Jordan, Robert M. 16–17
Jugement dou roi de Behaigne (Machaut) 25, 44, 62, 67, 78, 98, 146, 153
Jugement dou roy de Navarre (Machaut) 78, 98
Julian of Norwich
    A Revelation of Love 80, 101–2
    A Vision Showed to a Devout Woman 101
Justice, Steven 16

Kamath, Stephanie A. Viereck Gibbs 41
Kellogg, Alfred L. 31
Kingis Quair, The (James I) 6, 162, 167–9
Kittredge, George Lyman 8, 13, 38, 54, 70, 71–2, 121–2
Knight's Tale (Chaucer) 59, 70, 159
Kristeva, Julia 77
Kruger, Steven 38–9, 64–5

Lacan, Jacques 12, 62
laments 34, 46, 147–8; *see also* complaint
Langland, William: *Piers Plowman* 39, 80, 100–101, 164
Legend of Good Women (Chaucer) 11, 19, 28, 62, 83, 84, 90, 105, 107, 118–20, 156, 166, 177, 178
Lenvoy de Chaucer (Chaucer) 123–4, 126, 127, 129
Lenvoy de Chaucer a Bukton (Chaucer) 6, 114–30, 154–5, 174
Lenvoy de Chaucer a Scogan (Chaucer) 118

Lerer, Seth 3, 178
Lewis, C. S. 8
Life of Geoffrey Chaucer (Godwin) 8, 111
Livre dou voir dit (Machaut) 98–9
Lorris, Guillaume de: *Roman de la rose* 1, 36, 40, 41, 43–4, 71, 80, 88, 96, 97–8, 132, 137, 142, 145, 153, 164–5
lovesickness *see* melancholy; sickness
Lowell, James R. 62
Lowes, John Livingstone 11
Lydgate, John 28, 107, 114, 146, 178
    Beware of Doublenesse 126–7
    Complaynt of a Loveres Lyfe 6, 107, 110, 111, 138–45, 160, 161, 166
    Fall of Princes 19
    Floure of Curtesy 118
    My Lady Dere 140
    Siege of Thebes 159
    Temple of Glass 156
Lynch, Kathryn L. 18, 19, 42
lyric 34, 36, 45–6, 51–5, 75–6, 84, 85, 90–91, 96, 141, 144, 171, 172

Machaut, Guillaume de 8, 26, 36, 37, 41, 66, 71–2, 80, 81–2, 94, 176
    Dit de la fonteinne amoreuse 37, 54–5, 81–2, 85, 134, 135, 191 n. 133
    Dit dou lyon 85, 182 n. 12
    Jugement dou roi de Behaigne 25, 44, 62, 67, 78, 98, 146, 153
    Jugement dou roy de Navarre 78, 98
    Le Livre dou voir dit 98–9
    Remede de Fortune 37, 60, 98, 114
Man in Black (*BD*)
    age of 24, 190 n. 106
    chess analogy 11, 23–4, 39, 140, 143, 148–50

Man in Black (*BD*) (CONTD.)
  and consolation 55–7, 58–9,
    60–61, 173
  and debate 42–4
  identified with John of Gaunt 1,
    19, 22, 109
  lyrics 45–6, 51–5, 75–6, 90–91,
    141, 144, 147–8, 171, 172
  as projection of narrator 14, 15,
    30, 40, 161
  and writing symbolism 91, 93–4
Man of Law's Tale, Introduction
  (Chaucer) 28, 33, 82, 83, 89
Manciple's Tale (Chaucer) 99
Manly, J. M. 7
manuscript glosses (*BD*) 20, 112–13
manuscript preservation (*BD*) 6, 86,
  105–7
Margherita, Gayle 62–3
marriage 109–10, 116, 122, 123–30,
  131, 154–5
medical discourses 66, 68, 69
melancholy 1, 14, 35–6, 40, 55–6,
  65, 67–8, 93, 96, 139, 141,
  151–4, 170–73; *see also*
  sickness
memorialization *see* commemoration
memory 15, 43, 46, 57, 60, 61, 66,
  87–8, 172, 173
Metamorphoses (Ovid) 28, 37, 40,
  46–7, 82, 89–90, 132, 133–7,
  169, 173; *see also* Seys and
  Alcione story
Meun, Jean de: *Roman de la rose* 1,
  36, 40, 43–4, 71, 80, 88, 96,
  97–8, 132, 137, 142, 145, 153,
  164–5
Minnis, A. J. 51
Mirour de l'omme (Gower) 136
misogyny 125–30, 131
Morpheus 21, 40, 96, 113, 134, 135;
  see also Seys and Alcione story
Mother of Norture (anon.) 118,
  119–20
motivation 8, 11, 16, 31
multivalence 11, 16, 17, 38–9, 42, 68
Muscatine, Charles 8, 9, 14

My Lady Dere (Lydgate) 140
My Last Duchess (Browning) 174

narrative structure 1–2, 13–14, 57,
  143–4, 161, 173
narrator (*BD*)
  characterization 16–17, 53–5, 172
  and consistency 8, 11, 53–5, 162
  and debate 42–4
  identified with Chaucer 13
  and insomnia 1, 21, 53, 65, 68,
    95, 96, 129, 137–8
  Man in Black as projection of 14,
    15, 30, 40, 161
  motivation 8, 11, 16
  and queerness 64–5
  and sickness 13, 25–6, 28, 29, 31,
    65, 67–9, 105, 129
New Criticism 13, 184 n. 32
Nolan, Barbara 76
Notary, Julian 116, 117, 122
Nun's Priest's Tale (Chaucer) 34

occasion (*BD*) 5, 18–27, 108, 120
Octovyen, Emperor 23, 24, 95, 162
Of Theyre Nature (anon.) 127–9
Olson, Glending 66
Ovid: *Metamorphoses* 28, 37, 40,
  46–7, 82, 89–90, 132, 133–7,
  169, 173; *see also* Seys and
  Alcione story
Ovidius moralizatus (Bersuire) 133
Oxford group manuscripts *see*
  Bodley 638 manuscript;
  Fairfax 16 manuscript; Tanner
  346 manuscript

painted chamber motifs 40, 88, 90,
  158, 160, 163, 164
Palmer, J. J. N. 19–20
Palmer, R. Barton 37, 77–8
Paradys d'Amours (Froissart) 68, 72,
  75, 96–7, 98, 135, 137, 166,
  176, 207 nn. 9, 10
Parliament of Foules (Chaucer) 44,
  83, 105, 118, 119, 138, 144,
  164

parody 37, 58, 76
Partridge, Stephen 85
pastoral 34, 44–5
Patterson, Lee 3
Payne, Robert O. 14
Pearl (anon.) 39, 41, 57
Pearsall, Derek 20, 165
Pèlerinage de la vie humaine
  (Deguileville) 41, 110
Petrarch, Francis 142, 152
phenomenology 17
Philippa, of Hainault, Queen 19–20,
  30, 34
Phillips, Helen 23, 29, 68, 133
phoenix imagery 150–51
Piers Plowman (Langland) 39, 80,
  100–101, 164
Pinkhurst, Adam 85
plague 1, 19, 45, 65–8, 69
plain speech 22, 50–51, 75–6
polyglossia 74–6, 146
poststructuralist criticism 16–17
praeteritio 122, 151
psychoanalytic criticism 17, 62–3,
  91, 197 n. 72
Pynson, Richard 108

queer theory 17, 64–5

Regret Guillaume Comte de Hainault
  (Jehan de la Mote) 35, 72,
  73
Remede de Fortune (Machaut) 37,
  60, 98, 114
Remedy of Loue (anon.) 125–6,
  127
Retraction (Chaucer) 1, 28, 82, 83–5,
  90
Revelation of Love (Julian of
  Norwich) 80, 101–2
revision (*BD*) 5, 25–6, 29, 33, 120,
  187 n. 61
Riffaterre, Michael 77
Rimbaud, Arthur 176
Robertson, D. W., Jr 2, 15–16, 25,
  30, 34, 37, 51, 57–8, 59, 62
Robinson, Ian 13, 31–2

Roman de la rose (Lorris & Meun) 1,
  36, 40, 41, 43–4, 71, 80, 88,
  96, 97–8, 132, 137, 142, 145,
  153, 164–5
Roos, Richard: *La Belle Dame Sans
  Mercy* 118
Root, Robert Kilburn 8
Rosenthal, Constance L. 13
Rowland, Beryl 2
Rust, Martha Dana 88, 92

Salter, Elizabeth 74, 78
Sandras, Étienne Gustave 71
Scala, Elizabeth 9
Schibanoff, Susan 64
Schless, Howard 29
secularism 16, 58
self-consciousness, narrative 5, 6,
  17, 36, 74, 94–104, 162–4
Seys and Alcione story 28–9, 37,
  40, 46–7, 63, 82, 89, 90, 105,
  133–7, 173; *see also* Morpheus
Shannon, Edgar Finley 13
Shepheardes Calendar (Spenser) 170
Shirley, John 108
sickness 5, 13, 25–6, 28, 29, 31,
  65–9, 105, 129, 141, 144,
  153–4; *see also* melancholy
Siege of Thebes (Lydgate) 159
Skeat, Walter W. 119, 138
Solomon and Saturn (anon.) 43
Song of Songs 57, 58
Songe vert (anon.) 27, 72, 73, 155
sources (*BD*) 5, 8, 13, 18, 60, 67,
  70–74, 76, 77, 96
Spearing, A. C. 37–8, 139, 167
Speght, Thomas 108–10, 120, 121,
  124, 156–7, 159, 179, 210 n. 36
Spenser, Edmund
  Faerie Queene 169, 170
  Daphnaida 6, 169–74
  Shepheardes Calendar 170
Staley, Lynn 20
Stow, John 20, 108, 109, 112–13,
  120–21, 124, 125–6, 127–9, 156
Strohm, Paul 3, 121
subversion 76–7

supplementation 6, 111–13
Swynford, Katherine 21, 31–2, 109, 157, 159
Symons, Dana M. 139
Sypherd, W. Owen 13, 72

Tanner 346 manuscript 86, 105, 113, 120
Tatlock, J. S. P. 11
Temple of Glass (Lydgate) 156
temporality 12, 80, 81–2, 94–104, 163, 168, 175–6, 179–80, 202 n. 34
Testament of Cresseid (Henryson) 117, 118, 162, 168, 169
Testament of Love (Usk) 116–17
Thomas, Doreen M. 31–2
Thomas, William 110
Thundy, Zacharias P. 32
Thynne, Francis: Animadversions 116, 156, 190 n. 106
Thynne, William 6, 28–9, 105–6, 113, 114–20, 124–5, 127, 129, 138, 156, 178
translation 1, 59, 70, 84, 133–4, 176
transmission (BD) 6, 105–30, 138
Travis, Peter W. 18, 53
Trigg, Stephanie 9, 31, 122, 177, 178
Tripp, Raymond P., Jr 43, 140
Troilus and Criseyde (Chaucer) 10, 11, 12, 28, 38, 54, 58, 59, 65, 70, 84, 90, 92, 93, 105, 114, 118, 134, 136, 138, 141–2, 152–3, 182 n. 12, 209 n. 25
Tyrwhitt, Thomas 70, 115, 121

Urry, John 110, 120, 121, 124, 129, 142
Usk, Thomas: Testament of Love 116–17

Vaughan, Míceál F. 100
vernacular see English language
Vision Showed to a Devout Woman (Julian of Norwich) 101

Wallace, David 3
Walters, Lori 97
Watson, Nicholas 102
Watson, Robert A. 60
White (BD)
    and Christian symbolism 57–8, 62
    erasure of 62–4, 65, 91
    identified with Blanche of Lancaster 1, 18–19, 108, 109
    physical description of 57–8, 62, 64
    and sickness 65–6, 69
    and writing symbolism 91, 93
Wife of Bath (character) 115, 117, 123, 124, 189 n. 90, 195–6 n. 49
Wife of Bath's Prologue (Chaucer) 65, 122, 126, 130, 189 n. 90
Wilcockson, Colin 62
Williams, Deanne 18, 65, 75
Wimsatt, James 2, 14, 26–7, 36, 38, 46, 62, 70, 73, 99
Works (Chaucer)
    Anderson (1795) edition 121
    Bell (1782) edition 121
    Speght (1598) edition 108–10, 120, 121, 124, 156–7, 159, 179
    Speght (1602) edition 108, 110, 121, 124, 156–7, 159, 179, 210 n. 36
    Speght (1687) edition 121, 124
    Stow (1561) edition 120–21, 124, 125–6, 127–9
    Thynne (1532) edition 6, 28–9, 105–6, 113, 114–20, 124–5, 127, 129, 138, 156, 178
    Urry (1721) edition 110, 120, 121, 124, 129, 142
writing see authorship
writing symbolism 80, 91–4

Yvain (Chrétien de Troyes) 161
Yvernault, Martine 94

Zeeman, Nicolette 45